PRAISE FOR

Homeschooling Step-by-Step

"*Homeschooling Step-by-Step* is a treasure trove of honest and practical advice on everything from entertaining toddlers during school, to finding your child's learning style, to understanding state legalities. Complete with checklists, worksheets, and helpful Web sites listed in each chapter, this book is a must-have for the home educator's reference library!"

—*Lynn Foster, former preschool teacher and a homeschooling parent*

"This book takes you through the process of getting started step-by-step, or you can jump in wherever you need to. This would have helped me tremendously when I started homeschooling ten years ago."

—*Ruth Ann Lantis, former schoolteacher and homeschooling mom*

"My life as a busy mom will be much easier thanks to this book. With five children, ranging in age from infant to teens, this is a necessary book to have on my shelf."

—*Jeanie Zick, homeschooling mom*

"Interactive and provocative. The Strategies chapter is enough to keep any family going for a lifetime. I've never seen this kind of depth of understanding in a book for home educators; I finally feel like I've been treated like an intelligent person. *Homeschooling Step-by-Step* doesn't miss a single step!"

—*Rhonda Johnson, homeschooling mom*

"*Wow* is the best word I can use to describe this book! The section on confidence-boosting is just what many of the families in my homeschool support group need right now. I've already requested that my local library order a copy."

—*Ellen Doolin, Usborne book consultant
and homeschooling mom*

"Informative and all encompassing. A wealth of knowledge for everyone, from those interested in the possibility of homeschooling to the experienced homeschooler."

—*Saprina M. Bowman, manager of Home Education
Q's & A's in the MSN communities*

"What a terrific read! *Homeschooling Step-by-Step* is so thorough it could be used as a textbook about homeschooling."

—*Robin Goddard, former president of Teaching
Parents Association, homeschooling mom*

"There is no stone left unturned in this book. I wish I'd had this information when I was starting my family adventure in homeschooling!"

—*Alyeen Lim, homeschooling mom*

"This book should definitely be on the need-to-read list for all homeschoolers, regardless of their experience."

—*Pam VanLoon, homeschooling parent*

"This is an incredible resource for 'newbie' homeschoolers as well as those who have been homeschooling for years. The question-and-answer style creates an easy forum for looking up information quickly."

—*Kathy Lynch, homeschooling mom,
certified K–8 teacher*

Homeschooling
Step-by-Step

LAURAMAERY GOLD
JOAN M. ZIELINSKI

Homeschooling Step-by-Step

100+ Simple Solutions to
Homeschooling's Toughest Problems

PRIMA PUBLISHING

Published by Prima Publishing, Roseville, California. Member of the Crown Publishing Group, a division of Random House, Inc.

PRIMA HOME LEARNING LIBRARY is a trademark of Random House, Inc.

PRIMA PUBLISHING and colophon are trademarks of Random House, Inc., registered with the United States Patent and Trademark Office.

Graphics on pages 16, 65, 126, 150, 222, and 257 by Nathaniel Levine. All other illustrations courtesy of Original Country Clipart by Lisa.

Library of Congress Cataloging-in-Publication Data
Gold, LauraMaery.
    Homeschooling step-by-step : 100+ simple solutions to homeschooling's toughest problems / LauraMaery Gold, Joan M. Zielinski
        p. cm.
    Includes bibliographical references (p. 371) and index.
    ISBN 0-7615-3588-8
    1. Homeschooling—United States—Handbooks, manuals, etc.
I. Zielinski, Joan M. II. Title
LC40 .G645 2002
371.04'2'0973—dc21   2002022185

02 03 04 05 BB 10 9 8 7 6 5 4 3 2 1
Printed in the United States of America

First Edition

Visit us online at www.primapublishing.com

This book is dedicated to the parents everywhere who have the courage to be unconventional and to put their children first. You're making the world a better place. Thank you!

Contents

Acknowledgments

Our thanks to Prima Publishing for its ongoing interest in the homeschooling movement. This is our second homeschooling book with Prima, and we've been privileged to be associated with a company that honors education and the family.

Putting together a book is a team effort, and we want to thank the team that worked so hard at putting together *Homeschooling Step-by-Step*. Our continuing gratitude to acquisitions editor Jamie Miller and to production editor Tara Joffe, both of whom are wonderfully pleasant to work with and whose encouragement we treasure. To editorial assistant Erica Hannickel for keeping things moving. To copyeditor Rosaleen Bertolino, a master of the art. Also to Archetype, the compositor who so carefully assembled the manuscript into its present form. And to illustrator Nathaniel Levine, who is responsible for the superb electronic art. You're all talented and terrific, and we thank you!

Introduction

I'd been considering homeschooling for months, but it took a whispered conversation in the backseat for me to make up my mind.

As I drove down the street with a car full of public-schooled children, I overheard my oldest son tell his brother what he'd learned that day at school: "You can buy drugs on that corner," he said, pointing. "Officer Bob told us today in D.A.R.E. that it's the best place in town to buy pot."

I drove my giggling boys straight back to school, and withdrew them.

It's the best decision I've ever made.

Over the years, my children have grown into honorable, decent, loving people who care about one another and who work to make a positive impact on the world. They've turned into people whose company I enjoy.

I credit it all to homeschooling.

About four years ago, I began writing about home education, and since that time, I've responded to hundreds and hundreds of questions from families who are wondering how to teach their own children at home. Their questions have ranged from legal issues, to teaching approaches, to questions about how to juggle family and finances. In this book, you'll find answers to the most pressing problems encountered by teaching families.

This book is for every family that educates children, whether full-time or part-time, faithful or secular, traditional or nontraditional, newbies or old-timers.

In short, this book is the step-by-step guide to homeschooling that I wish *I'd* had when I got started—and it's also the handbook for teaching that I still use today.

We welcome inquiries from readers. If there's any question you'd like answered, please e-mail us at *<questions@homeschoolsteps.com>*. Readers are also welcome to visit us on our Web site at *<www.home schoolsteps.com>*, where you'll find updates, corrections, and news for homeschooling families.

Welcome to homeschooling! We look forward to hearing from you!

Homeschooling
Step-by-Step

Getting Started

What's This Book About?

You are holding in your hands a complete guide to homeschooling. In it are answers to all the questions you'll ever have about teaching your children at home.

How Is the Book Organized?

In this chapter, we introduce homeschooling. But this is primarily a reference book, so feel free to jump straight into:

Chapter 2: Legalities. How to run the legal gauntlet in your locality

Chapter 3: Strategies. Sixty ways to school your scholars

Chapter 4: Approaches and Philosophies. Fifty interesting approaches to family education

Chapter 5: Curriculum. Buy one, or build your own?

Chapter 6: Gaining Confidence. Practical advice for teaching effectively and staying on task

Chapter 7: Creating. Make your home a center for learning

Chapter 8: Balancing. Finances, organization, chores, and more: how to make homeschooling work financially and emotionally

Chapter 9: Challenges. How to cope with anything: objections, toddlers, distractions, and all the rest

Chapter 10: Support. Where to get assistance and backing

Chapter 11: Graduation. Getting your kids into college and adulthood

On Teaching

"The whole art of teaching is only the art of awakening the natural curiosity of young minds for the purpose of satisfying it afterwards."

—Anatole France
(1844–1924)

What Is a Homeschooler?

There's a broad definition, and a narrow one. Broadly speaking, a homeschooler is anyone who teaches children from—but not necessarily "at"—home. Within this broad definition are people who supplement homeschooling with private tutoring, cooperative classes, college courses, online classes, or even public or private schooling. It also includes unschoolers, deschoolers,[1] preschoolers, and the operators of very small private schools. It even includes older teenagers and young adults who educate themselves at home.

The narrow definition is parents teaching their own school-age children in their own home using a systematic curriculum.

In this book, we consider a homeschooler to be anyone who takes primary responsibility for the education of his or her own children, regardless of the method.

Why Do People Homeschool?

There are almost as many reasons for homeschooling as there are homeschoolers—and for most families the reasons change from time to time.

Families that homeschool do so for a combination of the following reasons:

Quality of Education. Homeschooling parents believe their children are educated better, and more thoroughly, than they would be in a traditional classroom.

Individualization. Some children simply do not learn well in a classroom setting. They may be bored or easily distracted. Some have learning disabilities that require one-on-one teaching. Some are gifted and cannot be challenged by the pace of traditional education. And homeschooled children have the freedom to pursue their academic interests when those interests arise, rather than when they fit into a curriculum.

Family. Families who homeschool are more tightly knit than those who don't. It's the simple, inescapable consequence of working and learning and spending time together. Moreover, homeschooled children have more time to develop relationships with grandparents and other members of their extended family.

On Education

"Aim for success, not perfection. Never give up your right to be wrong, because then you will lose the ability to learn new things and move forward with your life."

—Dr. David Burns, author

Positive Role Models. Homeschooling parents want their children to be raised with positive models of behavior. When children watch their parents and grandparents, learn from families in cooperative groups, and spend time in volunteer work, they are exposed to role models who are making a success of their families and work.

Interpersonal Skills. Because homeschooled children aren't segregated by age, they learn to work and learn with people of all different ages—notably, their siblings, but also those they interact within the community and their extended family.

Guided Development. Homeschooling parents want their children to be influenced primarily by adults, rather than by same-aged children who don't have the same maturity or wisdom of age.

Practical Skills. When children learn at home, they get hands-on "laboratory" exposure to the adult skills of home management, budgeting, comparison shopping, etiquette, child rearing, gardening, and operating a home business.

Specialization. Homeschoolers have the freedom to create a personalized curriculum to suit a particular child. As a result, a homeschooled child can follow his or her interests and learn to be an excellent gymnast, cook, musician, actor, technician, writer, computer programmer, or any of thousands of specialties that aren't available to those educated en masse.

Involvement. Parents want to be involved in the education of their children. Because the very nature of public schools excludes genuine parental involvement, homeschoolers find they have more interaction and influence over their children's education when they teach at home.

Belief. Many homeschoolers are committed to teaching their children from a particular worldview not shared by—or permitted to—educators in public schools. (Even when educators happen to share a parent's viewpoint on a controversial issue, they're prohibited by policy or law from sharing that viewpoint with students.) These parents

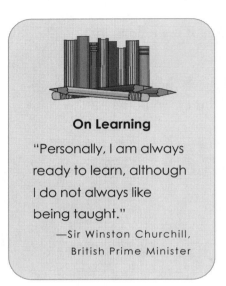

On Learning

"Personally, I am always ready to learn, although I do not always like being taught."

—Sir Winston Churchill, British Prime Minister

may have strong beliefs about theology, political issues, or academic approaches that they wish to integrate into their curriculum. For example, parents who are particularly sensitive to environmental issues might incorporate their beliefs into a science curriculum. Christian parents might use the Parables to illuminate a discussion of the metaphorical elements of literature. Classical homeschoolers might integrate Latin or logic and reasoning into every element of their teaching.

There are lots of other, less obvious, reasons for homeschooling:

Equality. Homeschooled children aren't at risk for gender bias[2] or educator prejudice related to political and religious beliefs, ethnicity, or disability.

Drug-Free Education. Children with attention or behavioral disorders are under heavy pressure from educators to use behavior-altering drugs.[3] Homeschooling parents are better able to focus on the individual needs and interests of their children, and teach one-on-one, without drugging their children into submission.

Service. Homeschooling families have the freedom to get involved in community service. Homeschooled children interact with adults as they volunteer at soup kitchens, nursing homes and other care facilities, the YMCA, art museums, churches, and political organizations.

Attention. In any group, the children who get the most attention are those who are either the most outgoing, or the most badly behaved. Children who are at neither extreme can "disappear" in large groups. When they're taught at home, however, they get all the nurturing

From the Front Lines

"I am homeschooling because I think I can spend more one-on-one with my children. I also want my children to have a positive social life. We love to home-school. I haven't found a downside, and I'm sure I won't."

—Teresa Redd, homeschooling mother of two, South Carolina

they need for a quality education, without having to act out to get attention.

Independence. When they become responsible for their own education, children learn important self-management skills that prepare them well for college and the workplace.

Free Thought. Homeschooled children have the freedom to disagree with the teacher, without ending up in detention. They can explore philosophies, political systems, social issues, and religious faiths without being told, "We don't discuss such things here." They have the sovereignty to become free thinkers, liberated from the tight boundaries of the traditional classroom.

Work. Children who are homeschooled also learn valuable employment skills. They're free to work with their parents in a home-based business, and, in most localities, older children have the freedom and flexibility to take jobs in the afternoons, when their traditionally schooled peers are still in class.

Parental Education. Parents who teach, learn. You don't have to know everything to teach. Part of the joy of the experience is finding the answers together.

Access. Families in rural areas, inner-city areas, and even many suburban areas simply don't have access to high-quality traditional classrooms, and so believe their children are better taught at home. In some areas, in order to attend public school, children would have to spend three or more hours per day riding a school bus. In other areas, the local schools are so badly operated—or so challenged by socioeconomic problems—that their only real function is warehousing children. Par-

From the Front Lines

"Our children's education is more important than the labels they wear . . . academically, or on their clothes."

—Ellen and Mark Latimer, homeschooling parents

ents in either situation would be almost irresponsible to send their children off to school.

Self-Esteem. Ever heard a child shout "Look, Mom! No hands!"? Children love having their parents see their accomplishments. And there's no better esteem builder than a high-five from Dad when a child works through a difficult math problem or a hug from Mom when that child masters a tricky chord sequence on the piano.

Scheduling. Some families simply don't mesh with the public-school year. Military families, families where a parent has vacation time that doesn't correspond with the school calendar, families that are frequently relocated, and families that spend time on the road for work or family commitments can't afford to bend their own obligations around the school's scheduling demands. Education simply is not "one size fits all." Homeschooling families range from migrant farm workers and long-distance truckers, to those raising Olympic gymnasts and Broadway stars. Their children's academic lives have to wrap around other commitments; the children are better off if they learn as they go.

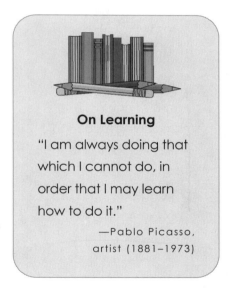

On Learning

"I am always doing that which I cannot do, in order that I may learn how to do it."

—Pablo Picasso, artist (1881–1973)

Finally, part of the motivation to homeschool arises out of a desire to escape the negatives of public education.[4] Some of the primary concerns include:

Class size. For decades now, public-school teachers have been complaining of overcrowded classrooms and unmanageable class sizes. Homeschooled kids have a student-teacher ratio that public schoolers can only dream about.

Understaffing. There's hardly a school district in the United States that has enough teachers to fill the classrooms. Emergency credentialing means teachers who don't meet even minimum standards of training are in front of classes of students. Public schools claim they are understaffed, underfunded, and overburdened. Why add to the problem?

Safety. Violence, weapons offenses, abduction, molestation, and other random acts against children don't occur when children are safe in their parents' care.

Socialization. There's no Lord-of-the-Flies negative socialization going on when parents maintain order and discipline in their homes. Homeschooled children are less susceptible to the tyranny of gossip, bullying, teasing, cruelty, cliquishness, hallway violence, racism, and bigotry. Their education is about academics, and about becoming adults. It has little to do with learning to appease the class bully.

From the Front Lines

"Why do I homeschool? I'm teaching my son to be *truly* social, to interact with people of all sorts and ages, not just thirty-some other kids his same age."

—Pamala Collins, homeschooling mother of one, Southern California

Indoctrination. One of the objectives of mass education—in any society—is to indoctrinate children with the "right" sort of thinking. Homeschoolers are less susceptible to those whose ambition is the social regulation of children. In fact, the original homeschoolers were the anti-establishment "flower children" of the 1960s who homeschooled—at least in part—to free their children from what they perceived as an oppressive "establishment" indoctrination.[5] Modern homeschoolers, no matter their political viewpoint, are unaffected by the mass indoctrination that eradicates creativity and free thought, and creates in its place unquestioning worker bees.

Peer Pressure. Homeschoolers aren't pressured to abuse drugs or alcohol. They aren't influenced by their schoolmates to cheat, commit crimes, wear unacceptable clothing, tattoo themselves, or pierce themselves. Dating is more carefully planned and supervised, and locker-room talk doesn't influence dating behavior. There are no homeschooling "gangs," and homeschooled children don't tend to get hysterical about not owning the "right" athletic shoes. In short, homeschoolers are already nonconformists, and don't need to shave their heads to demonstrate their individuality.

Assessment Culture. While public-schooled students spend hours and hours preparing for standardized, state-mandated examinations, homeschooled children are actually learning and growing.

Values. The teaching of morality may be the single most controversial aspect of public education. Fear of lawsuits, avoidance of controversy, and a simple disagreement about what constitutes "moral choice" leaves public education at odds with the values of many homeschooling families. It's a problem without a public-school solution, for even the avoidance of moral discussion teaches children that morality and values are unimportant—or unmentionable. Homeschoolers, believing otherwise, are free to incorporate their moral values into every academic subject.

On Education

"As for money, the relationship between it and effective schools has been studied to death. The unanimous conclusion is that there is no connection between school funding and school performance."

—John Chubb and Terry Moe, Brookings Institution scholars (1990)

How Many Families Homeschool?

There's no central government agency that collects homeschooling statistics, and homeschoolers—being an independent lot—aren't prone to volunteer them.[6] Moreover, lots of homeschooled children are involved in public or private schools at least part of the day, which skews any statistic. Nevertheless, several individuals and organizations have taken a stab at finding numbers. Brian Ray—who has been compiling homeschooling data longer than any other researcher—estimates that there were 1.5 to 1.9 million homeschoolers in the United States in 2001, a number that's growing by 7 to 15 percent annually.[7] Another researcher, Karl M. Bunday, has collected and analyzed homeschooling data from around the world, and estimates the U.S. homeschooling population at 2 percent of all school-aged children.[8] (In Canada, Bunday says, homeschoolers account for about 1 percent of the population, and he cites similarly high figures for other English-speaking countries.[9]) At the low end, a U.S. Department of Education study put the 1995–1996 total at nearly 750,000; a number that's questionable because it comes from figures provided by school districts themselves.[10] A newer study puts the number at 850,000.[11]

If Ray's numbers are accurate, at 1.7 million, homeschooled children make up a bigger segment of the U.S. population than all the school-age children in every U.S. state but eight.[12]

Research related to the number of home-educated children is available on the Numbers page of the Homeschool Steps Web site at *<www.homeschoolsteps.com/seealso/number.htm>*.

For More Information

For more information related to educational research and home education, visit the research section of the Homeschool Steps Web site, *<www.homeschoolsteps.com/seealso/research.htm>*.

Does Homeschooling Work?

Homeschooled children excel in every measure of educational success. They read more than public-schooled kids. They watch less television.[13] They win academic competitions.[14] They attend college.[15] They find jobs.[16] And even though vast numbers of children are homeschooled simply because they were failing to get an education in the public-school system, homeschoolers nearly always do better on standardized tests than do their public-schooled peers.[17] They progress more quickly.[18] And the longer they're homeschooled, the more they excel.[19]

The best evidence? Kids who are successfully homeschooled say they intend to teach their own children at home.[20] What better measure of success is there than having teenaged children who want to emulate their parents?

And How Much Does It Cost?

Relax. Homeschooling is free—or it can be. But if you have the interest or the resources, you can spend an awful lot. On average, homeschoolers spend $546 annually on each child for educational materials and services.[21] But the Internet and public libraries make it possible to build an effective, comprehensive curriculum at no cost.[22]

Self-Test

The first step to becoming a successful homeschooler is to think through your own beliefs about education, and to enumerate your reasons for teaching your children at home.

There's no "right" answer to these test questions. Each family will have different responses:

1. In general, what does "homeschooling" mean for our family?
    - ❏   A formal school-like educational program
    - ❏   A less-structured form of at-home education
    - ❏   A combination of public/private school and education at home

2. Why would we homeschool?
    - ❏   I think my child will get a better education at home.
    - ❏   My child needs or deserves individual attention.
    - ❏   I believe homeschooling will improve the quality of our family life.
    - ❏   I want my children to have more interaction with adult family members.
    - ❏   I want my children to develop the ability to interact with people of many ages.
    - ❏   I want to guide my children's development.
    - ❏   My child has skills or interests that can be better developed individually than in a group setting.
    - ❏   I want to be involved in my children's education.
    - ❏   I want my children to understand and practice our family's values and beliefs.
    - ❏   I am concerned that my children not be subject to bias or prejudice.
    - ❏   My child has attention-disorder or behavioral issues, and I don't want that child subjected to behavior-altering medications.
    - ❏   I want my children to be involved in our community.
    - ❏   My child is shy or disruptive, and I want that child to have positive individual attention.
    - ❏   I want my children to experience the independence of taking responsibility for their own education.
    - ❏   I want my children to learn to be independent thinkers.

❏ By studying at home, my children will be able to learn homemaking skills.

❏ My children need the flexibility of homeschooling for employment or other interests.

❏ I am excited about the possibility of learning alongside my children and improving or reinforcing my own education.

❏ Our family's location makes homeschooling a better choice than public school.

❏ My child thrives with parental attention.

❏ Our family's calendar requires flexibility.

❏ Other reasons:

_____

_____

_____

_____

3. We also have some concerns about public or private schools. Our family's concerns include:

❏ Class size

❏ Understaffing

❏ Safety

❏ Negative "socialization"

❏ Indoctrination

❏ Peer pressure

❏ Assessment culture

❏ Values we don't embrace

❏ Other concerns:

_____

_____

_____

Worksheet

Spend a few minutes thinking about your larger goals as a homeschooler. (This vision will provide encouragement for you on the days you feel discouraged about parenting and teaching.)

1. When you think about your child as an adult, what qualities would you hope to see in that person? (If you have more than one child, think about each child individually, and describe your hopes for each.)

   _____

   _____

   _____

   _____

   _____

2. In working toward those goals, do you envision your child being more positively influenced by you and your spouse, or by people outside your family?

   _____

   _____

   _____

   _____

   _____

3. You want your child to master academic basics, of course. What other interests or aptitudes does your child have? How could you help your child master those skills in a homeschool setting?

   _____

   _____

   _____

   _____

   _____

The Legal Gauntlet

Is Homeschooling Legal?

Practically speaking, homeschooling is legal. In some U.S. states, it's even recognized by statute or by judicial ruling as a fundamental right.[1]

In other states, though, parents still have to hurdle numerous, oppressive obstacles in order to legally teach their own children in their own homes. Worse, there are still people in positions of power who believe homeschooling is—or should be—illegal, and who wield that power to intimidate and harass homeschooling families.

In this chapter, you'll learn how to run the gauntlet of homeschooling laws in your state. You'll also learn how to organize the documentation you'll need to defend yourself against unwarranted accusations of educational neglect.

Is My State Friendly to Homeschoolers?

Alaska's homeschooling law is as wide open as its wilderness. New York's laws are so burdensome and time-consuming they actually compromise

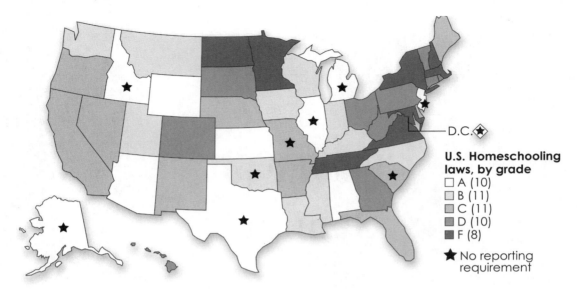

U.S. Homeschooling laws, by grade
- ☐ A (10)
- ☐ B (11)
- ☐ C (11)
- ☐ D (10)
- ☐ F (8)

★ No reporting requirement

Figure 2.1 *The Northeast has the most restrictive homeschooling laws; homeschooling is better accepted in the West.*

the ability of parents to educate their children. Laws in the other forty-eight states fall somewhere in the middle. We have graded each of the fifty states (and the District of Columbia) on the quality and openness of their homeschooling laws. Later in this chapter, and in Appendix A, we explain our rankings for each state.

How Did You Rank the States?

The grades we gave the states in Figure 2.1 were compiled using a matrix of factors, including a state's compulsory education ages, as well as its legal requirements for notification, parental qualifications, teaching format, required subjects, reporting, attendance, and testing and other academic assessments. In addition, we added points for a state's openness to allowing homeschoolers to participate—if they wish—in academic classes, activities, and interscholastic athletics through the public-school system.

States that impose fewer burdens and offer more academic opportunities score higher than states that have oppressive homeschooling laws and those that exclude homeschoolers from the public education resources available to other taxpaying citizens.

Why Worry About Compulsory Education Ages?

Each state requires children of certain ages to attend school. The later children are required to start school, and the earlier they are allowed to stop school, the more power you—as a homeschooling parent—have to teach your children as you see fit.

Compulsory education ages aren't much of an issue in states such as Idaho and Illinois where the laws aren't burdensome. But in states with oppressive laws (New Hampshire and Massachusetts, for example), a narrower age range gives parents more flexibility in the noncompulsory years.

Do All Homeschoolers Obey the Law?

Homeschooling Outside the United States

A large part of this chapter describes U.S. homeschooling laws. If you're homeschooling in Canada, Europe, Australia, or elsewhere outside the United States, you'll find legal help on our companion Web site, Homeschool Steps, at <www.homeschool steps.com/seealso international.htm>.

In states that have overly burdensome requirements, you'll find a number of parents who choose civil disobedience and refuse to cooperate with the law. These "underground" homeschoolers have to weigh the nuisance of cooperation against the possibility of being charged in court with educational neglect.

The case for civil disobedience is strengthened by the fact that, in many states, the legal demands placed on homeschooling families are little more than "nuisance" regulations that seem to exist solely to

On Compulsory Education

"The purpose of Compulsory Education is to deprive the common people of their commonsense."

—Gilbert Keith Chesterton

discourage parents from teaching their own children. In South Dakota, for example, state law rants on for several threatening paragraphs about how to deal with families that don't supply birth certificates for their children. New York law requires families to submit quarterly reports of the hours of instruction given to each child. In Hawaii, homeschoolers are required to produce a bibliography of all the books they use.

It's enough to make any reasonable person consider going underground. Think carefully, though, before you join the ranks of noncompliant homeschoolers. The penalty for breaking the law might be minimal (you'd be asked to cooperate with the homeschool law, for example) but it might also be ruinous. There is a remote possibility that failure to comply with the law could result in jail time for a parent or removal of children from the home. If you're considering breaking the law, remember the immortal words of Dirty Harry: "You've got to ask yourself one question: 'Do I feel lucky?'"

The advantage of compliance is that it gives you the legitimacy you need to work for change. Parents who practice civil disobedience tend to keep a low profile, and they make very poor advocates for creating better laws. Parents who stay scrupulously within the bounds of even the most outrageous laws have the legal standing to fight for better homeschooling conditions in their state.

What Kind of Notification Must I Give the State?

In several states, no notification is required. In these states (marked with a star in Figure 2.1), if you want to homeschool your child, you may go right ahead and do so, and you don't have to tell a soul. (If you're withdrawing children from public school, you will want, as a practical matter, to inform the school in writing that you're going to be teaching your children at home. Withdrawing without any notice might result in a visit from your state's child protective services workers and an accusation of educational neglect.) Other states have requirements that vary from a simple one-time declaration of intent, all the way to annual notarized applications requiring advance approval from local authorities.

What Is a Declaration of Intent?

It goes by different names in different states—affidavit of intent, request for exemption, application for excuse, or some similar designation. If you are required to notify the state of your intention to homeschool, it's wise to provide only the minimal information required by state or local law. If you provide more information, you're raising the bar for fellow homeschoolers who might be questioned for failing to give as many details as you gave.

If your state requires that you submit a particular form, contact your local school district office or your state department of education to obtain a form. If not, just write down the minimum information required by your state, sign the paper, and mail it in.

Consider going to the post office to send your notification "Return Receipt Requested." The return receipt costs less than two dollars and provides you with a dated confirmation notice, signed by the recipient.

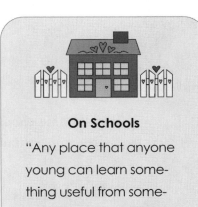

On Schools

"Any place that anyone young can learn something useful from someone with experience is an educational institution."

—Al Capp

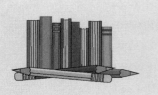

On Parental Rights

"We are opposed to state interference with parental rights and rights of conscience in the education of children as an infringement of the fundamental Democratic doctrine that the largest individual liberty consistent with the rights of others insures the highest type of American citizenship and the best government."

—Democratic National Platform (1892)

Am I Qualified to Teach My Child?

You probably meet the legal requirements to teach your children. Most states—thirty-two—set no minimum standard for parents to teach their own children. In ten other states, the requirement is only that the teaching parent have a high school diploma or some comparable academic qualification. (See the list later in this chapter to compare the different states.) Other states, though, require teaching certificates, bachelor's degrees, or supervision by various "qualified" people—onerous requirements that might motivate you to earn a college degree, if you don't already have one. The laws section of Appendix A describes parental qualification requirements for each state.

What you may really be wondering is whether you are *capable* of teaching your children. Worry not. Your children learned to walk and talk under your tutelage. You're entirely competent to teach them through their adolescent years. In fact, homeschooling researchers have found that parental "credentials" have no effect at all on how well homeschooled children perform on standardized tests.[2] We address concerns about effective teaching in more detail in Chapter 6.

Do I Have to Work Within a Particular School Format?

In about half of the states, there is no particular format to follow. Other states have a variety of restrictions and requirements, including registering or qualifying as a nonpublic school, a church school, or a private school, or educating under the auspices of an umbrella school or a homeschooling organization. Some states allow parents to choose from among two to four school formats, each with its own requirements. We describe format requirements for each state in Appendix A.

The most repressive school format law, in the state of New Hampshire, allows parents to teach only their own children, and then only by the agreement of educational authorities. Parents are required to teach using planned and supervised instructional activities, and must use a commercial curriculum and instruction.

Do I Have to Teach a Specific Sequence of Classes?

The vast majority of U.S. states have no requirements for the subjects you teach, or they require only a basic, generic list of academic subjects. In these states, you're pretty much free to teach whatever material you believe is best for your family.

At the other extreme, New York and Tennessee, and to a large degree, Pennsylvania, have extensive and highly detailed requirements for which subjects must be taught in the home at which times.

Even in states where there's no requirement, some families are more comfortable tracking their academic progress against state learning standards. If you wish to follow your state's academic requirements for public schools, you'll find a complete list of links to each state at our companion Homeschool Steps Web site, <*www.home schoolsteps.com/seealso/legal.htm*>.

What Reporting Requirements Must I Follow?

Reporting requirements are a close cousin to the school format requirement. Only eighteen states have no additional documentation requirements. In the other thirty-two states you are required to maintain or submit attendance or enrollment records, birth certificates, immunization records, calendars, assessment records, a portfolio of academic work, or various other records.

If you live in a state with reporting requirements, you'll want to set up a system for storing and maintaining documents.

For More Information

For more information on laws and legal issues related to home education, visit the legal section of the Homeschool Steps Web site at <www.homeschool steps.com/seealso /legal.htm>.

You'll save yourself headaches down the road if you keep all your homeschooling documentation safe in a single drawer or box that's kept on a high shelf, out of reach of little fingers. (Inexpensive, sturdy plastic file boxes are available at office supply and discount department stores.) Keep a separate file for each child's basic documentation: birth certificates, social security cards, immunization and health records, test results, and written assessments. (While you're at it, you might also wish to include fingerprint records and up-to-date photographs for each child. These documents are private, and needn't ever leave your possession.)

If you're required by your state to maintain attendance and/or curriculum logs, it's easy to add documentation to these folders as you progress through your homeschooling year. Alternatively, you might use specialized record-keeping software to track your homeschooling efforts by computer. (We list several of these software products at *<www.homeschoolsteps.com/seealso/records.htm>*.) Print out a weekly report for inclusion in your file.

Next, you'll want to create a yearly portfolio for each child. These portfolios do double duty: They give you and your child a sense of accomplishment as your homeschooling years pass by. They also provide persuasive documentation for school authorities, social workers, worried relatives, and others who question your child's academic progress.

How Do I Create a Portfolio?

There are three basic approaches to portfolio creation: files, notebooks, and electronic records. Some homeschoolers like to stick with one approach; others find that a combination of these methods works best.

The File Approach

The file approach is clean and simple: Each time your child produces a high-quality paper document, date it, and drop it into the file. Drawings, worksheets, essays, tests, math papers, reports—they all go in the file. Each school year, begin a new file for each child.

Photographs are another important component of the portfolio file. When your child creates a large piece of artwork (a wall mural, for example), cooks an unusually attractive meal, or makes a quilt, take a picture, and place the photographic record in the file portfolio.

You'll also want to include space in your file box for bulkier items such as audio- and videotapes of your child's performances and competitions.

The Notebook Approach

The notebook approach works well with older, more focused children who are able to take good care of their own documents. Provide your child with a sturdy notebook, a three-hole punch, and lots of markers and scrapbook materials. Work with your child to turn the portfolio into a work of art that organizes and showcases all the hard work he or she does throughout the year.

The Electronic Approach

The electronic approach is attractive to families with a high degree of computer literacy. You'll need the following tools: a personal computer,

a scanner, and a CD writer. Depending on your children's interests and your family's finances, you might also want to buy supplemental equipment such as an inexpensive digital camera, video recording and editing tools, and equipment and software for recording music.

Your child's electronic portfolio will consist of a homemade CD full of electronic documents such as research reports, essays, Web pages, musical compositions, video clips, photographs, and artwork.

The beauty of the electronic approach is that document storage is orderly, cheap, and permanent. The other advantage is that you can—quite inexpensively—send a copy of the CD to grandparents, college admissions offices, and anyone else who might want to know more about the quality of the education your child is receiving.

How Long Must I Homeschool Each Year?

In Chapter 4, we introduce fifty different homeschooling approaches, many of which operate under the theory that children are constantly learning and seldom require formal, traditional education. If you're an involved parent, there's technically no time when you're *not* educating your children.

Unfortunately, the law doesn't always take such a progressive view of education. All but a few states require that homeschools be in session a certain number of days and/or hours each year, or that you teach a period of time "equivalent" to the public schools—a vague requirement that could be interpreted by a hostile administrator or judge to mean that you must actually teach your children during the precise hours that children in your local public school are being taught.

In most locations, your school year need not correspond with the public-school calendar. You might, for example, homeschool formally from January through September, and take a break from October through December. You might school "year round," but teach only four days a week. You might teach by a two-weeks-on, one-week-off schedule. You might take an Unschooling approach (see Chapter 4) and *never* conduct a formal academic program. But operating under an unusual calendar can create paperwork problems if your state has strict reporting and notification requirements.

Failure to teach according to the local public-school calendar can present some additional problems—particularly in towns that have high truancy levels or few homeschoolers. A homeschooled child taking a midday walk risks being picked up by a truant officer in some locations. Attendance laws in the state of Georgia actually require children to be in the home during school hours unless they are carrying with them a written "excuse."

Fortunately, it's not all bad news. In most states there's little real enforcement of inflexible attendance laws, and most homeschoolers tend to treat them quite casually—even in locations that require the submission of attendance records.

Should I Have My Child Tested?

If state law requires it, you may have no choice but to have your kids tested. In states where you do have the option, there are several philosophical issues you should consider before signing your kids up for standardized tests. Testing gets a big thumbs-down from most people in the homeschooling community. Although homeschooled children tend to do better on standardized tests than their public-schooled counterparts,[3] many homeschooling families object to the very idea of standardized testing on several grounds:

* It doesn't test real-world knowledge.

* It requires all children to know the same information at the same time, and doesn't allow for individual children to develop different interests at different times.

* It's administered in an unfamiliar environment hostile to homeschoolers.

* Homeschoolers can't "teach to the test" (or flat-out cheat) as many public-schoolteachers have been found to do,[4] and so the tests inherently favor public-schooled children.

* The entire test culture is inimical to true education. Doing well on a test doesn't mean one is educated, and excessive reliance on testing edges out a more important emphasis on genuine learning.

In most states (New Mexico recently became the twenty-eighth) homeschooled children aren't required to take academic tests. Two others (Washington and North Carolina) require testing, but don't require parents to submit the test results to anyone. Some states require testing under one school format, but not under another.

In other states, children have to sit for standardized tests in at least three different years, and some states require homeschooled children to take a standardized examination every single year of their schooling.

Who Pays for the Tests?

In general, tests are administered through the school district at no cost to the parents. In some states, however, homeschooling parents are required to pay for the test, which is administered through the school district or through a private testing service located by the parent. In other states, parents can choose whether to test through the public-school system or through a private organization.

More information about private testing services is available on the Legal page of our companion Web site, <*www.homeschoolsteps.com/seealso/testing.htm*>.

What Happens If My Child Scores Poorly?

In ten states, the legal consequences of poor test scores range from remedial to draconian. In North Dakota and Minnesota, for example, a child who scores below a certain standard must undergo a professional assessment. North Dakota parents also are required to develop and adhere to a plan of remediation.

On Education by Government

"If the only motive was to help people who could not afford education, advocates of government involvement would have simply proposed tuition subsidies."

—Milton Friedman, winner of the 1976 Nobel Prize in economics

It could be worse. In Colorado, South Dakota, Oregon, Tennessee, New Hampshire, Virginia, West Virginia, and New York, a child who doesn't achieve sufficiently high marks on standardized examinations is required to enroll in public or private school. In our rankings, we called these the "Sword of Damocles" states (after the Roman courtier who sat at a banquet with a sword suspended over his head by a single hair, to show him the perilous nature of his fortunate life). Homeschooling families in Sword of Damocles states live with the fear of losing their "fortunate life" over a bad test score.

If you live in any of the other forty states, there is no legal consequence to having your child score poorly on standardized tests.

Is There an Alternative to Standardized Tests?

Alternatives to standardized tests exist—and sometimes the alternative isn't even optional. Connecticut, for example, doesn't test homeschoolers, but does require parents to submit an annual portfolio of their children's work for evaluation. Hawaii, Maryland, and Pennsylvania also require alternative assessments, and Minnesota requires additional assessments for parents who don't possess certain teaching credentials.

In most other states that require standardized testing, parents can choose instead to have their children professionally evaluated in lieu of testing. Generally, these evaluations must be conducted by a teacher who is certified in that state. The evaluations usually involve interviews with the children and portfolio reviews. Parents bear the cost of these evaluations, and teachers who conduct them typically charge from $35 to $75 per child per year.

Am I Allowed to Use Public Schools as a Resource?

Iowa is the model state for public-school access. It allows something called "dual enrollment," meaning that children there can officially be classed as homeschoolers, and still have pick-and-choose access to public-school resources. A spokesman for the state department of education told us that some Iowa homeschoolers dual-enroll their children for recess and lunch only! Washington and Wyoming have similarly liberal access policies.

Other states permit dual enrollment in only some, or none, of the three major resources: academic classes, extracurricular activities, and interscholastic sports. South Dakota's access law is unexpectedly helpful to homeschoolers: Public schools there are required to lend textbooks comparable to those used in public schools to homeschooled students.

There is a growing trend across the United States for alternative-education programs, which are not, technically, homeschooling, but which do provide a separate and distinct alternative to standard public schools. When children enroll in these programs, the district receives state and federal funding, and students are generally subject to the same testing and attendance requirements as mainstream public-school students. When these programs are flexible, and when they permit a high degree of parental involvement, they can be an attractive supplement to traditional homeschooling programs.

A few states allow homeschooled students to earn diplomas when they enroll for their senior year, or when they earn sufficient college credit.

And sometimes—even in states that are generally hostile to homeschooling—you'll find administrators at your local public school who are supportive, and who will bend rules to lend out textbooks, educational materials, and other resources to aid you in teaching your child at home.

What Is the Homeschooling Law in My State?

The following list gives a brief summary of the law in each state. Letter grades are based on a combination of several factors, including requirements for testing, parental qualifications, notification, access, and reporting. (For a detailed look at each state's homeschooling laws, and an explanation of how we assigned grades, see Appendix A or visit <*www.homeschoolsteps.com/seealso/states.htm*>.)

Legally Speaking

Appendix A contains a breakdown of home-schooling laws in each state, along with complete grades, and an explanation of how we ranked each factor in arriving at our grades.

You'll find this information, and more, at <www.homeschool steps.com/seealso /states.htm>.

Alabama   A

Alabama is the state least deserving of its high grade, because while it permits families to "sneak into" homeschooling under a vague "church school" format, it doesn't openly acknowledge homeschooling. Families that wish to homeschool without affiliating with an existing church must either invent a church of their own in order to homeschool, or conform to untenable private school laws that are strict enough to put Alabama into the bottom 5 percent of homeschool-friendly states.

Alaska   A+

The model state. Alaska's homeschooling law was an after-the-fact acknowledgment that families are going to homeschool no matter what the law says. Legislators decided the best course is to just leave homeschoolers alone. Bravo!

Arizona   A

Arizona law simply does most things right: No testing, no loathsome parental qualifications, no nuisance regulations.

Arkansas   C+

Interesting take on testing: In Arkansas, you can test under the auspices of an approved homeschooling cooperative, rather than through the public schools. And it's required for only three years. The state also awards high school graduation diplomas to anyone who public schools for their senior year. The downside? Nuisance regulations related to notification.

California   C

California's nuisance legislation is structured to pressure families into "independent study" programs through the auspices of public schools.

Colorado   D+

It's that Sword of Damocles testing law that brings Colorado's score down. As a matter of fairness, will someone force poorly performing public-school students into homeschool?

Connecticut   D

Submit a mandatory annual portfolio for evaluation, and hope that whoever is looking at it finds the portfolio acceptable.

Delaware   C

Delaware imposes burdensome regulations related to the format of your homeschool.

District of Columbia   B

The district is actually contemplating lowering its compulsory education age from the worst in the nation to worse yet: compulsory preschool. Fortunately, homeschooling laws are fairly progressive.

Florida   C–

It's that annual testing thing. Luckily, there's a "certified teacher evaluation" alternative—but still, you have to play along year after year.

Georgia   D+

Test every three years, and submit monthly attendance forms to the local superintendent. Like you have nothing better to do.

Hawaii   D

Bizarre documentation laws. Not only do you have to keep records of everything you do; you're also required to keep a bibliography of the books you use. Who came up with that one?

Idaho   A–

The only downside: a vague requirement that homeschooled children receive an "equivalent" education. Otherwise, Idaho is a great state for homeschooling.

Illinois   A+
Near-perfect homeschooling laws. Minor glitch: excessive regulation of the subject matter. But since the regulation is unenforced, live with it. Illinois is a homeschooling oasis in the northern Midwest.

Indiana   B
Access laws are hostile to homeschoolers. Otherwise, Indiana has fairly moderate homeschooling laws.

Iowa   B–
Model access laws—you can enroll your child in Lunch, if you wish—but the notification laws are vexatious.

Kansas   A–
Operate as a non-accredited private school and you're home free.

Kentucky   B+
Not too hot; not too cold. Compliance is fairly easy, and there's no testing requirement.

Louisiana   B
Operating as a private school requires approval, but it's better than any of the alternatives.

Maine   C+
Operation as a private school is vastly less oppressive than the home-schooling option, but it requires teaching "at least two unrelated students." Homeschoolers in Maine organize as private schools with classrooms in each home to comply with this nuisance regulation.

Maryland   F
Maryland has an oppressive homeschooling law, one that has the effect of shutting out families who don't have the money or the inclination to teach via approved correspondence or church schools. All

Maryland unschoolers are engaging in civil disobedience. The only redeeming feature of the Maryland homeschooling law is that families aren't subject to mandatory testing or parental qualification standards.

Massachusetts   F
And you thought filling out the state income tax return was painful! Massachusetts's notification regulations are the worst in the nation. And failure to get approval from an unregulated power-mongering local authority could force your child into the school system.

Michigan   A+
Virtually no homeschooling restrictions. It's hard to fault this law!

Minnesota   F
Parental qualifications, notification, reporting, testing . . . Minnesota strikes out on almost every count. Elect some legislators from Michigan.

Mississippi   B+
Barely misses an A because of the annual notification requirements.

Missouri   C+
No testing, but record-keeping requirements are a nuisance.

Montana   B
No testing, but numerous minor compliance laws keep Montana out of the A range.

Nebraska   C-
Reporting requirements are onerous. The bright side? No testing.

Nevada   C-
Nevada's parental qualification law seems ridiculous on the face of it, but the option of consulting with a three-year veteran homeschooler

is, frankly, a good idea. Most homeschooling families are happy to lend a helping hand.

New Hampshire   F

Tote that barge; lift that bail. New Hampshire's homeschooling laws are oppressive. Testing, documentation, approvals . . . Yes, you can comply, but it'll take a lot of energy.

New Jersey   A

New Jersey's access policy is hostile to homeschoolers who wish to take advantage of public-school programs and classes. Otherwise, it's one of the most homeschool-friendly states in the nation.

New Mexico   C

Woo-hoo! No more standardized testing! Beyond that, state homeschooling regulations are still dismal.

New York   F

Sshhh! Don't tell 'em about parental qualification laws! It's the only thing New York *doesn't* regulate.

North Carolina   B+

Annual standardized testing, but test results are not submitted or inspected. Sleep soundly.

North Dakota   F

Those parental qualifications are an outrage. If you don't meet stringent requirements, you're subject to weekly monitoring!

Ohio   D–

Too bad you have to start so young and continue for so long. Compulsory ages in Ohio are six to eighteen. At least you get an alternative to annual standardized testing.

Oklahoma   **B**

Oklahoma is least deserving of its weak score. Homeschoolers are mostly left alone, and a wide compulsory age range doesn't cause much trouble for homeschoolers who needn't report in.

Oregon   **C–**

Oregon has a subjective standard for passing test scores, which brings its rating down dramatically.

Pennsylvania   **D–**

Only one thing to be thankful for: Compulsory schooling doesn't begin until age eight. Whatever you do, *don't* move to New York!

Rhode Island   **D–**

Local school authorities have the power to make capricious and oppressive demands of homeschooling families. There is, fortunately, an appeals process, but lack of statewide standards gives local authorities broad power to harass and restrict homeschooling families.

South Carolina   **C**

Document, document, document. And yes, you really must join a large homeschooling organization.

South Dakota   **D–**

South Dakota law has an unnatural obsession with birth certificates. Better have one. The state also has a subjective "less than satisfactory" standard for passing exams.

Tennessee   **F**

Tennessee's "nuisance" homeschooling laws virtually demand civil disobedience of homeschoolers. The three recognized homeschooling options are unduly burdensome for the average American homeschooling family. The Home School Legal Defense Association outlines a fourth option: Operate as a satellite campus of a nonrecognized church school based on the assertion that the church-related school option unconstitutionally excludes certain religions.

Texas   A–
It's the subjective "bona fide homeschool" requirement that keeps Texas from being an A+.

Utah   B+
No mandatory testing is a big plus. Use the free time to hike a canyon.

Vermont   D
Approval? I need approval to homeschool? Thumbs way down.

Virginia   F
If you qualify to school under the tightly defined church school option, you're home free. For everyone else: bummer. Virginia needs to take a lesson from Alabama in the concept of freedom of religion.

Washington   B–
Washington State's testing requirements are unenforced. Interviews with homeschoolers suggest a high degree of compliance, nevertheless.

West Virginia   D–
It's the testing thing. If your kids' scores fall into the 40th percentile for three consecutive years, you're required to enroll them in school.

Wisconsin   B–
Wisconsin's restrictive compulsory school ages and annoying annual notification forms keep it from being an "A" state.

Wyoming   A
Full access to public-school resources guaranteed by law. And no testing!

If I Run into Legal Problems, How Do I Get Help?

You might encounter legal problems from three sources:

* Public-school administrators
* Law-enforcement agencies and social workers
* Disgruntled family members, neighbors, or acquaintances

Conflict with public-school administrators is unlikely if you're in full compliance with state homeschooling laws. Disputes arise when you and the administrator disagree about whether or not you're complying. Some parents have had problems, for example, when they've withdrawn a child from public school, and the administrator has demanded that the child continue to attend. Parents and administrators also butt heads when states have oppressive legal requirements for documentation, testing, and notification, and the two parties disagree about whether a family's documentation is in compliance with the law.

Law-enforcement agencies, truant officers, and social workers can be a source of difficulty when they believe that a child is truant or that a family is failing to properly educate a child. More than a few parents have had to answer legal charges of educational neglect when, in fact, they've been faithfully teaching their children in the home.

The most common legal problem for homeschoolers today is having a noncustodial parent or a grandparent dispute a parent's decision to homeschool. It's also possible to face legal problems with neighbors, coworkers, or others who don't like to see your child out of school during school hours.

In any of these situations, you and your family could find yourself facing a judge or a law-enforcement officer if you haven't taken reasonable precautions to protect yourself.

Obviously, preventing legal trouble is better—and cheaper—than battling it. Protect your family by preparing in advance for the possibility of legal difficulties. You have several options:

1. Start with a good offense. Be friendly with your neighbors, make social contacts with local school authorities, get politically active, volunteer in your community, know your local law-enforcement officers, and be involved in your church, temple, or mosque. The wider your social circle, the more support you'll have if things ever get difficult for you or your family.

It's also to your benefit to maintain the exterior trappings of a functional, socially involved family. Keep a reasonably clean home and yard. Be sure your children are appropriately dressed and reasonably clean. Maintain at least minimal educational records. Have your children receive regular physical examinations and dental care. Cover all the basics. No matter how kind and decent you are, there'll be someone, somewhere, who doesn't like you or your lifestyle. Don't give anyone a ready-made excuse to complicate your life.

2. Know the law. Spend time learning about your legal rights and responsibilities. As part of this effort, we strongly advise that you become involved in both a statewide and a local homeschooling support group, and that you participate in a strong online support group. You can find out more about your legal rights and your responsibilities in Appendix A and also on our companion Web site, <*www.homeschoolsteps.com/seealso/legal.htm*>. You'll find more about support groups in Chapter 10.

3. Be prepared. Locate a local attorney who is supportive of homeschooling and who understands educational and family law. Consider finding a lawyer who shares your religious faith, your po-

The Politics of Education

"In all countries, in all centuries, the primary reason for government to set up schools is to undermine the politically weak. . . . The core is religious intolerance. The sides simply change between the Atheists, Catholics, Protestants, Unitarians, etc., depending whether you are talking about the Soviet Union, the Austro-Hungarian Empire, America, etc."

—Marshall Fritz (1999), founder, the Separation of School & State Alliance

litical views, or any other factor that might make your family subject to questioning by people who have a different set of values. If home-schooling ever becomes a legal issue for you, you don't want to have to defend yourself to your own lawyer!

As part of your research, you should also keep on hand contact information for reporters or editors at your local newspaper, news radio station, and television stations. Not only is this information useful if you're thinking of promoting a homeschooling event; it's also useful if you ever get an unwelcome knock on the door from a zealous visitor who wants to enter your home, interview your children, or examine your files.

4. **Have backup.** Consider joining the Home School Legal Defense Association <*www.hslda.org*> or getting involved with other organizations that defend civil liberties.[5] In recent years, the HSLDA has been at the forefront of changing and clarifying laws related to home education, as well as defending families whose right to homeschool is challenged by educational authorities. Membership is an investment; as of 2002, membership costs $100 a year.

There are a couple of things you'll want to consider, however, before sending in your membership fee. First, the HSLDA has fairly rigid standards for whom it will accept as a member. The membership application requires you to certify that you are using "a clearly organized program of education to instruct [y]our children," and that you will "keep records of each child's educational progress." If you are unschooling, or educating under any sort of philosophy that doesn't fit the "clearly organized" standards of the HSLDA, you're not eligible for membership. Moreover, the HSLDA does not defend homeschooling in custody disputes between parents—the legal area that causes problems for the largest number of homeschoolers.[6]

The second consideration is this: The HSLDA is prominent politically and in the media as a mouthpiece for the homeschooling movement. This high-profile position has embroiled it in a great deal of controversy with parents who argue that the Association's conservative politics are not representative of the wide spectrum of homeschoolers. If you'd like to know more about the debate surrounding the HSLDA, you'll find an extensive collection of information at *<www.homeschoolsteps.com/seealso/hslda.htm>*.

Self-Test

This test is not a "to-do" list, nor is it a recommended approach to homeschooling. It's only an evaluation of how likely it is that your family might encounter legal difficulties over your homeschooling choices.

1. In general, how familiar are you with your local homeschooling laws?
   - ❏ A. I don't know what the homeschooling law is in my locality.
   - ❏ B. I've talked with people and asked questions, but I've never read the law.
   - ❏ C. I've read the law, but don't remember all the details.
   - ❏ D. I'm well versed in our local homeschooling laws.

2. How would you evaluate your family's vulnerability to legal problems? (Check all that apply)
   - ❏ A. We have already had some encounters with social workers or law enforcement over our decision to homeschool.
   - ❏ B. We have already had difficulties with family members, neighbors, coworkers, or other people about our decision to homeschool.
   - ❏ C. We have already encountered problems with local school authorities over homeschooling.
   - ❏ D. We have a pretty good working relationship with all of the people listed above, and don't anticipate any problems.

3. How would you describe your family's current or expected homeschooling approach? (Chapter 3 discusses this topic in detail.)
   - ❏ A. We believe in unschooling, child-led learning, or other approaches that don't bear much resemblance to traditional school.
   - ❏ B. We use an eclectic homeschooling approach that is somewhat casual and undocumented, but also involves some structure and use of traditional curriculum materials.
   - ❏ C. We use a strict "school-at-home" approach with commercial curriculum and well documented records.
   - ❏ D. We are, or will be, enrolled in an alternative education program through the public schools, or working through the auspices of a state-approved umbrella school or organization, and we're fully compliant with all their requirements.

(continues)

4. How carefully does—or will—your family comply with local homeschooling laws?

❑ A. Our state has burdensome laws that conflict with our belief about the duty of parents to educate their own children, and we don't intend to comply at all.

❑ B. We will notify local educational authorities that we're homeschooling, but won't have any other interaction with the state.

❑ C. We will try to comply with the law completely.

❑ D. Our jurisdiction has progressive homeschooling laws, and there's virtually nothing to comply with.

Scoring: For each A response, give yourself 3 points; for each B response, 2 points; for each C response, 1 point.

8 to 15: Your family is at high risk for legal difficulties. Be sure all your documentation is in order, and have at hand contact information for your attorney, local media, and the HSLDA. Give serious consideration to moving to a location that has laws more in line with your philosophies.

4 to 7: You're at some risk. Take reasonable precautions, put effort into developing strong social contacts, and be sure to maintain good records.

0 to 3 points: Your risk of encountering legal problems related to homeschooling is low. Take a deep breath, and focus all your energy on your kids.

Worksheet

If you scored from 6 to 15 points on the self-test, the following legal worksheet will assist you in keeping useful information in one place, and help protect you and your family from legal complications.

1. Laws: Summarize the requirements of your state's homeschooling laws (see Appendix A for a rundown of laws in every state).

_____

_____

_____

_____

_____

_____

_____

2. Records: What documents and records must you maintain, and where are they now being kept? (Consider birth certificates, immunization and medical records, academic records, etc.)

_____

_____

_____

_____

_____

_____

_____

_____

(continues)

3. Legal advisors: If your family doesn't have a homeschooling-friendly attorney, place some phone calls over the next few days to make inquiries. Begin by contacting your local bar association referral service (it's in the yellow pages). In addition, ask for referrals from one of the support groups listed in Chapter 10. Ask potential attorneys about their experience with family law, education law, and the local social services agency. When you have located an attorney who expresses an interest in homeschooling families, record contact information below. If you are a member of the HSLDA or any other legal support service, include that contact information here as well:

_____

_____

_____

_____

_____

4. Support contacts: List names and phone numbers of supportive relatives, neighbors, and friends who would provide backup in the event your family ever confronted legal problems with homeschooling. Include contact information for successful homeschooling families of your acquaintance, supportive educators, and clergy. In addition, list contact information for local media outlets and homeschool-friendly journalists and reporters, who can assist you in the unlikely event your family is ever confronted with hostile social workers, police officers, or school administrators.

_____

_____

_____

_____

_____

_____

Teaching Strategies

How Can I Teach Effectively?

Good teaching is three parts enthusiasm, one part strategy, and one part knowledge. In this and the following chapter, we help you get enthusiastic about teaching by presenting a wide variety of teaching strategies, approaches, and philosophies. Between the sixty teaching strategies in this chapter and the fifty approaches and philosophies in Chapter 4, you'll soon be tripping over yourself in your excitement to try them out on your own family.

What Are "Teaching Strategies"?

Simply put: Strategies are tools for teaching. They're the building blocks for the fifty teaching approaches we discuss in the next chapter. These sixty teaching strategies, listed below by category, will provide all kinds of interesting twists to the way your family educates.

How Do I Use These Strategies?

We introduce each of the strategies below and then explain how to implement each strategy in your educational program. We also list related strategies, along with related approaches and philosophies, which will be covered in depth in Chapter 4.

The sixty strategies are grouped into six categories, which are listed below and shown in more detail in Table 3.1.

* Administrative Strategies: How to administer an education at home. The focus is on planning and developing your homeschool program.

* Cognitive Strategies: Help your children work their brains. These strategies are mind expanding.

* Experiential Strategies: These are the strategies that get your hands dirty. Learn how to get out and experience the world.

* Input Strategies: Give the brain something to remember. These strategies focus on ways to get information into your kids' minds.

* Output Strategies: Show me the learning! These fun strategies for generating visible results will give your kids something to brag about.

* Motivational Strategies: Finally, three terrific ways to motivate your children to learn!

Adjust your bifocals. It's time to strategize!

Administrative Strategies

The first three strategies in this category describe ways to homeschool in spite of scheduling problems. These strategies are especially helpful to families that spend a great deal of time outside of the

Table 3.1   Sixty Teaching Strategies for Homeschooling Families

Administrative Strategies (pages 46–59)	Cognitive Strategies (pages 59–72)	Experiential Strategies (pages 72–82)
After-Schooling	Concept Mapping	Case Studies
Family Nights	Creativity	Field Trips
Road School	Critical Reading	Interviewing
Build-It-Yourself	Graphic Organizers	Kitchen Science
Collaborative Learning	Listening Skills	Labs and Demos
Correspondence Courses	Logic and Rhetoric	Learning Centers
Learning Environments	Metaphors	Library Skills
Lesson Planning	Outlining and Note-Taking	Manipulatives
Online Classes	Scientific Method	Research Techniques
Placement Testing	Socratic Questioning	
Rubrics	Writing to Learn	
Scope-and-Sequence		
Traditional Curriculum		
Umbrella Schools		
Input Strategies (pages 83–92)	**Output Strategies (pages 92–105)**	**Motivational Strategies (pages 105–108)**
Copywork	Evaluations	Awards
Dictation	Broadcasting	College Prep
Discussions	Journaling	Competitions
Expert Resources	Narration	
Forums	Nature Diaries	
Lectures	Notebooking	
Literature-Based Learning	Portfolio Building	
Media-Supported Learning	Presentations	
Memorization	Scrapbooking	
Web-Based Education	Self-Publishing	
Worksheets	Theses and Dissertations	
	Timelining	

home, as well as to single-parent families, two-earner families, or families with a sick or disabled parent who feel compelled to enroll their children in public or private school.

The other administrative strategies in this section will be of most interest to conventional homeschoolers who are focused on traditional academics, lesson planning, and curriculum design.

After-Schooling

For families that must private- or public-school their children, After-Schooling—the practice of educating your children outside of school hours, on holidays and weekends—may be your only home-school option. Some families homeschool after school hours; some limit their homeschooling to school holidays and vacations.

Methods: When children work hard during the day, after-schooling time needs to be fun and joy-filled. Consider using informal and un-schooling approaches in order to keep it light. If your children are in school full-time, you may want to focus your After-Schooling on a single subject. Fill in academic gaps, share your religious faith, or en-rich your kids' education with additional investigations into their current topic of study. You might want to begin with a flexible corre-spondence course, or supplement the education of your gifted child with intellectually stimulating activities.

Related Strategies (explained elsewhere in this chapter): Corres-pondence Courses, Family Nights

Related Approaches (explained in Chapter 4): Hybrid, Scouting, Scripture Study, Unit Studies, Values

Family Nights

A change of pace for homeschoolers, and a boon to part-time, After-Schooling, and holiday homeschoolers, Family Nights are a fun way to teach your children and strengthen your family.

Methods: Set aside one night a week for fun and learning. No in-terruptions from phones, computers, television, or PlayStation al-lowed. Family Night is the chance for the kids to shine. They can teach a lesson, show off their educational progress, practice a presen-tation, or simply share a new idea. Use this night to try out a new recipe, play family board games, or practice a song. Don't let it become "family fight night"; keep things upbeat and happy. As a supplement to Family Nights, also consider family councils, marriage councils, and private interviews. Bonus: Any of these practices keep working parents involved in their children's education.

Related Strategies: After-Schooling, Discussions, Evaluations (Forensics), Presentations (see also Chapter 8's discussion of fathers and homeschooling)

Related Approaches: Cognitivism, Peer Tutoring, Scouting, Scripture Study, Values

Road School

School on the road is the strategy of choice for everyone from soccer moms to families who live on the road full time. Being away from home—even if only for the afternoon—can still be educational.

Methods: In the car, reading is the natural choice. Other educational automobile activities to keep your kids actively learning: spelling practice, oral book reports, discussions, a bag full of beads and yarn to string together for math problems, audiotapes (books on tape, biographies, and other educational tapes can be borrowed from most public libraries), activity books, educational card games, verbal games, and games that promote fitness. Have kids read spelling words and other problems into a tape recorder and play it back on the road. Make maps to all your destinations. One family of successful "roads scholars" uses individual binders with pockets for worksheets, writing tools, research notes, spelling lists, and math pages. Mom organizes these binders early in the week, and every time they're out the door, the binders travel along. The kids keep extensive journals filled with drawings and notes about the family's travels.

Related Strategies: Field Trips, Notebooking, Umbrella Programs

Related Approaches: Constructivism, Contract Learning, Eclectic

Build-It-Yourself

There's no need to spend buckets of money on one-size-fits-all commercial curricula. Customize your children's learning experience, at a fraction of the cost of commercial curricula, by building your own.

Proponents: Your authors didn't found the Build-It-Yourself movement, but our popular how-to book, *Homeschool Your Child for Free* <*www.hsfree.com*>, certainly gave it a boost. The book describes more than 1,200 free educational resources for homeschooling families, fully reviewed and sorted by academic subject area, and includes a suggested academic scope-and-sequence for every year from preschool to college.

Methods: Some families design a program completely on their own, based on their personal beliefs about what their children should be learning. Others are guided by published "scope-and-sequence" plans or by the standards of learning documents promulgated by the public schools. Homeschooling can be done on a shoestring using homemade teaching materials, the public library, and the Internet! See Chapter 5 for instructions on finding and creating your own teaching materials.

Related Strategies: Evaluations, Research Techniques, Rubrics, Scope-and-Sequence

Related Approaches: Eclectic, Layered Curriculum, Purpose-Based Learning, School-at-Home, Scouting, Self-Directed

Collaborative Learning

Collaborative homeschoolers work with other homeschooling families to share resources and teaching.

Methods: Work with a local or an online group of homeschooling parents who share your interest in collaborative learning. In a cooperative group, parents or older teenagers teach classes in subjects in which they have a high degree of knowledge or interest. Collaboration can also involve sharing resources—such as a traveling library—so that each parent is better equipped to teach her own children. We discuss support groups and learning cooperatives in more depth in Chapter 10.

Related Strategies: Web-Based Education

Related Approaches: 4MAT, Hybrid, Learning Cycles

Correspondence Courses

This homeschooling strategy relies on commercial correspondence courses for curriculum materials and guidance.

Methods: Correspondence schools—some accredited, some not—offer curricula for all grade levels. This strategy also includes college courses offered via independent study for college credit. Some correspondence programs offer a full curriculum; others offer individual classes. Correspondence programs are administered two ways: over the Internet and traditionally, through the mail. These programs come in both tightly scheduled and unscheduled versions. The unscheduled versions give your child a year or more to finish the course. We review these correspondence programs as part of our Curriculum Review project (see Chapter 5 for details).

Related Strategies: Lesson Planning, Online Classes, Placement Testing, Rubrics, Scope-and-Sequence, Traditional Curriculum, Umbrella Programs

Related Approaches: Accelerated Learning, Frienet, School-at-Home

Learning Environments

Research[1] and anecdotal evidence suggest that environment has a dramatic influence on education.

Methods: A number of environmental strategies have a direct impact on learning. These strategies include:

* Adequate lighting: A child who doesn't have to strain to read or write learns better than one who does.

* Alpha environment: Some educators believe that children learn best in an environment that produces an "alpha" brain state, where the brain is alert and receptive, without being either agitated or drowsy. This theory suggests that the alpha state is induced through low-volume music set at forty to sixty beats per minute (Researchers[2] advise setting the stage for learning with Gregorian chants, alternative or Celtic music, or slow (largo) Baroque music—all of which have a tempo of about 60 beats per minute, rather than rock music, which accelerates the heartbeat, or slow rock, which depresses it.); deep breathing and meditation; and an environment of love and acceptance.

* Freedom from distractions: Despite teenaged assertions that studying is easier with the television turned on, a distraction-free environment is more conducive to learning.

* Reading: Homes with reading parents and shelves stuffed with reading material produce readers. And parents who read to their children have smarter children. It's that easy.

Learning environment strategies are addressed in more detail in Chapter 7.

Related Strategies: Learning Centers

Related Approaches: Child-Led, Christian Unschooling, Delayed Schooling, Desuggestive, Integrated, Montessori, Moore, Natural Learning, Play, Reggio Emilia, Relaxed, School-at-Home, Self-Directed

Lesson Planning

Many families find success using traditional lessons. Lessons are an efficient way to provide systematic instruction, which helps children acquire skills and addresses deficiencies in learning. Sometimes these lessons are taught as lectures; other times they involve hands-on learning or other experimental strategies.

Methods: Lesson-plan development is covered in detail in Chapter 7.

Related Strategies: Correspondence Courses, Experiential Strategies, Online Classes, Placement Testing, Rubrics, Scope-and-Sequence, Traditional Curriculum, Umbrella Programs

Related Approaches: Behaviorism, Classical, Classical Christian, Desuggestive, Layered Curriculum, Learning Cycles, Objectives-Based, Peer Tutoring, School-at-Home, Scripture Study, Values

Online Classes

The Internet is teeming with free classes, both instructor-led courses and interactive self-study classes.

Methods: Classes are delivered online or via videotape, video-conferencing, satellite, and other new technologies. Some classes include parental reporting tools. Some classes are open-ended and have an unspecified or long-term completion period; some are highly scheduled. We list dozens of resources for free online classes on the Classes page of the Homeschool Steps Web site, *<www.home schoolsteps.com/seealso/classes.htm>*. (Commercial classes are discussed under the Correspondence Courses strategy.)

Related Strategies: Correspondence Courses, Lesson Planning, Placement Testing, Rubrics, Scope-and-Sequence, Traditional Curriculum, Umbrella Programs, Web-Based Education

Related Approaches: Accelerated Learning, Contract Learning, Frienet, New Media, Purpose-Based Learning, Religion-Based, School-at-Home, Scripture Study, Self-Directed

Placement Testing

A strategy for parents who want to:

*   Assess school readiness, in order to determine when a child should begin formal academic studies.

*   Evaluate appropriateness of curriculum materials. This strategy is particularly helpful when determining an appropriate textbook for mathematics, reading, or other sequenced subjects.

*   Compare a child's academic progress against a scope-and-sequence/standards-of-learning document.

*   Conduct IQ testing. (We discuss this subject in more detail in Chapter 7.)

*   Administer quizzes

*   Assess college readiness

This strategy differs from Assessment Testing (part of the Evaluations strategy), which determines primarily whether or not a child has met a state standard for a particular grade.

Methods: Many commercial curriculum providers offer placement testing. Alternatively, your local public-school district may administer standardized tests for any of the above purposes, or you may self-administer tests using online resources. (We discuss this strategy in more detail in Chapter 7, and list hundreds of free and low-cost placement testing resources on the Placement page of our companion Web site, *<www.homeschoolsteps.com/seealso/placement.htm>*.)

Related Strategies: Correspondence Courses, Evaluations (Assessment Testing), Lesson Planning, Online Classes, Rubrics, Scope-and-Sequence, Traditional Curriculum, Umbrella Programs

Related Approaches: 4MAT, Delayed Schooling, Hybrid, School-at-Home

Rubrics

A rubric is a set of guidelines for evaluating student work. Rubrics provide clear expectations for the child and help parents establish quality standards. Generally, rubrics contain a point scale that assigns varying numbers of points for varying levels of achievement. When a rubric is well defined, learners know exactly what is expected of them, and know how to produce a high-quality project or document.

Methods: Rubrics are a great stress reducer. Parents establish standards without nagging, and children know what's expected before they begin. In a homeschool setting, you may or may not choose to include a point scale. If you do assign letter grades[3], the point scale enables you to say without argument that a certain project earns only a C, or that it meets all the standards and has earned your child an A. The Internet is awash in rubrics and rubric-generators, making your task as a rubric-using parent much simpler. (We discuss rubrics in more detail in Chapter 7 and provide rubric resources, including self-generating rubrics, at our companion Web site, *<www.homeschool steps.com/seealso/rubrics.htm>*.)

Related Strategies: Correspondence Courses, Evaluations, Lesson Planning, Online Classes, Placement Testing, Scope-and-Sequence, Traditional Curriculum, Umbrella Programs

Related Approaches: Contract Learning, Frienet, Layered Curriculum, School-at-Home, Unit Studies

Scope-and-Sequence

A scope-and-sequence is a document that outlines the academic sub-jects to be covered at each age or grade level. (The public-school equivalent is a standards-of-learning document, which may be devel-oped by the state department of education or an individual school district, or a curriculum outline, which may be developed by an individual teacher, department, school, or district. The scope-and-sequence for an individual subject or course is called a syllabus.) The scope-and-sequence is useful for knowing when your children are ready to move to the next grade level, planning lessons and unit studies, choosing curriculum materials, tracking achievement, pro-ducing a transcript for college and scholarship applications, and re-assuring yourself and others that your children are making academic progress in line with other schoolchildren.

Founder: Author and educator E. D. Hirsch is a leading proponent of scope-and-sequencing. His popular *What Your X-Grader Needs to Know* series of books created a sea of change in the educational estab-lishment, and fomented the current emphasis on learning standards.

Methods: Use the scope-and-sequence as a model, not a mandate. Don't let it take precedence over your family's basic homeschooling goals. Using the scope-and-sequence as a guideline, work on two or three objectives at a time, and move on as each subject is mastered. Finding a scope-and-sequence is easy. You can ask your local school district for its standards of learning document if you want to follow your state's guidelines, or you could go online and choose from a multitude of excellent scope-and-sequence outlines. We discuss this strategy in more detail in Chapter 5. The Sequence page of our com-panion Web site *<www.homeschoolsteps.com/seealso/sequence.htm>* has a large collection of scope-and-sequence documents, including the standards of learning for each state.

Related Strategies: Correspondence Courses, Lesson Planning, Online Classes, Placement Testing, Rubrics, Curriculum, Umbrella Programs

Related Approaches: Accelerated Learning, Behaviorism, Contract Learning, Desuggestive, Eclectic, Hybrid, Inquiry-Based, Layered Curriculum, New Media, Objectives-Based, Principle-Based, Religion-Based, School-at-Home, Values

Traditional Curriculum

The traditional approach to homeschooling uses commercial curriculum packages. Curriculum packages are available new or used. They may include individual textbooks, workbooks, teaching guides, schedules, answer books, software, video- and audiotapes, or other items required for a particular course. Some of these packages cover an entire school year; others cover a single subject or multiple subjects, without claiming to be complete. (We discuss the use of individual items, such as textbooks and workbooks, under the Build-It-Yourself strategy, above.) Curriculum packages can be administered by an umbrella school, by a correspondence school, or, most commonly, by an individual family. Reasons for using curriculum packages include:

* **Simplicity:** Curriculum packages require no teacher preparation and comparatively little parental interaction.

* **Scope:** Commercial packages provide complete coverage of the standard academic course of study.

* **Clarity:** When children finish one year's worth of curriculum, they've finished a grade, and can move along to the next grade.

* **Administration:** Curriculum packages are relatively easy to administer. The child simply sits at a desk and does the work.

* **Legality:** The use of traditional curriculum can be a safety net in states that have onerous homeschooling laws.

Traditional curriculum packages have several drawbacks as well:

* **Cookie-cutter approach:** Like the traditional public-school curricula, commercial packages tend to be one-size-fits-all.

* **Expense:** The more complete packages are comparable in cost to college tuition.

* **Interest level:** Many families report bad experiences with commercial curricula. Sitting around reading textbooks and doing workbooks is tedious, and involves very little hands-on learning. Bottom line: Kids find them boring.

Methods: Families that have the most success with traditional curriculum use it in one of two ways: as the foundation for an accelerated approach, or as a supplement to hands-on learning. We discuss Accelerated Learning in Chapter 4. And we review hundreds of commercial curriculum providers, including providers of traditional packaged curricula, in the Curriculum Review Project, described in more detail in Chapter 5.

Related Strategies: Correspondence Courses, Lesson Planning, On-line Classes, Placement Testing, Rubrics, Scope-and-Sequence, Umbrella Programs

Related Approaches: Accelerated Learning, Behaviorism, Contract Learning, Eclectic, Hybrid, Layered Curriculum, Learning Cycles, Objectives-Based, Peer Tutoring, School-at-Home, Unit Studies

Umbrella Programs

Umbrella schools, a category that includes satellite learning programs and charter-school home-education programs, provide legal cover for homeschooling, and may additionally provide accreditation, transcripts, attendance documents, curriculum recommendations, and supervision. Some umbrella schools even provide curriculum packages, at which point they become difficult to distinguish from correspondence schools.

Methods: Depending on your location, umbrella schools may be available locally or on a statewide level, or you may wish to get involved with a national umbrella school. Local programs may offer field trips, activities, homeschooling support, and educational programs, and may be virtually indistinguishable from a homeschool support group. Some umbrella programs provide the bare legal minimum of service and charge only a nominal membership fee. We review umbrella programs in the Curriculum Review Project, discussed in Chapter 5.

Related Strategies: Correspondence Courses, Lesson Planning, On-line Classes, Placement Testing, Rubrics, Scope-and-Sequence, Traditional Curriculum

Related Approaches: Accelerated Learning, Eclectic, School-at-Home

Cognitive Strategies

The eleven strategies in this section develop higher-level thinking skills. Kids who master these strategies end up smart. *Very* smart!

Concept Mapping

Use concept maps to turn passive learning into active learning. Concept Mapping is a strategy for graphically illustrating the relationships between ideas. Like brainstorming or note-taking, concept mapping requires children to use high-level critical thinking about new information. But unlike these linear techniques, concept mapping is unrestricted and helps the learner see information in a creative, organic, networked relationship.

Applications: Concept Mapping is useful in a number of applications, including reading comprehension, case study development, essay prewriting, planning, problem solving, and as an aid to memorization. Use Concept Mapping in discussions, field trips, forums, lectures, lessons, movies, reading, television shows, and other learning events. Completed concept maps are an ideal component for portfolios.

Founder: Joseph D. Novak, a retired Cornell University professor of biological science and science education.

Methods: To create a concept map, a learner actually maps ideas onto a sheet of paper. Use a clean, unlined sheet of paper to avoid visual distractions. Write the main idea or ideas in the center of the paper. The main idea can be single words or longer phrases, but train your children to keep it concise. (Distilling complex ideas into basic concepts is a learned skill, and demonstrates a thorough grasp of information.) Use arrows, lines, and words to link additional ideas into a connected web, and to draw branches and spokes that link concepts. The more connections that can be made between concepts, the more thinking is taking place. Work quickly, without stopping to consider where in the map an idea belongs. It's better to simply write ideas down anyplace on the paper, and try to find links after the ideas have been recorded. Make use of color to distinguish the original ideas from your own interpretations and comments.

Related Strategies: Case Studies, Collaborative Learning, Critical Reading, Discussions, Field Trips, Forums, Graphic Organizers, Lectures, Literature-Based Learning, Media-Supported, Memorization, Notebooking, Portfolio Building

Related Approaches: 4MAT, Classical, Classical Christian, Cognitivism, Learning Cycles, Values

Creativity

Creativity is the ability to generate novel and interesting ideas. As a teaching strategy, creativity means encouraging your children (and yourself) to dive into their own minds to generate wonderful works of art or any other manifestation of their inherent talents and interests. Creativity could relate to the fine arts, but in the left-brained portion of the population, it might relate to more practical creations: research, engineering, design, scientific discoveries, or solutions to social problems.

Methods: Creativity is both a cognitive skill and a practical one. On the cognitive side, teach your children to be aware of their innate creativity by encouraging them to maintain creativity journals— pocket-sized notebooks in which they jot down creative ideas as they occur. Have them record ideas for research, for a poem, or for anything else that piques their interest. Teach your children that creative ideas arise through three processes: inspiration (another person's creative work might inspire their own), meditation, and serendipity (a child might be washing dishes and thinking about nothing in particular, when suddenly he is struck with a brilliant creative idea). Another technique for encouraging creativity: Ask your children meditative questions and have them use their creativity journals to actually sit down to answer those questions. Sample questions: What motivates me? How could I fix the world? What would I like to do? What could I be really good at? These introspective questions about their own gifts, talents, and interests can generate hundreds of creative ideas. On the practical side, creativity involves actually carrying through with creative ideas. Until your children are self-motivated, get them involved in crafts that involve the simultaneous use of hands and brain. We recommend paper crafting, sewing, and quilting, all of which use fine motor skills and both sides of the brain.

Related Strategies: Graphic Organizers, Metaphors, Scrapbooking

Related Approaches: Child-Led, Christian Unschooling, Contract Learning, Delayed Schooling, Hierarchy of Needs, Integrated, Logotherapy, Mediated, Montessori, Moore, Natural Learning, Play, Relaxed, Waldorf

Critical Reading

For younger children, this strategy involves narrating the plot of a story or writing a book report. For older children and teenagers, it involves in-depth analysis of works of literature. This strategy is also useful for analyzing poetry, plays, movies, and other fictional works.

Methods: As your children grow older, it becomes increasingly important to expose them to different ways of appreciating literature. Young children learn about plot by telling a story. Older children should not only know the plot of a piece of literature; they should also be able to discuss how the plot illustrates the theme and have an opinion about whether or not the plot advances the story effectively. Is the plot well paced? How does it set the mood? The same kinds of analytical questions can be posed about every element of a creative work: How is symbolism used? What is the genre of a poem or a story? If you're feeling a little "out of your element," relax. We describe more than a hundred literary devices on the Literate Folk Web site, *<www.literatefolk.com/literarydevices.htm>,* and provide dozens of resources for book report forms, as well as advice about teaching critical reading, on the Critical page of our companion Web site, *<www.homeschoolsteps.com/seealso/critical.htm>.*

Related Strategies: Concept Mapping, Graphic Organizers, Literature-Based Learning, Logic and Rhetoric

Related Approaches: Classical, Classical Christian, Contract Learning, Discipleship, Inquiry-Based, Logotherapy, Mediated, Principle-Based, Problem-Based, Project-Based Learning, Religion-Based, School-at-Home, Scripture Study, Self-Directed

Graphic Organizers

Graphic organizers are ways to graphically organize thoughts. There are dozens of permutations. Concept maps, described above, are one example of graphic organization. Some other useful Graphic Organizer strategies are Semantic Maps, Story Maps, and Venn Diagrams, each of which we'll describe individually.

Semantic Maps. Sometimes called "idea maps," semantic mapping is an exercise to help kids visualize the relationships between topics and categories. They're great for brainstorming and prewriting exercises, for producing research plans, and for solving problems. At the conclusion of this exercise, each child will have created an internal scheme of a topic, and be prepared to think about inquiry or research into specific areas.

> **Method:** Select a one-word topic for mapping (i.e., puppies, automobiles, or the book of Genesis). Quickly generate a page full of associations, examples, and connectors to the topic (i.e., if the topic were "automobiles," I might write the following words: Ford, Model T, Detroit, transportation, cars, taxis, SUVs, minivans . . .). Once the page is full, go to the next step: Begin grouping items. Work either as a family or as individual learners. Learners should justify why they place each item under a particular heading. If an item belongs under multiple headers, try to think of a way to divide the item— perhaps with a parenthetical comment (Ford, Henry, and Ford Company). Ask each child to graphically represent— with colors, symbols, or stick figures—each category. Some people change this step to concept mapping, by putting the main topic in a circle in the center of a large page, with lines showing relationships between ideas, topics, and heading.

Story Maps. A way for readers to think about the structure of their reading.

> **Method:** For younger readers, you might supply a worksheet with open boxes that they fill in with step-by-step descriptions of story events. Older readers might create their own more-complex maps, graphing the development and eventual resolution of

one or more story conflicts, graphing the development of a character, or tracing the development of several themes.

Venn Diagrams. A familiar graphic device, Venn diagrams are two or more overlapping circles where the overlaps describe similarities between categories.

Founder: English priest John Venn (1834–1923)

Method: Teach the Venn diagram model by drawing two overlapping circles. At the top of each circle, write the name of one of your children, or the name of your child and a neighbor child. In the non-overlapping portion of each circle, list some unique characteristics of each child. In the overlapping portion, list some characteristics shared by both children. Once the concept is understood, add a third circle and a third child, and try to find characteristics to place in each of the three overlap areas, as well as in the central three-way overlap. Finally, apply the model to a more philosophical topic (see Figure 3.1). Perhaps you'd like to compare your family's rules with a neighbor family's, or compare your religious faith with two other faiths. You could also use Venn diagrams to compare books, math concepts, historical events, or virtually any subject at any level of thinking.

Other Applications. It's easy to develop graphic organizers of your own. Organize thoughts by using flow charts, matrices, numbered lists, and side-by-side lists. Break down a complex idea by comparing its parts to the parts of stick people, a house, a chair, or a religious icon. Enumerate ideas by mapping them onto shapes, floating clouds, the spots on a cow, or stones on a path.

Related Strategies: Concept Mapping, Creativity, Critical Reading

Related Approaches: Classical, Classical Christian, Inquiry-Based, Logotherapy, Mediated, Problem-Based, Project-Based Learning, Scripture Study, Self-Directed

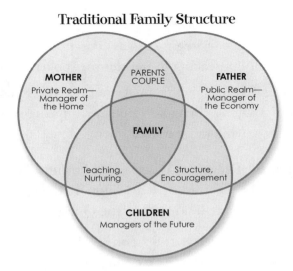

Figure 3.1 *Sample Venn diagram showing traditional family structure*

Listening Skills

One way to teach effectively is to train your children to *listen* effectively. At its root, the skill of listening is simply the discipline of paying attention and processing information.

Methods: There are dozens of ways to improve poor listening skills. Practice these techniques with your children during lessons and family nights and in other formal learning situations.

* **Ask.** If you're in a dialogue, ask questions during the conversation. If you're in a lecture situation, write down questions to be asked later. Rather than dead-end "yes/no" questions, ask the speaker to describe, explain, or share ideas.

* **Find personal application.** In other words, assume that everyone—even a younger sibling—has at least one thing to teach you. Ask yourself what positive thing you can learn from what you're hearing to improve your own life.

* **Observe.** Watch body language and gestures.

* **Repeat.** Restate the speaker's words, either aloud or internally.

* **Take notes.** Use strategies such as Graphic Organizers or Outlining and Note-Taking to transfer the spoken word to paper.

* **Visualize.** Create a mental image or even a sketch of what the speaker is saying. Imagine implementing the speaker's suggestions or living the speaker's story.

Related Strategies: Dictation, Discussions, Forums, Graphic Organizers, Interviewing, Lectures, Media-Supported Learning, Narration, Outlining and Note-Taking, Socratic Questioning

Related Approaches: Delayed Schooling, Desuggestive, Foxfire, Logotherapy, Mediated, Moore, Natural Learning, Play, Relaxed, Religion-Based, School-at-Home, Scripture Study

Logic and Rhetoric

Rhetoric is the art of persuasion, in writing, in formal speech, or in everyday conversation. (It's also the third stage of Classical Education's Trivium. See Chapter 4 for more information.) There are three ways to persuade: appeal to reason (logos), to emotion (pathos), or to ethics/credentials (ethos). Logic—the art of reasoning—falls under the first category.

Methods: Want to teach rhetorical skills? The Greeks had a simple program for teaching basic rhetoric that you can easily emulate at home. The program, called *progymnasmata,* involves fourteen exercises (see Table 3.2), taught in sequence, as a precursor to studying formal logic and formal oration.

The second part of this strategy—the study of formal logic—involves learning about two kinds of reasoning (inductive and deductive), several argumentative structures, and a multitude of sophisms (or fallacies). Find dozens of resources for teaching the progymnasmata and formal logic, as well as resources for critical thinking, im-

Table 3.2   The Progymnasmata

The Progymnasmata is a series of fourteen rhetorical exercises. Teach each component, in the following order, then encourage your child to communicate about the component. At each step, your child should write or talk about the component by paraphrasing, giving examples or applications, comparing and contrasting, and supporting or refuting the component.

1. **Fable.** Aesop's fables work nicely.
2. **Narrative.** Retell a factual or fictional story.
3. **Chreia.** Explain an anecdote. Use *Reader's Digest* as a resource.
4. **Proverb.** The book of Proverbs makes an excellent source.
5. **Refutation.** Attack an opposite view. Begin by considering a political or social issue on which your child may already have strong opinions.
6. **Confirmation.** Defend a point of view.
7. **Commonplace.** Discuss a virtue or vice.
8. **Encomium.** Praise the virtue of a person or thing.
9. **Vituperation.** Revile a particular subject's vice.
10. **Comparison.** A double encomium (compare virtue A to virtue B) or an encomium compared to a vituperation.
11. **Impersonation.** Dramatize a speech or dialogue that might be spoken by a real subject.
12. **Description.** Describe, completely, a person or action.
13. **Thesis or Theme.** Prove a political or theoretical argument by defending a position and refuting the opposition.
14. **Defend or Attack a Law.** Appeal to ethics, reason, and emotion.

proving memory, problem solving, propaganda, and the history of rhetoric, on our Rhetoric page at *<www.homeschoolsteps.com/seealso/rhetoric.htm>*.

Related Strategies: Critical Reading, Discussions, Evaluations (Forensics), Memorization, Metaphors, Outlining and Note-Taking, Scientific Method, Socratic Questioning

Related Approaches: Classical, Classical Christian, Discipleship, Foxfire, Frienet, Heart of Wisdom, Mediated, Objectives-Based,

Principle-Based, Problem-Based, Reggio Emilia, Scripture Study, Waldorf

Metaphors

Metaphorical thinking is the ability to make connections between two unlike things, by finding an inherent similarity or a common trait. Use this strategy to help your children think creatively and intelligently.

Methods: As parents, we use metaphors almost unconsciously to explain ideas, insights, and abstractions. When children learn to find and use metaphors, they build a foundation for learning about symbolism, logic, abstract thinking, and imagery. This strategy includes teaching not only how two things compare, but also how they contrast. Don't limit yourself to finding and using the usual literary metaphors (allegories, parables, and similes) in writing; develop analogies in everyday life ("Feeding the dog is like. . . ?"). Teach your children to avoid mixed metaphors ("You're skating on hot water"), clichés ("mad dogs and Englishmen"), false analogies (if two things share characteristic A, they must also share characteristic B), and overextended metaphors ("She's as dangerous as a snake, and needs to be soothed with a snake charmer's music, kept in a basket, and fed mice.").

Related Strategies: Creativity, Critical Reading, Logic and Rhetoric

Related Approaches: 4MAT, Cognitivism, Hierarchy of Needs, Logotherapy, Scripture Study

Outlining and Note-Taking

A child who takes notes gets involved visually, tactilely, and auditorily. Outlining helps a child think logically and understand the relationship between ideas.

Methods: This strategy is useful when listening to formal lectures and presentations, and when watching high-quality documentaries and educational programs. The standard format for outlining is:

I.
II.
    A.
    B.
        1.
        2.
            a.
            b.
                i.
                ii.

Related Strategies: Interviewing, Lectures, Media-Supported, Presentations, Research Techniques

Related Approaches: Classical, Classical Christian, Contract Learning, Foxfire, Inquiry-Based, New Media, Problem-Based, Project-Based Learning, Religion-Based, School-at-Home, Scouting, Scripture Study

Scientific Method

The recognized method of studying a subject scientifically.

Methods: The traditional scientific method has five steps:

1. State a hypothesis.
2. Design an experiment to test the hypothesis.
3. Collect data.
4. Analyze data.
5. Draw conclusions.

In reality, scientists don't always follow these restrictive steps. Often, real-life science focuses on observing, collecting data, and measuring, rather than actual experimenting. Science also tends to make new discoveries through luck, determination, inductive reasoning, guessing, collaboration, and sometimes even dreams and intuition. Nevertheless, children who understand and can use the scientific method are freed to modify the method to fit their own scientific investigations.

Related Strategies: Case Studies, Kitchen Science, Labs and Demos, Logic and Rhetoric, Nature Diaries, Research Techniques, Theses and Dissertations

Related Approaches: Contract Learning, Inquiry-Based, Learning Cycles, Mediated, Montessori, Problem-Based, Purpose-Based Learning, Scouting, Waldorf

Socratic Questioning

This strategy involves asking a series of questions so that the respondent gets logically from point A to point B simply by answering the questions. Socratic questioning arouses interest and gets learners involved in solving a problem.

Methods: A pure Socratic dialogue would involve *no* explanations. Instead, a teaching parent would continue asking questions until her children landed on the correct conclusion through their own answers. In practice, most users of the Socratic method will sometimes resort to a simple explanation when their listeners have trouble puzzling out answers. One proponent of the Socratic method says that effective questions will meet these four criteria: "(1) They must be interesting or intriguing to the students; they must lead by (2) incremental and (3) logical steps (from the students' prior knowledge or understanding) in order to be readily answered and, at some point, [must be] seen to be evidence toward a conclusion, not just individual, isolated points; and (4) they must be designed to get the student to see particular points."[4] Learn more about Socratic questioning on the Socratic page, <*www .homeschoolsteps.com/seealso/socratic.htm*>.

Related Strategies: Case Studies, Evaluations (Forensics), Interviewing, Logic and Rhetoric

Related Approaches: Classical, Classical Christian, Inquiry-Based, Learning Cycles, Mediated, Peer Tutoring, Principle-Based, Problem-Based, Project-Based Learning, Religion-Based, Scripture Study, Self-Directed

Writing to Learn

If you want to really learn a subject, try writing about it. As children "write to learn," they not only improve their writing skills; they also discover new understanding, find intellectual connections, generate questions, learn high-level thinking skills, and internalize their learning so that they understand better and retain longer.

Methods: Begin by assigning a small report on, say, pet grooming or some other subject that's unfamiliar but interesting to your children. Using this method, they will research and read about the topic until the material feels familiar, taking only sketchy notes. They will then attempt to generate a written report without using notes. Encourage children to refer back to their original material or note cards only to fill in blanks. The majority of the report should be produced strictly from memory. A basic report format is a five-paragraph essay: introduction, three support paragraphs,

On Moral Education

"Whom do I call educated? First, those who manage well the circumstances they encounter day by day. Next, those who are decent and honorable in their intercourse with all men, bearing easily and good naturedly what is offensive in others and being as agreeable and reasonable to their associates as is humanly possible to be . . . those who hold their pleasures always under control and are not ultimately overcome by their misfortunes . . . those who are not spoiled by their successes, who do not desert their true selves but hold their ground steadfastly as wise and sober-minded men."

—Socrates, philosopher (469–399 B.C.)

and a conclusion. Be sure your children understand this basic format before beginning their research, so that they can formulate the three support points in their minds as they read.

Related Strategies: Journaling, Library Skills, Media-Supported, Notebooking, Research Techniques

Related Approaches: Accelerated Learning, Contract Learning, Foxfire, Heart of Wisdom, Inquiry-Based, Logotherapy, Mediated, Principle-Based, Problem-Based, Scouting, Self-Directed

Experiential Strategies

In this section, we offer nine strategies for encouraging your children to interact with the world. These strategies will give your kids hands-on experiences with people and things.

Case Studies

The case study asks learners to draw on real life and their own experiences and observations. Case studies are highly participatory. The key to a successful case study is selecting a problem to study that is relevant to both the interests and experience level of the learner. As your children develop concerns about the world around them, the Case Studies strategy will help develop a positive, solutions-oriented view of the future.

Methods: For your case study, consider a large-scale problem or concern—disappearing wetlands, poverty, divorce, or education, for example. Locate an individual or organization that appears to have found a solution to the problem. Conduct interviews, observations, surveys, and other research to discover how—and whether—the solution has had any impact on solving the problem. Produce a case report, which should include facts regarding the original problem, the environmental context of the study, and the people involved in the case. Finally, theorize about how the individual solution could be extrapolated to a larger scale. Once a case study has been completed, consider publishing it, or using it as the foundation for a more extensive thesis or dissertation.

Related Strategies: Expert Resources, Interviewing, Research Techniques, Scientific Method, Self-Publishing, Socratic Questioning, Theses and Dissertations

Related Approaches: Constructivism, Contract Learning, Foxfire, Hierarchy of Needs, Inquiry-Based, Logotherapy, Problem-Based, Project-Based Learning, Religion-Based, Self-Directed, Unit Studies, Values, Values-Based Eclecticism

Field Trips

For hands-on learning, nothing beats a field trip. But when you can't afford a real-life trip to the Musée du Louvre, consider the next best thing: virtual field trips. Most major attractions have Web sites with complete tours, historical information, and exhibits for distant viewers.

Methods: Stumped for inspiration? Check out our list of more than 250 hands-on field trip ideas, located in Appendix B. These ideas are usable nearly anyplace in the world, so there's sure to be something here to keep your family busy and active. And look into virtual field trips on the Field page of the Homeschool Steps Web site, <*www.homeschoolsteps.com/seealso/virtual.htm*>. There you'll find listings for a multitude of well known international educational destinations, so that your children can learn "in the field" without leaving home.

Related Strategies: Notebooking, Road School

Related Approaches: Constructivism, Contract Learning, Discipleship, Foxfire, Identity-Directed, Inquiry-Based, Logotherapy, Moore,

New Media, Problem-Based, Project-Based Learning, Purpose-Based Learning, Religion-Based, Scouting, Scripture Study, Self-Directed, Unit Studies, Values-Based Eclecticism

Interviewing

Interviewing is a way to acquire new perspectives, build interpersonal skills, conduct research, and prepare for adult interview situations. The focus here isn't so much on learning how to *be* interviewed (as in preparation for a job interview), but rather on learning how to *conduct* interviews for research, for recording oral histories, for case studies, and for investigating a story for print or broadcast.

Methods: Preparation and practice are key to conducting effective interviews, whether chatting with someone familiar or interviewing a perfect stranger. There are several techniques your child should know before heading out to interview a neighbor for gardening tips, grandma for an oral history, a police officer for a case study, or a scientist for medical research:

* **Be prepared.** As you write questions, leave space to record answers.

* **Ask good questions.** Ask leading, open-ended questions (How? Why? What happened when . . . ?) rather than questions that require only a yes or no response. (Did you . . . ?)

* **Be flexible.** Expect to stray from the written list if the answers you hear bring up unexpected new questions.

* **Wait for answers.** Sometimes the interviewee has to stop and think. Don't worry about awkward pauses. Likewise, don't cut off the response until you're certain it's completely finished.

* **Be courteous.** An interview is not the time to explain your own opinion or show off your knowledge. Keep the focus on the interviewee.

* **Take notes.** Assume that your written notes will be the only record of what transpired during the interview. Tape interviews only as a backup to written notes. Too many interviewers have lost priceless material because of mechanical failures.

Related Strategies: Broadcasting, Case Studies, Expert Resources, Outlining and Note-Taking, Research Techniques, Socratic Questioning

Related Approaches: Contract Learning, Foxfire, Hierarchy of Needs, Identity-Directed, Inquiry-Based, Logotherapy, Moore, Problem-Based, Project-Based Learning, Purpose-Based Learning, Scouting, Scripture Study, Self-Directed, Unit Studies, Values, Values-Based Eclecticism

Kitchen Science

Your children can create all sorts of fabulous crafts and materials right in your own kitchen: edible finger-paint, colored pasta, crazy putty, sidewalk chalk, goop, homemade stickers, baker's clay, crystal gardens,

Recipe for Sticker Glue

One of our favorite recipes.

    Dissolve four envelopes of unflavored gelatin into two cups of boiling water. Stir until dissolved. Add 1 teaspoon flavoring (root beer, peppermint, vanilla, or any other food flavoring). When mixture cools to room temperature, paint "glue" on the backs of pictures, homemade stamps, and anything else you might want to "lick and stick." Allow stickers to dry overnight. Store dry stickers between sheets of waxed paper or in sealed plastic bags.

play dough, peanut-butter play dough, play slime, salt clay, bubbles, paper airplanes, homemade volcanoes, papier-mâché, and more.

Methods: Collect kitchen science recipes the same way you collect food recipes—in a recipe box on your kitchen counter. Gather new ideas from library books, magazines, and on the Internet, then share those recipes with other parents in your homeschooling group.

We discuss this strategy in more detail in Chapter 6. There is also a list of dozens of other recipes and lab ideas on the Kitchen page of the Homeschool Steps Web site at *<www.homeschoolsteps.com/seealso /kitchen.htm>*.

Related Strategies: Labs and Demos, Scientific Method

Related Approaches: Inquiry-Based, Learning Cycles, Moore, Problem-Based, Project-Based Learning, Scouting, Self-Directed

Labs and Demos

The easiest strategy of all for homeschoolers—but one we sometimes overlook. Home is the best laboratory for family sciences, chemistry, agriculture, and every other sort of practical science.

Methods: Teach laboratory sciences with a garden in your backyard, an electronics workbench in your garage, a photo studio in your bathroom, or an astronomy lab on your deck. Teach chemistry by investigating the chemicals you use to clean your hair, your clothes, your dishes, and your bathtub. Teach physics by exploding bubbles and balloons, skipping rocks, flying kites, and skating uphill. Teach biology and geology by digging around your backyard, the neighboring pond, and the closest cave. Teach the social sciences by going to the mall and observing how people behave. Science is better taught through observation and experimentation than it ever could be through textbook studies in a sterile classroom.

Related Strategies: Kitchen Science, Scientific Method

Related Approaches: 4MAT, Cognitivism, Inquiry-Based, Learning Cycles, Moore, Peer Tutoring, Problem-Based, Project-Based Learning, Self-Directed, Unit Studies

Learning Centers

Learning centers are an alternative to the classroom-at-home method some families use. When a home is set up with learning centers, children have regular and orderly access to every available tool for a particular project, but the centers are in physically separate locations. Learning centers encourage "learning binges," where a child might ask to spend hours or days working on a single project, with easy access to every necessary tool. (See pages 78–79 for learning center ideas.)

Methods: Learning centers can be set up in box windows, in corners, on desktops, in plastic tubs, in fabric bags hung on hooks, in the corner of a large closet, in utility rooms, in baskets, in large bathrooms, and under a large table. (We're big fans of gallon-sized self-sealing kitchen bags for storing almost anything.) Leave learning-center materials out in the open, rather than closed away in cupboards or hidden on high shelves. It takes discipline to train toddlers to respect learning centers and keep materials neatly organized, but families who use this strategy say it's worth doing.

Related Strategies: Learning Environment, Manipulatives, Media-Supported Learning, Worksheets

Related Approaches: Inquiry-Based, Learning Cycles, Montessori, Moore, Problem-Based, Project-Based Learning, Reggio Emilia

Library Skills

Learning to navigate the public library gives your child a leg up on conducting research and instills a love of books and literacy that may carry over into adult life.

Ideas for Learning Centers

Here are several ideas for elementary-age learning centers, and suggestions for the type of items you might put in each center:

* **Art Center:** art books, clay, paints and brushes, sculpting tools, sketch pads

* **Building Center:** workbench, hand tools, nails, screws, safety goggles, wood scraps

* **Computer Center:** keyboarding software, learning games, Internet access for doing research projects and Web quests

* **Construction Center:** building blocks, cardboard, Legos, Lincoln logs, markers, tape

* **Crafting Center:** cutters, embossing tools, fabric, glitter, glue, glue gun, markers, papers, ribbon, rubber stamps, sewing machine, sewing supplies, stickers, templates

* **Discovery Center:** books about inventors and designers, graph paper, wire, batteries, motors, drafting tools

* **Drama Center:** props, costumes, stage makeup, dolls, child-sized kitchen, puppets

* **Games Center:** backgammon, board games, chess set, dice, playing cards, Yahtzee game, timers

* **Math Center:** old-fashioned adding machine, calculator, calendar, countables (beads, beans, coins, marbles), dice, estimation station, fraction manipulatives, graph paper, magnetic numbers, math games, math textbooks, measuring cups, measuring instruments, measurables

(beans, dried peas, popcorn, rice, or other items in sufficiently large quantities to be measured by the cup), metric conversion tables, number blocks, play money, timer, worksheets

* **Music Center:** stereo, classical music, sheet music, instruments (including homemade instruments of rubber bands, boxes, foil, lids, popcorn, spoons), tape recorder

* **Poetry Center:** poetry books, models of various kinds of poetry, poetry textbooks, blank notebooks, paper, calligraphy pens

* **Reading Center:** books, books on tape, comic books, flannel board with stories, magazines, magnetic letters, child-made story books, vocabulary charts

* **Research Center:** dictionaries, foreign-language dictionaries, encyclopedia, Bible or other scriptures, style and citation guide (APA, MLA, Chicago, or Turabian), thesaurus

* **Science Center:** bucket, safe "chemicals" (baking soda, cornstarch, dish soap, powdered drink mix, sugar, yeast, vinegar, water), flashlight, fulcrum (long board and something to balance it on), lenses, magnets, magnifying glass, microscope, mirrors, ramps, sand and other things to mix, scales, sensory boxes with items to investigate various senses (the tactile box, for example, might contain carpet samples, a plastic bag of play dough, a piece of silk, and a toothbrush), springs, wheels

* **Writing Center:** handwriting samples, alphabet charts, calligraphy pens, gel pens, notebooks, cards, journals, stationery, typewriter

Methods: You can help your children get familiar with your local public library in several ways. If they're young, sign up for reading hour and other library events for young children. Help them get their first library card, use the computers in the children's section, and choose their own books and recordings. For older children, arrange a guided library tour during the library's slow period. Ask for a guide who is particularly knowledgeable about the library's reference section and who will spend time teaching your children how to look for information using a variety of resources. Sign up for reading programs offered through the library, and enroll your family in courses and programs offered by the library. If you live near a college or university, inquire about the college's policies regarding community use of the library. Many institutions of higher learning open their libraries (and other facilities) to community members for a nominal administrative fee.

Related Strategies: Research Techniques, Writing to Learn

Related Approaches: Contract Learning, Scouting, Scripture Study, Self-Directed, Unit Studies

Manipulatives

Primarily a math and science strategy, manipulatives are anything that a child can manipulate for learning: beads, string, blocks, coins, and an unlimited number of other possibilities.

Founder: Italian early-childhood educator Dr. Maria Montessori (1870–1952)

Methods: Dr. Montessori believed that there was a close relationship between the hand and the mind. Manipulatives help children learn through observing and handling objects that teach about relationships and cause and effect. When gathering your own manipulatives, think in terms of objects that teach a child to compare color,

Dramatic Play

For preschool-aged children, dramatic play means something different from stage acting. Dramatic-play centers for preschoolers might take the form of a child-sized kitchen, a huge cardboard box designed as a fire station, or a small workshop with plastic tools. Dramatic-play centers give young children experiences that encourage social, cognitive, emotional, and language development. One way you might encourage dramatic play is to set up a miniature version of whatever real-life job the working parent holds. Is mommy a piano teacher? Create a child-sized music studio. Is daddy a lawyer? Create a miniature courtroom where your preschooler can play judge and jury.

number, size, shape, weight, magnetic properties, and volume. For mature children consider objects that allow comparision of properties, such as acidity, combustibility, conductivity, convectivity, elasticity, flexibility, mass, melting point, refractivity, sublimability, solubility, toxicity, transparency, and viscosity.

Related Strategies: Learning Centers

Related Approaches: Learning Cycles, Montessori

Research Techniques

Strong research skills will serve your children well in college and in most professional careers. Research must have a purpose. In academics, the purpose of research is to understand an issue, find support for a hypothesis, or solve a problem. In the adult world, attorneys research laws, physicians research medical journals, journalists research background information for a story, and professionals in occupations from aircraft maintenance to zoology study new developments in their fields. Research skills are equally important in the home, where your children will one day need to know how to research home mortgage rates, compare home appliances, track tax law changes, and make hundreds of other informed decisions about their health, finances, and family.

Methods: There are several ways to conduct research. Traditional library research and online research are the most common techniques, but encourage your middle-school-aged and older children to broaden the scope of their thinking to include original research. Interviews and correspondence with experts, surveys, case studies, observation, experimentation, and data analysis are terrific ways to add to the body of human knowledge. Find more information about conducting original and secondary research, writing research papers, citing sources, and plagiarism on our Research Web site, *<www.literatefolk.com/research .htm>*.

Related Strategies: Case Studies, Expert Resources, Interviewing, Library Skills, Outlining and Note-Taking, Scientific Method, Theses and Dissertations, Writing to Learn

Related Approaches: Classical, Classical Christian, Contract Learning, Discipleship, Foxfire, Inquiry-Based, New Media, Principle-Based, Problem-Based, Project-Based Learning, Purpose-Based Learning, Religion-Based, Scouting, Scripture Study, Self-Directed, Unit Studies

On Purposeful Education

"If education is always to be conceived along the same antiquated lines of a mere transmission of knowledge, there is little to be hoped from it in the bettering of man's future. For what is the use of transmitting knowledge if the individual's total development lags behind?"

—Dr. Maria Montessori, educator

Input Strategies

There are eleven strategies for getting information into your kids' heads. Yes, several of these tactics involve rote learning and repetition—but who can argue with thousands of years of success?

Copywork

Children learn to speak through imitation. Advocates of copywork believe children can likewise learn to emulate great writers and thinkers—while improving their spelling, grammar, vocabulary, punctuation and handwriting—by copying selections from great literature.

Methods: Shakespeare? Write it. The Gettysburg Address? Write it. The Declaration of Independence? Write that, too. Maintain copybooks so that children have at hand their copies of the best of human thinking. Some families expand this strategy by asking children to analyze what they've copied. This analysis can take the form of illustration or narration for younger children, vocabulary research for intermediate ages, and complete research themes for teenagers.

Related Strategies: Dictation, Literature-Based Learning, Narration, Notebooking

Related Approaches: Behaviorism, Charlotte Mason, Classical, Classical Christian, Scripture Study, Unit Studies

Dictation

Dictation is a useful tool for teaching language. This strategy teaches grammar, handwriting, listening, punctuation, proofreading, spelling, and anything else that has to do with language arts.

Methods: The strategy is simple: Dictate a passage of literature—a sentence, a paragraph or more, depending on age—while your children

Research Techniques

No matter what the purpose, research generally follows the same basic procedure:

* Choose a topic. ("buying a dog")
* Frame a central research question. ("How do pet shops affect the health and well being of dogs?")
* Survey the topic by reading and interviewing.
* Develop your thesis and supporting arguments. ("The legislature should ban the sale of dogs in pet shops. Shops encourage overbreeding, dogs are kept in inhumane conditions, and shop conditions exacerbate health problems in dogs.")
* Locate and evaluate resources.
* Work with your sources.
* Develop your written document.
* Cite your sources.

write it down. During copywork time, allow them to correct their errors and rewrite the passage perfectly. Use high-quality literature for dictation so that your children are exposed to good examples of writing and vocabulary that extend their learning.

Related Strategies: Copywork, Listening Skills, Literature-Based Learning, Narration

Related Approaches: Behaviorism, Charlotte Mason, Classical, Classical Christian, Unit Studies

Ideas for Stimulating Discussion

Use textbook questions as a jumping-off point. Engage in role-playing and brain-storming, and debate both sides of social and political issues. Teach leadership skills by allowing your children to plan and conduct the formal discussions.

Discussions

As a teaching strategy, Discussions are both informal and purposeful conversations between parents and children about a particular academic subject.

Methods: Mealtime is perfect for informal discussions of the day's academic study. Consider using a more structured discussion format for family nights and during school hours. Formality encourages children to analyze alternative ways of thinking and acting, and helps them explore their own experiences so they can become better critical thinkers. Use the structured format to discuss the content of books and other media, to share ideas, and to solve problems. Teach your children to share their own ideas, as well as consider ideas put forth by other family members.

Related Strategies: Concept Mapping, Family Night, Forums, Logic and Rhetoric

Related Approaches: 4MAT, Aesthetic Realism, Logotherapy, Peer Tutoring, Scouting, Scripture Study, Unit Studies, Values

Expert Resources

One of the pleasures of homeschooling is that your children have the freedom and flexibility to meet face-to-face with scientists, doctors, farmers, musicians, clergy, politicians, and other experts in a particular field or profession. These interviews provide valuable learning for your children and could even result in a mentoring situation where your children are invited back to receive further feedback on their creative projects, research, or other academic endeavors.

Methods: Help your children call or write locally based experts and ask for an interview. When the expert you want to meet is located at some distance, you still have options. Some homeschooling families actually pack up the family car and travel cross-country to meet with people whom they believe will positively influence their children's education. If you don't have the time and money to make long trips, consider the large number of online "expert" resources where professionals in every field volunteer to answer questions from students and educators. We list numerous "ask-an-expert" resources on our Experts page, *<www .homeschoolsteps.com/seealso/experts.htm>*.

Related Strategies: Case Studies, Field Trips, Forums, Interviewing, Research Techniques

Related Approaches: Contract Learning, Foxfire, Logotherapy, New Media, Peer Tutoring, Problem-Based, Scouting, Scripture Study, Unit Studies

Forums

A forum is an open discussion between one or more experts or resource people and an entire group of learners.

Methods: The Forums strategy is particularly effective with homeschooling groups or large families. A moderator guides the discussion—consider asking an older child to do the honors—and learners raise and discuss issues, make comments, offer information, or ask questions of the resource people and one another. (Close cousins of the forum are the panel discussion, the seminar, the fireside, and the symposium.) A forum requires a great deal of preparation from all participants, including the audience, and so tends to be a very productive way of teaching.

Related Strategies: Discussions, Expert Resources, Listening Skills

Related Approaches: Aesthetic Realism, Logotherapy, New Media, Scouting, Scripture Study

Lectures

Lecturing's gotten a bad rap. It doesn't mean tirade, rant, or harangue. *Lecture* comes from a Latin root meaning "to read or interpret." It's the root of such English words as *intelligent, select, legend, legible,* and *lesson.*

Methods: In the homeschool setting, lectures might consist of a reading, an interpretation, or even a prepared lecture using a white board or chalkboard as a visual aid. Lecturing is also effective for imparting information to co-op classes, and within large families.

Related Strategies: Listening Skills, Outlining and Note-Taking, Presentations

Related Approaches: Learning Cycles, Logotherapy, Peer Tutoring, Scripture Study

Literature-Based Learning

Classical homeschoolers call it the "great-books strategy"; in Charlotte Mason it's called "living" books. Either way, it's all about reading great works of classic literature as a foundation for serious education. Rather than reading *about* Plato, Benjamin Franklin, or

Sigmund Freud, children actually *read* Plato, Franklin, and Freud—if not in their original languages, then certainly in translation.

Methods: Use one of dozens of lists of great classic literature, and work your way through. One good source for reading lists is your public library. Commercial study guides are widely available; numerous online literature study guides are available for free. Lists are long, and nobody can read everything, so pick and choose the works that fit your family's educational goals. We offer our own classical reading list at *<www.literatefolk.com/readinglist.htm>*.

Related Strategies: Critical Reading, Narration

Related Approaches: 4MAT, Aesthetic Realism, Charlotte Mason, Classical, Classical Christian, Contract Learning, Logotherapy, Objectives-Based

Media-Supported Learning

This strategy involves supplementing teaching with high-quality radio and television, prerecorded media (educational videos, DVDs, CDs, and audiotapes), periodicals (newspapers, magazines, and academic journals), and the Internet.

Methods: These media can be very powerful tools for informing learners, supplementing textbook learning, and stimulating discussion. Interesting research about gifted children and television suggests that certain kinds of television watching are actually beneficial to intellectual development.[5] To be an effective teaching tool, the researchers say, television programs must challenge the child's intellect. Their findings suggest that cable television and videos are the most reliable for quality. Moreover, children must avoid prime-time commercial television and infomercials, and parents must be actively involved in choosing purposeful programming and co-viewing with the child. We discuss additional research, and other techniques for purposeful media use in the homeschool environment, on the TV page of our companion Web site, *<www.homeschoolsteps.com/seealso/tv.htm>*.

Related Strategies: Concept Mapping, Listening Skills, Notebooking, Outlining and Note-Taking, Writing to Learn, Web-Based Education

Related Approaches: Frienet, Logotherapy, New Media, Unit Studies

Memorization

Memory is the capacity to retain and recall information. This strategy attempts to add data to the mental "storage unit" in the belief that children need to be able to instantly recall certain information in order to function in the world, and to be well educated. Proponents argue that knowing information is more valuable than being able to find information.

Founders: Kohler and Koffka, Max Wertheimer

Methods: Things are committed to memory in three ways: (1) through repetition (practicing or reviewing the material several times); (2) through association (relating new information to things already known); and (3) through connection—or what we call "pop!" You're already familiar with the first two; the tip on page 90 describes the sorts of information that should be memorized using these two techniques. The third technique, connection, may be less familiar. It describes intense, unforgettable Gestaltic flashes of insight that arise out of contemplation and intimate understanding of or interaction with a subject. It's the Eureka! moment when, all of a sudden, you "get" something you've never understood before. Learning that occurs through this third mechanism involves deep study, personal interest, and time to contemplate. So while teaching via memorization, don't neglect the secondary learning. All learning is an aid in creating context for new knowledge and can become a foundation for subsequent memorization, analysis, and growth in wisdom.

Related Strategies: Copywork, Logic and Rhetoric, Narration

Related Approaches: Classical, Classical Christian, Desuggestive, Peer Tutoring, School-at-Home, Scouting, Scripture Study, Unit Studies

Web-Based Education

This exciting strategy is the online version of collaborative teaching. It involves teaching over the Internet in a collaborative effort. A

Memorization Tip

Rather than asking your children to memorize spelling words, vocabulary, or parts of speech, try focusing on things that will have long-lasting impact on building wisdom. Information worth memorizing: poetry, passages from literature, scripture, and political documents (the Bill of Rights, the Magna Carta, the Constitution, the Declaration of Independence), jokes, stories, songs, and passages from important speeches.

Place secondary emphasis on the "trivia" of academics: significant historical dates, lists (U.S. presidents, names of books of scripture, names of wars, countries in South America, names of cloud formations, and anything else that will build cognitive maps).

And as far as possible, completely shelter your children from memorizing information that has no long-term beneficial impact on learning. Advertising jingles, trivia contests, fluffy pop music, game shows, daytime television, most nighttime television, celebrity gossip, and sports trivia are all corrosive to the human spirit. (Sports trivia may be especially damaging. The irony of "spectator sports" shouldn't be lost on your children. Remind your sports fans that actually getting up and running laps around a sports stadium is vastly more entertaining and productive than sitting in that same stadium—or lying on the couch—watching strangers exercise.)

teaching parent creates an online class, and learners participate from home.

Methods: Your real-life homeschooling co-op group can supplement teaching with the Internet, or you can form a teaching cooperative with families anywhere in the world. Online classes can take either of two forms. In the synchronous format, class members meet online in real time and hold discussions and exchange information. In the asynchronous format, the teaching parent posts information to a central location, and each class member has a limited amount of time to access the information and report back. Non-teaching parents may be involved at any level, from cooperative learning alongside the child, to receiving reports and logs, to complete hands-off involvement. There are plenty of free and low-cost tools for Web-based teaching: electronic white boards, mailing lists, streaming video, chat tools, ftp software, instant messaging, message boards, cooperative project tools, publishing tools, free Web space, online quiz makers, storage areas, and videoconferencing. Our companion Web site *<www.homeschoolsteps.com/seealso/webed.htm>* lists dozens of these Web-based education tools and gives lots more information about developing and administering online classes.

Related Strategies: Collaborative Learning, Online Classes, Self-Publishing

Related Approaches: Frienet, New Media, Scouting

Worksheets

Make your own worksheets or choose from the tens of thousands of worksheets available from commercial providers and on the Internet. Worksheets are an easy way to introduce a topic or reinforce learning. Even committed unschoolers sometimes find themselves using worksheets, usually at the request of their kids. Some children enjoy doing worksheets almost as a hobby—much like adults who enjoy doing crossword puzzles. While worksheets are commonly thought of as a tool for elementary-school-aged children, 60 percent of middle- and secondary-level teachers in public schools say they use worksheets every week.[6] Worksheets are also a good way to keep preschoolers focused while parents are working with older children.

Methods: Older children can work independently, of course. You might even want to provide an answer key so they can check their own work. With children who are not yet writing, you might permit them to dictate their worksheet responses. And work alongside elementary-school-aged children to encourage progress and respond to questions. As you generate worksheets, try to encourage creativity and problem-solving skills. Rather than asking children to name the primary colors, for example, you might ask them to draw a picture using only primary colors and then reverse the drawing using tertiary colors.

Related Strategies: Learning Centers

Related Approaches: Behaviorism, Frienet, School-at-Home, Scripture Study

Output Strategies

All that information flowing into your children needs someplace to go! These twelve strategies will give kids a creative outlet—and will give them tangible reminders of their homeschooled lives, to boot.

Evaluations

This strategy entails providing creative ways for children to demonstrate the results of their learning.

Methods: Pick and choose from a whole list of creative ways to evaluate your kids' academic progress. These ideas will give your children an outlet for their artistic talents, as well.

  * **Animations.** More fun than the flipbooks you made as a child, inexpensive computer software allows kids to animate short movies on their own. Animations make a terrific collaborative project for homeschooled kids, who could live on opposite sides of the globe and still work together to develop more elaborate animation projects.

  * **Assessment Testing.** The traditional way of monitoring progress, assessment tests are administered by the local public-school system or by private testing services. Test results may provide you with quantifiable evidence of educational attainment, and give your kids practical experience in test taking. Chapter 2 addresses legal and practical issues related to assessment testing.

  * **Artwork.** Encourage your child to create a gallery or portfolio of artwork. Artwork includes not only the usual media of painting, drawing and sculpture. Your child's art gallery can also include displays of quilts, sewing projects, and crafting projects. Take pictures of three-dimensional or oversized artwork for inclusion in a portfolio.

  * **Dance.** From ballet to modern interpretative dance to clomping around the house in mommy's high heels, kids love to dance. Encourage them to use dance as a form of intellectual expression by choreographing an interpretation of literary or historical events.

  * **Demonstrations.** An approach that teaches children to think on their feet, demonstrations require little preparation. A child demonstrates a product, a process, or a technique before a group, and then attempts to teach group members to repeat the demonstrated information independently.

  * **Documentaries.** Urge your kids to plan, research, and film exposés, historical accounts, tributes to heroes, or any other nonfiction

subject that captures their interest. (We discuss the making of amateur documentaries on our Documentaries page, at *<www.homeschool steps.com/seealso/documentaries>*. Learn about research and interviewing techniques, filmmaking tips, and places to submit your documentaries for competitions and for public viewing.)

* **Dramatic Presentations.** Whether they script their own theatrical productions or produce a play or a musical from an existing script, your kids will enjoy showing off their dramatic side to a room full of friends and family. On a smaller scale, your children may be interested in doing interpretive dramatic readings, mimes, or other individual dramatic presentations at home, in meetings of their homeschooling coop or youth group, or at religious services.

* **Essays.** The mark of an educated person is the power to develop passionate, well reasoned written arguments supporting or opposing a subject. As a model of the essay form, have your child read, or use as copywork, essays by Thomas Paine, Ralph Waldo Emerson, and John Stuart Mill. Visit our Essays page at *<www.homeschoolsteps.com/seealso /essays.htm>* for examples of historically significant essays, as well as useful instructions for teaching the essay form of writing.

* **Forensics.** Public speaking and debate provide the opportunity to investigate, analyze, and defend important issues. Many homeschoolers participate in organized forensics tournaments, where they debate or get involved in a variety of individual events (extemporaneous, persuasive, informative, or impromptu speeches; rhetorical criticism of essays, speeches, books, and the like; humorous after-dinner speeches; and various interpretive events, such as dramatic interpretations of prose, theatre, or poetry). Informally, your children can present their speeches to their family, their homeschooling group, or their youth group or club meetings. Formal opportunities for public speaking abound. Public meetings and hearings organized by governmental organizations, Toastmasters clubs, and youth organizations are just a few of the unlimited number of places your children can

speak out. Our Forensics page lists organizations that sponsor forensics tournaments and compiles resources describing the format and rules for formal debates and for individual events. Check it out at *<www.homeschoolsteps.com/seealso/forensics.htm>*.

* **Movies.** When they were younger, our boys used the family video camera to film battle scenes and car chases using clay, dirt, and toys scrounged from the bottom of their toy box. Now that they're older, we expect a little more thought to go into the scripting. See the Documentaries strategy, discussed earlier, for help on moviemaking techniques.

* **Musical Compositions.** Set Robert Frost to music, write lyrics about the Civil Rights movement, or perform nineteenth-century folk music. They're all valuable ways to express learning.

* **Performance Art.** Not quite drama, not quite dance, not quite art and not quite music—though it may incorporate elements of all four. Performance art is an unprecedented—and unrepeated—interaction between a performer and an audience. Because the audience is small, the performer can involve the audience's senses. Performance art occupies a space with specific objects and actions for a specific amount of time, at a low cost with minimal sets and props. Performance art is brief, usually about 15 minutes long. Performance art festivals are a good way to showcase these short performance pieces. The audience receives a flyer or handbill introducing each piece.

* **Reports.** Reports—oral or written analyses of an academic subject—are usually brief and can be researched and completed in an afternoon.

Other outlets for creative expression include Broadcasting, Journaling, Narration, Nature Diaries, Notebooking, Portfolio Building, Presentations, Scrapbooking, Self-Publishing, Theses/Dissertations, and Timelines. We explain each of these strategies individually below.

Related Strategies: Interviewing, Learning Centers, Research Techniques

Related Approaches: 4MAT, Contract Learning, Discipleship, Frienet, Learning Cycles, Objectives-Based, Peer Tutoring, School-at-Home, Scouting, Scripture Study, Unit Studies

Broadcasting

With the right tools, your children can broadcast anything from their own musical performances and radio dramas, to interviews and speeches, to panel discussions and debates. Let them tell the world what they believe about politics, religion, or any subject at all.

Methods: Unless you've had the good fortune to be fabulously wealthy, you and your family will have to do what the rest of us do: Take the cheap route. Modern technology and great laws give you and me access to the public airwaves. The Federal Cable and Telecommunications Acts of 1984, 1992, and 1996 require your local cable provider to give you free airtime on public-access television. In many locations, you also have the right to use their equipment and facilities to produce your public-access show. Another approach is to use Internet radio to broadcast from the Web. Our Broadcasting page *<www.homeschoolsteps.com/seealso/broadcast.htm>* tells how to find Internet radio resources and provides pointers for public-access shows.

Related Strategies: Evaluations (Documentaries), Interviews

Related Approaches: Foxfire, Problem-Based, Unit Studies

Journaling

Involving a written record of notes and ideas, the strategy of Journaling is a more writing-intensive form of Notebooking (see below).

Methods: Homeschooling journals might include copywork of subject-related passages, questions and answers about the subject under study, observations, and thoughts and feelings about the topic. The written word is the primary focus in journals, so unlike other forms of notebooking, graphics play a far lesser role as learners work to master writing skills.

Related Strategies: Nature Diaries, Notebooking, Portfolio Building, Scrapbooking, Writing to Learn

Related Approaches: 4MAT, Aesthetic Realism, Charlotte Mason, Heart of Wisdom, Identity-Directed, Inquiry-Based, Logotherapy, Principle-Based, Problem-Based, Project-Based Learning, Purpose-Based Learning, Religion-Based, Scripture Study, Unit Studies

Narration

The Narration strategy encourages learners to assimilate information and then retell it. Readers and listeners pay close attention when they know they're going to retell what they've heard. Because children have to select the particular details they'll relate back, narration teaches memorization, as well as the skills of classifying and connecting information.

Methods: Read aloud to children from a variety of quality books. Avoid textbooks. Young children orally retell the story they've heard; older children write it. Oral narration begins at around age six; written narration begins at about age ten. With loquacious or reluctant children, "model" narration by saying a sentence, suggesting a shorter way to say the same thing, and then asking them to repeat after you.

Related Strategies: Literature-Based Learning, Dictation, Memorization

Related Approaches: Charlotte Mason, Classical, Classical Christian, Inquiry-Based, Problem-Based, Project-Based Learning, Scripture Study

Nature Diaries

Also called nature notebooks, these diaries encourage the study of nature through firsthand observation. Maintaining a nature notebook is both an artistic and a scientific undertaking.

Methods: This strategy calls on children to closely observe the things they discover in nature and "picture narrate" them in their notebooks. Drawings are lifelike representations of birds, insects, rocks, reptiles, plants, and mammals, with accompanying text describing what was found, and the date of its discovery. Sometimes the representations are painted or colored. Typically, the accompanying text will include common names, Latin names, and taxonomic classifications. It might also include a brief narration of how the specimen was found, and a poem, a quote, or a very brief story. At the back of the nature diary, a child might maintain a classified list of all the items described in the book.

Related Strategies: Journaling, Notebooking, Portfolio Building, Scientific Method, Scrapbooking

Related Approaches: Aesthetic Realism, Charlotte Mason, Unit Studies

Notebooking

A compilation of everything that fits in a binder, arranged by subject, Notebooking is a form of Portfolio Building (see next strategy), but it's far more extensive, and more day-to-day. Bound books, make-your-own books, and three-ring binders all make a good foundation for notebooking.

Methods: Any subject can be used as the subject of a notebook. Start with three-ring notebooks and page protectors, or make your own using papercrafting and bookbinding techniques (see Scrapbooking, below, for details). Have your children create separate notebooks for each subject. A single notebook might contain any or all of the following items: index, reading logs, assignment tracking sheets, research logs, goal sheets, story maps, illustrations, spelling and vocabulary lists, worksheets, copywork, fiction, essays, reports, correspondence, and certificates and awards.

Related Strategies: Journaling, Nature Diaries, Portfolio Building, Scrapbooking, Writing to Learn

Related Approaches: Aesthetic Realism, Discipleship, Foxfire, Frienet, Heart of Wisdom, Inquiry-Based, Learning Cycles, Principle-Based, Problem-Based, Project-Based Learning, Scripture Study, Unit Studies, Waldorf

Portfolio Building

A portfolio is a carefully assembled collection of work that exhibits a child's efforts or achievement in one or more areas. It's more focused than notebooking, because a portfolio is intended to be seen by others—a college admissions committee, a scholarship committee, a potential employer, or, if local law mandates it, a public-school administrator.

Methods: Gather together the best representations of your child's work, along with certificates, awards, and other items of recognition. A serious portfolio should contain an index with brief commentary about what material appears in the portfolio and why it was chosen. Physically, a portfolio should be large enough to display your child's best work unfolded. If your child is an artist, you might consider using an oversized art portfolio to display the work. If your child's work is all letter-sized, consider using a binder or having copies of the work bound at a local copy center. Kinkos and most office supply retailers have binding facilities. If your child's best work is three-dimensional or performance-related, try to create two-dimensional representations for the portfolio. Photographs and CDs are impressive additions to a portfolio, and make it easier for the reviewer to assess the contents.

Related Strategies: Journaling, Nature Diaries, Notebooking, Scrapbooking, Theses and Dissertations

Related Approaches: Classical, Classical Christian, Inquiry-Based, Problem-Based, Project-Based Learning, Self-Directed

Presentations

A child skilled in giving presentations is well equipped for future college courses and for future employment. Encourage your children to give reports in the form of presentations. Presenters should be very clear about what information they want to convey, limit their presentations to two or three key points, and present information in small chunks. (For example, if you're using text on a visual aid, limit each visual to about twenty-five or thirty words.)

Methods: The key difference between a presentation and a lecture is the use of audio and visual aids. Where a lecture might be supplemented with just a chalkboard, a presentation might use charts, demonstrations, diagrams, drawings, graphs, handouts, models, murals, music, overhead transparencies, paintings, performances, posters, slides, or video clips.

Related Strategies: Family Nights, Lectures

Related Approaches: Inquiry-Based, Problem-Based, Project-Based Learning, Religion-Based, Scripture Study, Unit Studies

Presentation Suggestions

If you're trying to teach your children computer literacy, you might want to encourage the use of digital audio and visual aids. Here are some inexpensive ways to produce and use presentation graphics using your home computer:

* **Graphics.** If your children are artistic, they can produce their own graphic art and animations using the software that probably came free with your computer, or any of the free or inexpensive programs available over the Internet. If they'd rather work from pre-drawn artwork, there are thousands of clipart resources available online for free or at a very low cost.

* **Sound.** Add music and speech to your presentations with one of dozens of music and sound editors. You may have sound editors installed on your computer already. If not, there are plenty of freeware and shareware editors available online.

* **Slide show.** If you have presentation software such as PowerPoint, Freelance, or Harvard Graphics, you're all set. If not, several free or low-cost software programs provide many of the same features.

* **Video.** The newest versions of Microsoft Windows (ME, and later) and all new Macintosh computers feature built-in video editing tools. These tools require lots of disk space and lots of memory, so if your home computer is elderly, you might want to skip the frustration.

* **Display.** Many PCs have a video output jack that allows you to connect the PC to a television set. Cables can be purchased for five dollars or less from electronics retailers.

We list dozens of resources for each of these methods on our companion Web site at <www.homeschoolsteps.com/seealso/presentations.htm>.

Scrapbooking

Scrapbooking is more craft-oriented, and more artistic, than its word-oriented counterpart, Journaling, but both involve the same basic elements. Use archival-quality materials and assemble memory albums detailing your personal and family history, or use Scrapbooking as a creative outlet for schoolwork.

Methods: Get creative with rubber stamps, stickers, stencils, templates, embossing tools, custom-made papers, and markers, all of which are available at local craft and stamping stores. One scrapbooking technique you might want to investigate is bookmaking and papercrafting, where you actually create the book itself by making and binding paper using traditional papermaking techniques. We describe papercrafting and other scrapbooking techniques on the Scrapbooking page of the Literate Folk Web site at *<www.literate folk.com/scrapbooking>*.

Related Strategies: Journaling, Nature Diaries, Notebooking, Portfolio Building, Self-Publishing

Related Approaches: 4MAT, Heart of Wisdom, Inquiry-Based, Problem-Based, Project-Based Learning, Unit Studies

Self-Publishing

This homeschooling strategy uses paper documents and Web site creation as a gallery for schoolwork. Use this strategy to publish your children's artwork, correspondence, creative writing, editorials, essays, journals, magazines, newsletters, poetry, political campaigns, school projects, reading lists, research, screenplays, and transcripts.

Founders: Several well known nineteenth-century teachers reproduced their pupil's texts (Dumas in Paris, 1730; Oberlin in the Vosges c. 1800; and Robin at Cempuis, c. 1900). In 1921, the Polish educator Janus Korczak used a school newspaper as an educational tool.

Methods: Consider making multiple copies of your child's best work for grandparents and other family members, for scholarship applications and college admissions applications, and—if the work is of sufficiently high quality—for sale. Copy centers and office supply stores are able bind published documents inexpensively with coil, comb, wire, tape, or velo bindings, and can drill manuscripts to be stored in ring binders. Or produce handmade books using the techniques discussed under the Scrapbooking strategy, above. Digital publishing is an inexpensive alternative to traditional paper publishing. Your children can publish their work on CD-ROM using a CD writer, which can be purchased for as little as $100 from computer and discount retailers. Blank CDs typically cost around 40 cents apiece. Or publish directly to the Web. If your children do the publishing on their own, they'll become familiar with computers, work with graphics, learn design principles, improve their writing and computer programming skills, research subjects that interest them, and interact with people who read their work. We explain marketing techniques, Web publishing, and other self-publishing techniques on the Publishing page of our companion Web site, *<www.homeschoolsteps.com/seealso/publishing.htm>*.

Related Strategies: Case Studies, Notebooking, Scrapbooking, Theses and Dissertations, Web-Based Education

Related Approaches: 4MAT, Aesthetic Realism, Constructivism, Foxfire, Frienet, Inquiry-Based, Layered Curriculum, Logotherapy, New Media, Problem-Based, Project-Based Learning, Religion-Based, Scripture Study, Unit Studies

Theses and Dissertations

For your serious student, consider assigning a thesis or dissertation—an extensive research and writing project for publication. A thesis is a lengthy scholarly analytic paper; a dissertation is a lengthy scholarly analytic paper that makes an original contribution to human knowledge. A project-in-lieu-of-thesis is a unique contribution (any hands-on demonstration of knowledge), accompanied by a written analytical document. For example, if your child were to produce a business project, she might set up an actual business and then write a monograph describing the experiment.

Methods: To qualify as a thesis or dissertation, the written document must adhere to certain rigid guidelines. Numerous organizations will print and bind copies of the final document, and even assign it an ISBN number for permanent cataloging. We provide in-depth guidance for thesis and dissertation development, including citation and manuscript preparation guidelines and publishing tips, on the Thesis page of our companion Web site, *<www.homeschool steps.com/seealso/thesis.htm>*.

Related Strategies: Case Studies, College Prep, Research Techniques, Scientific Method, Self-Publishing

Related Approaches: Accelerated Learning, Inquiry-Based, Problem-Based, Project-Based Learning, Religion-Based, Scripture Study

Timelining

Do your children ask whether you remember the Civil War? Help kids compile a mental map of history—and your place in it—using timelines.

Methods: Adherents of the Charlotte Mason approach advise making a "Book of the Centuries"—a timeline in a notebook with two pages per century. Our family likes an approach that's more accessible to the entire family, and so we have created a wall-sized timeline with canvas hung on dowels. A ribbon line runs the length of the canvas, and we use a contrasting color of ribbon to mark the centuries. Non-bleeding Sharpie markers are used to add information as we study history, literature, and religion. Some families paint elaborate murals directly on their walls; some limit their large-scale timelines to temporary sheets of butcher paper.

Related Strategies: Notebooking

Related Approaches: Charlotte Mason, Foxfire, Heart of Wisdom, Inquiry-Based, Problem-Based, Project-Based Learning, Religion-Based, Scripture Study

Motivational Strategies

Get your kids excited about their educations. At least one of three strategies in this section will motivate kids in every age group to focus on learning.

Awards

Eventually, kids learn to work for intrinsic awards . . . but everyone likes a public pat on the back for a job well done.

Methods: You can award your children's homeschooling achievements in several ways. The following techniques can be done on an individual basis, or on a group basis with children from your homeschooling cooperative or support group:

   * **Certificates.** Consider providing your hardworking kids with documentation of their successes in the form of certificates that can be maintained as part of their portfolio. We provide award certificates in our homeschooling cooperative to kids who complete one of our quarterly classes. Make and print customized coupons, announcements, diplomas, and achievement awards from your word processor. Certificate forms are available at your local office-supply

store and from the variety of award-making resources available for free on the Internet. The best of these award sites are list on the Awards page of the Homeschool Steps Web site at *<www.homeschool steps.com/seealso/awards.htm>*.

   * **Events.** Plan recitals, talent shows, demonstrations, and end-of-year parties to showcase your children's talents. Invite grandparents and other family members, neighbors, fellow churchgoers, and anyone who has ever expressed an interest in homeschooling. If it's an especially large and well organized event, invite a reporter from your community newspaper and television station.

   * **Exhibitions.** Arrange for a public showing of your children's photography, artwork, sculpture, or film creations. Your kids might not rate space in a commercial gallery or a prominent museum, but that shouldn't stop you. Solicit wall or lobby space from banks, public libraries, hospitals, medical clinics, community centers, or places of worship. Submit photos and a news article to local media.

Related Strategies: Competitions, Portfolio Building

Related Approaches: Behaviorism, Eclectic, Frienet, Logotherapy, New Media, Peer Tutoring, Scouting

College Prep

When your child senses college looming on the horizon, take advantage of that apprehension by focusing your homeschooling effort on college preparation.

Methods: When your child turns fourteen, begin working with these strategies:

   * **Improve basic academic skills.** Rocket science isn't required. But be sure your child has mastered basic skills such as factoring,

conversions, fractions, decimals, and percentages, as well as practical grammar, basic spelling, Aristotelian logic, and the fundamentals of a foreign language.

* **Specialize.** University admission requires a balance of depth and breadth. Help your child become the world's leading expert in two or three different disciplines. A black belt in karate, a semester living abroad, raising pigs in 4-H, and publishing research on the wildlife in the pond in your backyard would make your child the most popular candidate in the college admissions office.

* **Document learning.** Your college-preparation program should include the development of an extensive portfolio of your child's best academic work. If your children were also to produce theses or dissertations for publication, it would guarantee serious consideration by every research university to which they applied.

* **Teach to the test.** Advise your children to go over and over the material in several college test prep books. These books are available at the public library, college libraries, and large bookstores. Encourage mastery of every question format, and study of the sections on how to take the test. Counsel your children to take the test for practice during what would be their junior year of high school, and to take a practice test again early in the senior year.

* **Take some credit.** Help your children enroll in college classes during their high school years. Investigate advanced placement and other early college credit programs, as well as independent-study college courses.

We explain each of these techniques, and other college-admission tips, in great depth in Chapter 11. Master these techniques and your children are virtually guaranteed a spot in their favorite university.

Related Strategies: Correspondence, Logic and Rhetoric, Portfolio Building, Theses and Dissertations

For More Information

For more information on any of the homeschooling strategies described in this chapter, visit the Strategies section of the Homeschool Steps Web site at *<www.home schoolsteps.com/see also/strategies.htm>*. There you'll find additional tips and advice, recommended books, and readings related to each homeschooling strategy.

Related Approaches: Accelerated Learning, Classical, Classical Christian, Eclectic, Logotherapy, Religion-Based, Self-Directed

Competitions

Participate in national academic competitions available to homeschoolers.

Methods: While nobody advocates that academic competition become the focus of homeschooling, it's indisputably a good tool for piquing the interest of a self-motivated learner. Many academic competitions require that children enter as part of a sponsoring group, so consider joining or forming a learning cooperative with other families that share your child's interest. We discuss competitions in Chapter 7 and list more than 350 national academic competitions at *<www.homeschoolsteps .com/seealso/compete.htm>*.

Related Strategies: Awards

Related Approaches: Behaviorism, Eclectic, Scouting, Self-Directed

4

Approaches and Philosophies

What Are Teaching Approaches?

Teaching approaches are basic philosophies about how education should be structured. They arise out of fundamental beliefs about discipline, freedom, responsibility, and the relationship between children and parents. As you read here about a variety of educational theories, you'll choose an approach that suits your family's habits, beliefs and schedule.

This chapter will not address learning styles; those are discussed in great depth in Chapter 7. Nor will it discuss picking a curriculum or finding materials, which are covered in Chapter 5. And it doesn't address specific teaching techniques, which are found in Chapter 6.

What it does is survey a large number of educational approaches and address their strengths and weaknesses. When you're finished with this chapter, you'll have a strong opinion about the ideal educational approach for your own family and will be able to speak authoritatively about how it compares to every other major approach.

How Do These Approaches Differ from the Strategies in Chapter 3?

The average human being doesn't know the difference between judo, karate, and tae-kwan-do, let alone the differences between the other four hundred–plus types of martial arts. That's not surprising. All the martial arts overlap and borrow from one another. If you were to study, say, kung fu, you'd learn to use a specific set of tools—blocks, pressure points, and leverage, for example. And several of those tools would be useful to you if you later decided to study shotokan, kenpo, or jujitsu.

The same principle applies to teaching strategies. Each of the fifty teaching approaches we discuss in this chapter (see Table 4.4, page 119) relies on certain strategies to be effective. Now that you've reviewed the strategies, it's time to learn how to combine them in in a variety of approaches to education.

Do I Need a Chalkboard?

Some homeschooling families operate like small-scale versions of conventional schools, with textbooks and tests and traditional grades.

Other families freely adapt ideas from alternative educational philosophies such as Waldorf or Montessori. Many give their children near-total control over what is learned and how learning takes place.

So yes, you may need a chalkboard, if you choose an approach that involves lectures, demonstrations, or other strategies with a visual component. But you may also choose an approach that involves any of dozens of other ideas about how to teach children effectively.

In this chapter we introduce our "Ages and Stages" homeschooling model. Use it to analyze your family's basic beliefs, needs, and habits so that you can choose or develop the ideal teaching approach for your family. The Ages and Stages model is used to group our fifty different homeschooling approaches into eight categories.

What Are the Categories of Teaching Approaches?

In the past, the debate over educational philosophies has focused rather narrowly on Unschooling versus School-at-Home, and on sharp disagreements over secular and religious approaches.

The pitfall in debating these limited alternatives is that a whole world of options has been virtually ignored by homeschooling writers—and parents who could have chosen from an entire menu of options are stuck, instead, with an ill-fitting approach that discourages both parents and children.

Our eight categories of educational approaches, listed roughly in order of the degree of parental direction required, encompass:

1. **Psychology-Based Philosophies.** The public-school system is still entrenched in the psychology of 1950s. Are you up-to-date on information that might change your assumptions about how children learn? We discuss three psychological models for education.

2. **Directed Approaches.** Enthusiastic, take-charge parents who are deeply involved in leading their children's education get justifiably excited about these ten Directed approaches to homeschooling. See if your kids don't find a new spark of enthusiasm when Mom and Dad try new ways of teaching.

3. **Faith-Based Values Approaches.** No separation of Church and State for your family. You're homeschooling because you want your children to develop a deep and abiding understanding of morality, Divinity, and your family's religious faith. Our eight Faith-Based teaching approaches will infuse all your teaching with a

religious worldview and help you raise up your children in the way they should go.

4. **Secular Values Approaches.** You became a parent because you wanted to make the world a better place and raise good, honorable people who act with confidence and stand up for what's right. Yes? These five values-oriented educational approaches will teach your children to interact with the world on a high moral plane. Religious homeschoolers will likewise find much to ponder in these approaches. Right is right, no matter what model you use to teach it.

5. **Informal Approaches.** Push the chair away from the desk. These seven Informal approaches let you pick and choose from a wide variety of hands-on resources. Select a philosophy, then create a home education program to match. In this section, we show you how.

6. **Questioned Learning.** Who said you needed to know all the answers? Our collection of five different approaches to Questioned Learning will send your kids searching for answers to all their questions.

7. **Undirected Philosophies.** Tie up your trainers and strap on your fanny pack. Each of these three Undirected homeschooling philosophies will have you racing to keep up with your children's enthusiastic learning. This is *fun* stuff!

8. **Unschooling Philosophies.** No, it's not a case of the inmates running the asylum. It's a collection of nine different approaches based on a philosophy of trusting in the natural desire of children to take on the world and learn everything there is to know. What these approaches have in common is a belief that the enthusiastic participation of children is the single most important factor in their education.

How Do I Choose an Approach?

While there's no absolute correlation, in general, families that are highly structured and organized tend to favor the formal approaches to homeschooling, while those that are more informal tend to gravitate toward the unstructured approaches.

There's no reason, though, that a very structured family couldn't incorporate the most unstructured approach to homeschooling. As you'll see from the results of the self-test at the end of this chapter, your basic beliefs about how parents and children should live together in a family will be a stronger indicator of the approach you should take than will your family's current level of organization and structure.

An additional caveat: Your children will thrive under any approach. If, after reading this chapter, you're still undecided, just pick an approach and give it a try. If tackled with good humor, lots of love, and a cheerful attitude, even the most incompatible approach will work just fine. Whether your children earn master's degrees at the age of thirteen, or just schlep around in pajamas reading Dr. Seuss for thirteen years, they'll always know they were loved and cared for and that your family values learning.

How Does the Ages and Stages Model Work?

In life, there are an infinite number of ideas, notions, philosophies, strategies, and hypotheses. To attempt to understand them all would be overwhelming—particularly if you were trying to learn them without the benefit of any sort of structure.

In this section, we introduce our Ages and Stages model, an integrated framework for understanding the world. The model applies not only to education but also to parenting, religion, writing, law, business, and virtually any other discipline you can contemplate.

Ages and Stages integrates various teaching strategies, learning styles, and educational approaches into a single model. The model is a useful way of thinking about the world because it considers a large number of variables and categorizes them in a simpler way.

Table 4.1   The Ages and Stages Integrated Model

Alpha Philosophies	Iota Philosophies	Omega Philosophies
A	I	Ω
The first letter of the Greek alphabet. In astronomy, it denotes the brightest star of a constellation. Equivalent to the Hebrew letter Aleph. The **Animated** (beginning, hands-on, or introductory) level of a discipline	The first letter of the second triad of the Greek alphabet. Iota is the smallest letter in the Greek alphabet. The word "jot" derives from "iota." The **Intermediate** (central, transitional, or moderate) level of a discipline.	The last letter of the Greek alphabet. In Greek, it means "large." Omega denotes the ending of a series or sequence. Omega correlates with the English letter "W." The **"Wise"** (mature, advanced, or more hands-off) level of a discipline.

Ages and Stages is a three-part model. We label the three categories Alpha, Iota, and Omega—the beginning, middle, and end of the Greek alphabet. Table 4.1 describes these categories and explains why we chose these labels.

To understand Ages and Stages, consider how it applies to a "discipline" you're already familiar with: parenting. In Table 4.2 we consider Ages and Stages as it applies to the cognitive stages of human development.

Notice that we don't apply specific age groupings to the model. We have a good reason: The stages aren't strictly linear. They're cyclical, and have both macro and micro applications. The categories could have several different meanings, depending on the context of the idea to which they're applied. For example, the Iota phase (Middle age/Intelligence stage) might apply to children of middle-school age (roughly ages eleven to fourteen) as they grow toward adulthood and begin the process of emotional separation from their parents. The model predicts that children in the Iota phase thrive under a somewhat more relaxed form of parenting, which complements their increasing independence while honoring evidence of maturity and intelligence.

But the Iota phase might also apply, microcosmically, to the early years of childhood. It describes the "terrible twos" stage where children begin to assert their independence and assemble a worldview.

At the same time, the Middle age could apply in a larger sense to *adults* of middle age as they question the meaning of their lives and seek to realign their priorities. It could also apply in a macro sense to the entire history of Western civilization, where the Middle age applies, literally, to the medieval period of history. Finally, it could be applied in a transcendent, supramacro sense to all of eternity, where human mortality comprises the Iota phase of Ages and Stages.

Table 4.2   The Ages and Stages of Parenting

	Alpha Philosophies	**Iota Philosophies**	**Omega Philosophies**
Categories	A	I	Ω
Ages	Younger	Middle	Older
Stages	Affinity	Intelligence	Wisdom
Explanations	When children need direct affiliation with parents and learn to adapt to the world. This stage requires more interaction, supervision, intervention, training, and association than do later stages. The child seeks, above all else, approval, affinity, acceptance, and security. Advice is freely accepted.	Cognitively, the child is acquiring information and beginning to make intellectual connections among disparate pieces of data. Data is more significant than approval. Advice is questioned.	At this stage, the child is integrating new information into a largely completed map and can apply the new learning to other settings. Symbolism is more significant than data. A person at this stage acquires new information relatively slowly, but integrates it, filters it, and applies it at a rapid pace. Advice is routinely rejected unless it adds meaning to the existing worldview.
Structure	Structured	Relaxed	Unstructured

Table 4.3 The Ages and Stages of World Views

	Alpha Philosophies	Iota Philosophies	Omega Philosophies
Categories	A	I	Ω
Community Stages	Family	Neighborhood	World
Behavioral Motives	Preservation	Convenience/Comfort	Joy
Pathological Counterparts	Fear	Competition	Imposition of Ethics—Terrorism, Arrogance
Philosophical Values	Animalistic/Primal	Humanistic	Moral/Ethical
Christian Worldview	Tribal/Feudal	Mosaic/Covenantal	Benevolent/Agape

As you seek begin to assimilate the Ages and Stages model, you'll find support for it nearly everywhere you look (see Table 4.3). Plato (in Chapter 17 of *The Republic*) described what he called the three parts of the soul, each of which corresponds neatly with the Ages and Stages model: the love of money (a desire to satisfy our natural appetites), the love of knowledge (a desire to learn), and the quality of passion or spirit (a desire to fulfill our emotional potential).

To an Old Testament believer, the Ages and Stages model is supported by scriptures that advise parents to "train up a child in the way he should go," so that "when he is old, he will not depart from it" (Proverbs 22:6). Similar support is found in the New Testament. In fact, the end of the 13th chapter of the book of Corinthians describes the model three times in three verses: "When I was a child, I spake as a child, I understood as a child, I thought as a child," the Apostle Paul writes, "but when I became a man, I put away childish things." "For now we see through a glass, darkly; but [in the future] face to face: now I know in part; but then shall I know even as also I am known. And now abideth faith, hope, charity, these three; but the greatest of these *is* charity." John understood the model implicitly: In several places in the book of Revelations, he describes Jesus

Christ as "Alpha and Omega, the beginning and the end, the first and the last."[1]

How Does the Model Apply to Education?

In Chapter 3, we described a teaching strategy called Memorization and suggested it had three components: repetition, association, and a factor we called "Pop!"—the sudden Gestaltic, Newtonian understanding of something that falls into place instantaneously. Now that you're familiar with Ages and Stages, consider how those three strategies fit the model.

Ages and Stages of the Memorization Strategy		
A	I	Ω
Repetition	Association	Pop!

If you're suddenly seeing connections between memorization strategies, Plato, and parenting, you're probably having a Pop! moment of your own right now. For this moment at least, you're an Omega parent!

Now consider the eight categories of teaching approaches outlined earlier in this chapter, and see how they fit the Ages and Stages model:

Ages and Stages of Teaching Approaches		
A	I	Ω
Parent-Directed Traditional Models (Psychology-Based Philosophies, Directed Approaches, Faith-Based Approaches)	**Parent-Monitored Eclectic Models** (Secular Values-Oriented Approaches, Informal Approaches, Questioned Learning)	**Parent-Observed Unstructured Models** (Undirected Philosophies, Unschooling Philosophies)

If you're still following along, you're beginning to see how fifty different teaching approaches might have individual meaning for your family's educational program.

How Do I Use These Approaches?

You learned about the sixty supporting teaching strategies in Chapter 3. The remainder of this chapter follows a similar format. We introduce each of the fifty teaching approaches below, along with descriptions of the founders, advice about how to implement each approach as part of your educational program, and a list of related teaching strategies.

The fifty teaching approaches are categorized in Table 4.4.

Psychology-Based Philosophies

Two of these psychological models have become so much a part of the way we think and believe as a modern society that it's difficult to imagine Western civilization without them. These models are the foundation of beliefs about public education, rewards and punishments, left- and right-brain theories, the tax system, social justice, and virtually everything about the way you were reared as a child of the Dr. Spock revolution. The third model, though, is modern psychology at its peak. It sees children not as large animals to be disciplined into learning, and not as blank slates to be written on by an omniscient professional teacher, but rather as individual artists and constructors of their own personal maps of the world.

Ages and Stages of the Psychological Models		
A	I	Ω
Behaviorist	Cognitivist	Constructivist

Table 4.4   Fifty Teaching Philosophies

Psychological (pages 118–123)	Directed (pages 123–137)	Faith-Based Values (pages 137–145)	Secular Values (pages 145–152)
Behaviorism Cognitivism Constructivism	Classical 4MAT Method Accelerated Desuggestive Layered Curriculum Learning Cycles Montessori Objectives-Based School-at-Home Unit Studies	Scripture Study Purpose-Based Religion-Based Classical Christian Discipleship Heart of Wisdom Identity-Directed Principle-Based	Moral Development Aesthetic Realism Values-Based Eclecticism Hierarchy of Needs Logotherapy
Informal (pages 152–158)	**Questioned Learning (pages 159–163)**	**Undirected (pages 163–168)**	**Unschooling (pages 169–178)**
Charlotte Mason Contract Learning Eclectic Hybrid New Media Peer Tutoring Scouting	Project-Based Inquiry-Based Problem-Based Foxfire Mediated	Waldorf Reggio Emilia Frienet	**Directed** Delayed Schooling Moore Natural Learning Integrated Relaxed **Undirected** Play Child-Led Self-Directed Christian Unschooling

Behaviorism

The original psychological model, the science of Behaviorism seeks to observe and control behavior and learning through "conditioning." Behavioral scientists study the human mind by introducing a stimulus and then observing the response. Behaviorism goes well beyond mere observation, of course, which is why it appears in this chapter. Behaviorists look for the stimuli that will *induce* people—children, in this instance—to produce a desired behavior.

For More Information

It must be noted that the descriptions of teaching approaches in this chapter are only perfunctory explanations of some very complex theories. Many of these approaches are supported by libraries of research, theory, investigation, and commentary. These explanations touch only on the most significant points as they affect home education. To learn more about each of these approaches, visit the Theories page on our companion Web site, where we review related publications, Internet resources, and applications for the approaches and philosophies described in this chapter. The Theories page is found at <www.homeschool steps.com/seealso/theories.htm>.

Founders: John B. Watson (1878–1958), Ivan Pavlov (1849–1936), and B. F. Skinner (1904–1990) are the best-known founders of the behaviorist approach.

Methods: Watson suggested in 1913 that social scientists should study only observable behavior. Pavlov (remember the slobbering dogs?) theorized that behavior is simply a response to a stimulus. Ring a bell and feed a dog. The dog associates food with the bell. Ring the bell again, the dog salivates in anticipation of more food. Skinner—a man who, as part of his research, raised his own daughter in a box so that he could observe her behaviors—expanded the theory with the concept of "reinforcement." His studies suggested that you can cause behavior to reoccur by rewarding it. Interestingly, Skinner discovered that it's far more effective to reinforce behavior intermittently than it is to reinforce it regularly and frequently. Behaviorists believe that information exists separately from individuals and that it can be taught by breaking it into small components so that the learner can be "shaped" with behaviorist techniques into learning. Behaviorist techniques tend to be successful if the goal is to produce low-level learning—recalling facts, making generalizations and associations, and chaining (automatically performing a procedure.) You might, for example, choose to use behaviorist psychology to teach your children how to fold laundry, or to help them memorize a list of spelling words.

Related Strategies: Awards, Competitions, Copywork, Dictation, Lesson Planning, Scope-and-Sequence, Traditional Curriculum, Worksheets

Cognitivism

Cognitivism rejects the simplistic stimulus-response model of Behaviorism and suggests, instead, that there is a mediator—human cognition—between stimulus and response, giving individuals control over how they respond to stimuli. The theory argues that people are not "programmed animals" that respond to environmental stimuli in the same way. Information goes in to the brain, is processed, and results in an outcome—but the outcome depends on the way the individual processes the information.

Founder: Although his work is built on a foundation laid by others, Albert Bandura (1925), a professor of psychology at Stanford University, is considered the most prominent of the early founders.

Methods: Like behaviorists, cognitivists believe information is "out there," and that it can be transmitted to the "black box" called the human brain, if you simply discover the key to putting it there. The goal of instruction is the communication or transfer of knowledge to learners in the most efficient, effective manner possible. To transmit information, a cognitive scientist would analyze a task, break it down into smaller "chunks," and use that information to develop instruction that moves from simple to complex. Bandura suggested the idea of vicarious learning, or modeling, as a teaching approach. He also introduced the idea that there can be a significant time lapse between input and learning. Cognitivists believe people can learn by observing others, as well as by participating in an act personally. They also believe learners are most likely to model behavior observed in people they "identify with"—in other words, those to whom they have a high degree of attachment or those with whom they believe they share a similarity; in other words, one might argue, parents or peers.

Related Strategies: Concept Mapping, Family Nights, Labs and Demos, Metaphors

Constructivism

Constructivism is based on the premise that we all construct our own perspective of the world. Radical Constructivism says that reality doesn't even exist. The only thing that's "real" is what we create in the mind. The less radical form—Social Constructivism—asserts only that we construct our personal realities out of our own experiences. Unlike the two previous approaches, Constructivism focuses on preparing the learner to solve problems in ambiguous situations.

Founders: Jean Piaget (1896–1980), Lev Vygotsky (1896–1934)

Methods: Since children learn from their experiences, the constructivist says, it's critical that they have a multitude of real-life learning experiences. Note two different philosophies: Piaget's theories are the foundation for "discovery learning models," in which the teacher plays a limited role. In Vygotsky's social learning theories, on the other hand, parents and older children play very important roles in learning. The teaching parent taking a constructivist approach would provide for active, self-regulating, reflective learning opportunities. A child's mental map of the world expands and evolves as new situations recast it in a different, more densely textured form. A constructivist would avoid any teaching that took learning out of its natural context, in the belief that no transfer of knowledge occurs if learning doesn't take place in a real-world context. Learning a list of random Spanish vocabulary words, for example, has no long-term impact, but learning an equal number of words off a menu at a Mexican restaurant provides context and builds the learning map. Constructivism is a particularly useful approach when it comes to teaching high-level thinking skills, such as language development, problem solving, inference generating, and critical thinking.

Related Strategies: Case Studies, Field Trips, Road School, Self-Publishing

Directed Approaches

These are the hands-on, involved-parent approaches that attempt to mold and train children, and imbue them with a large body of knowledge.

Classical

The Classical approach originated in twelfth-century England, and served as the curriculum for Western education from the medieval age until the twentieth century. The Classical approach is grounded in the "liberal arts" of ancient Greece. In the medieval university, the seven liberal arts were grammar, rhetoric, and logic (known collectively as the Trivium) and geometry, arithmetic, music, and astronomy (the Quadrivium). Classical homeschoolers organize their educational program largely on the Trivium element of classical education, teaching the three elements in progressive stages. The Grammar stage (roughly corresponding to early elementary-school ages) focuses on memorizing facts and learning a classical language (Greek, Latin, or, for Jewish and Christian classical schoolers, Hebrew). The Dialectic or Logic stage (middle-school years) is focused on understanding the logic and meaning of memorized facts and asking questions. Finally, the Rhetoric stage (high-school years) teaches composition, oratory, and debate.

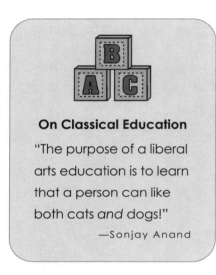

On Classical Education

"The purpose of a liberal arts education is to learn that a person can like both cats *and* dogs!"

—Sonjay Anand

Founders: Influenced by Roger Ascham, tutor to Queen Elizabeth I and author of *The Scholemaster* (1570). In modern times, the classical homeschooling movement was given its impetus by the reprinting of Dorothy Leigh Sayers's 1947 essay "The Lost Tools of Learning" in a homeschooling publication. It continues to be promoted by several well-known authors, including Jessie Wise and Susan Wise Bauer, Douglas Wilson, and Laura M. Berquist.

Methods: In the Grammar stage, a teaching parent might employ a variety of strategies to teach basic facts: Copywork, Dictation, Lesson Plans, Literature-Based Learning, Memorization, and Narration are all popular. The Dialectic stage involves formal instruction in logic, which can be taught through Socratic Questioning, Concept Mapping, and Outlining and Note-Taking. At the Rhetoric stage, learners continue to read extensively, but also are involved in College Prep, guided Research Techniques, and Portfolio Building.

Related Strategies: College Prep, Concept Mapping, Copywork, Critical Reading, Dictation, Graphic Organizers, Lesson Planning, Literature-Based Learning, Logic and Rhetoric, Memorization, Narration, Outlining and Note-Taking, Portfolio Building, Research Techniques, Socratic Questioning

Ages and Stages of the Classical Approach		
A	I	Ω
Grammar	Dialectic or Logic	Rhetoric

4MAT

The second Directed approach, the 4MAT model, is based loosely on learning styles, which you'll read about in Chapter 7. The 4MAT model suggests that learners can be distinguished two ways: by the way they *perceive* information (Concrete learners perceive primarily through the five senses; Abstract learners perceive via intuition, imagination, visualization and other intangible means) and by the way they *process* information (a Sequential learner organizes information in a linear, step-by-step form, while a Random learner thinks about information in small pieces with no particular order). The 4MAT model sorts learners into four quadrants based on their learning preferences: Concrete-Random learners want to know Why; Abstract-Sequential learners wants to know What; Concrete-Sequential learners ask How; and Abstract-Random learners ask If. (See Figure 4.1.)

Founder: Author/lecturer Dr. Bernice McCarthy, who drew heavily on the theories of researcher Anthony F. Gregorc, PhD, and of David A. Kolb (1939–), a professor of organizational behavior.

Methods: In the 4MAT method, the focus is on teaching not just to the preferred style, but also to all four learning styles. While a lesson is being taught in a strong area, the learner shines. During the portion of the lesson that addresses the learner's weaker areas, the child stretches to develop and learns to use the entire brain. Children in the first (Concrete-Random) quadrant are highly social. They like group discussions, care for others, and cooperate. They need to understand why a particular subject is relevant. Provide lots of context

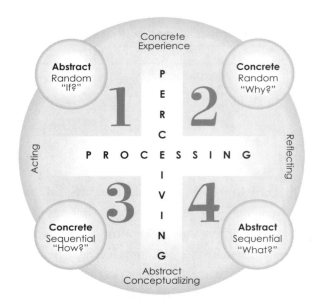

Figure 4.1 *McCarthy's 4MAT System*

Adapted from the 4MAT System, developed by Dr. Bernice McCarthy *<www.aboutlearning.com>*.

for a first-quadrant learner. Second quadrant (Abstract-Sequential) learners are highly analytical. They seek content, accuracy, logic, and competence. Provide a second-quadrant learner with intellectually challenging materials and access to expert opinions. (We discuss building an intellectually stimulating learning environment in Chapter 7.) The quadrant-three (Concrete-Sequential) learners are problem solvers. They enjoy experimenting, practicality, strict scheduling, consistency, and task completion. Learners who lean toward the fourth quadrant (Abstract-Random) are risk takers. They want to do it themselves, make their own discoveries, and fix the world. These learners are dynamic and thrive on change.

Related Strategies: Collaborative Learning, Concept Mapping, Discussions, Evaluations, Journaling, Labs and Demos, Literature-Based Learning, Metaphors, Placement Testing, Scrapbooking, Self-Publishing

Accelerated Learning

Speed teaching! The Accelerated Learning approach focuses on teaching a specific body of knowledge in the shortest possible time. One educator calls it a "substantial increase in the tempo of content presentation and acquisition." Accelerated learners aren't necessarily gifted learners, although they progress much faster than average.

Founders: Sidney L Pressey, the founder of programmed learning, described Accelerated Learning in 1949. Dr. Brian Smart, emeritus professor of education at Melbourne University, has conducted extensive research on learning rates and pacing. In the homeschooling arena, Joyce Swann is the "poster mom" of Accelerated Learning.

Methods: For homeschoolers, Accelerated Learning describes a philosophical concept developed around 1975 by Joyce Swann, the mother of ten homeschooled children. Each of the Swann children finished high school by age eleven, college by age fifteen, and an advanced college degree through home study by the age of sixteen. The Swanns' Accelerated Learning philosophy is the most formal and structured of the approaches to homeschooling. Teaching with the Accelerated Learning method requires discipline and organization. The teaching parent and the homeschooled children focus on moving through the curriculum as though it were a "line of progression," without taking "meandering forays" into unrelated projects. The Swanns use commercial curricula[2] to teach their children, and school three hours a day, five days a week, year-round, taking breaks only on weekends and government holidays when Dad is home from work. Each day's lessons take place around the breakfast table, all children are required to work through their day's lessons efficiently, and no outside interruptions are permitted. School is completed by 11:30 each morning, after which the children are free to play, finish their chores, and pursue their own interests.

The Accelerated Learning approach requires unswerving commitment to completing a standardized curriculum, maintaining accurate records, and fulfilling prerequisites to college admission at a young age. To get started, you might want to read through the background material on the Accelerated page of the Homeschool Steps Web site at *<www.homeschoolsteps.com/seealso/accelerated.htm>*. This page contains information about Accelerated Learning, gifted education, Advanced Placement classes, and distance learning.

Related Strategies: College Prep, Correspondence Courses, Online Classes, Scope-and-Sequence, Theses and Dissertations, Traditional Curriculum, Umbrella Programs, Writing to Learn

Desuggestive

The name "Desuggestive" describes the belief of its founder that children typically learn slowly because it has been suggested to them that they aren't capable of learning quickly and completely. Suggestopedia is a teaching method that relies on a highly structured environment and intense memorization techniques. Its proponents assert that children taught by this method learn at rates twenty-five times faster than through conventional methods.

Founder: Bulgarian psychiatrist-educator Dr. Georgi Lozanov (1926–)

Methods: Desuggestive teachers approach education with authority and optimism. Children are taught in a rapid-fire manner by educators who attempt to teach the subconscious mind. This approach has been compared with hypnosis and is achieved in part through information-rich visual aids, a round or horseshoe-shaped seating arrangement in which children and teacher can interact face-to-face, classical background music, and the confident, authoritative behavior of the teacher—all designed to soothe learners into a state of physical relaxation and mental alertness. As a teaching parent employing desuggestive techniques, you'd use vocal rhythms, movement, and an authoritative (meaning, "confident," not "authoritarian") style to impart large volumes of information to your children.

Related Strategies: Learning Environments, Lesson Planning, Listening Skills, Memorization, Scope-and-Sequence

Layered Curriculum

The Layered Curriculum approach is custom-made for large homeschooling families or co-op groups with children of different ages. Layering means that the teaching parent designs a single learning experience—a unit study, say—with different expectations for different children.

Founder: Educator Kathie F. Nunley

Methods: The Layered Curriculum method was created for the classroom, but is easily adapted to homeschooling. Create a lesson plan or unit study with several "layers" of understanding, learning objectives, and responsibilities. Each child receives a copy of the parent's learning objectives and is encouraged to work through as many objectives as the parent considers age appropriate. The parent helps learners set goals, organize material, and assess their learning. While the entire family studies, say, Chinese history, a younger child might learn to count to ten in Chinese and draw the numbers. An older child might focus on social customs, and a high-school aged child might learn the names and characteristics of the various dynasties. At some point in the study, each child would take responsibility for teaching his "specialty" to his siblings, younger and older. In this manner, children can work together while working independently.

Related Strategies: Build-It-Yourself, Lesson Planning, Rubrics, Scope-and-Sequence, Self-Publishing, Traditional Curriculum

Learning Cycles

The Learning Cycles model works almost backwards from what you're probably accustomed to. The model begins with an exploration of new phenomena, is followed by an explanation, and concludes with an application. Progressing from the concrete to the abstract is consistent with Piaget's view of intellectual growth. Moreover, research—and common sense—suggests that learners are more receptive to understanding a concept if they have first engaged directly in a concrete experience that raises a question in their minds. The Learning Cycles model has been used successfully for learners of every age, and can be adapted to virtually any topic—although science tends to be the most natural application.

Founder: Robert Karplus (1927–1990), professor of physics at the University of California

Methods: In the Exploration stage, students perform activities with physical objects before the teaching parent gives a formal presentation. The parent may provide a simple instruction about the goal of the exploration stage, or the activity could be completely open-ended. In this stage, children might be encouraged to observe, measure, record data, make predictions, create tests, or otherwise formulate explanations. For example, you might place an egg in a bowl, and then allow your child to examine the egg, break it, manipulate it with wooden skewers, heat it, freeze it, or devise other experiments. The second stage is the Introduction of the Concept. In this "guided discovery" stage, the teaching parent takes an active role in presenting the concept. This more formal stage could also include instruction using textbooks, audiovisuals, demonstrations, or laboratories. The final stage, Concept Application, occurs after children are familiar with the new concept. In this stage, the teaching parent introduces a new application activity where the concept is used in a slightly different setting than was originally developed, thereby demonstrating the concept in a wider frame of reference. Overall, the Learning Cycle approach is easy to use. Most teaching materials are ready-made for the Exploration stage, and many activities that textbooks and commercial materials suggest "for further study" are ideal for the Concept Application stage.

Related Strategies: Collaborative Learning, Concept Mapping, Evaluations, Kitchen Science, Labs and Demos, Learning Centers, Lectures, Lesson Planning, Manipulatives, Notebooking, Scientific Method, Socratic Questioning, Traditional Curriculum

Ages and Stages of the Learning Cycles Approach		
A	I	Ω
Exploration	Concept Introduction	Concept Application

Montessori

The Montessori method is all about practical life skills, taught through the tools of sensory stimulation, a prepared learning environment, individual attention, and modeling of ideal behavior. The approach is generally employed at the preschool level, but some believers teach with the Montessori approach through the eighth grade.

Founder: Italian early childhood educator Dr. Maria Montessori (1870–1952)

Methods: The Montessori approach can be very rigorous, with formal teacher training and the purchase of commercial Montessori products and manipulatives. But the theories are still valid even if you apply them in a customized, do-it-yourself format. Look for opportunities to teach practical skills by involving your children in meal preparation, house cleaning, gardening, laundry, home repair, and every other preparation for eventual independence. Providing opportunities for independence has a positive effect on children's self esteem—another important factor in Montessori theory.

Sensory stimulation is a major factor in Montessori education. Look for ways to refine motor skills with activities such as tying, pouring, stirring, cutting, pasting, eating with chopsticks, playing an instrument, sports, and dance. Teach kinesthetically wherever possible. For example, you might cover wooden alphabet letters with various materials—velvet, sandpaper, satin, wax—so that your children get sensory feedback while learning. Teach size and color discrimination, as well as math skills, with different-sized cylinders or blocks that can be lined up from largest to smallest, lightest to darkest, or grouped by color or other categories. Look for other items that allow children to group, sort, categorize, and distinguish. Concentration—a memory game where a child tries to match up identical cards—is an ideal Montessori game because it involves concentration, cognitive skills, and kinesthetic learning.

It's critical to Montessori theory that the learning environment be conducive to education. There is no junk food and no television. Books, toys, and other educational materials are carefully chosen and of the best quality. A Montessori classroom is bright, clean, well organized, child-sized, filled with cultural, artistic, and scientific activities, and very accessible to children. It encourages exploration while insisting on courtesy and kindness. Parents can model these behaviors by, for example, never forcing a child to attend a lesson or do a piece of work, and by refraining from interrupting a child who is working on an activity. A Montessori parent learns to observe children and follow their interests in suggesting work.

Related Strategies: Creativity, Learning Centers, Learning Environments, Manipulatives, Scientific Method

On Trivial Pursuits

"Nothing in education is so astonishing as the amount of ignorance it accumulates in the form of inert facts."

—Henry Brooks Adams,
*The Education
of Henry Adams*

Objectives-Based

The Objectives-Based approach is all about the destination, rather than the journey. In short, you begin with the end in mind. The theory applies on a small scale to tasks such as cleaning the kitchen or teaching children to tie their shoes, and on a large scale to objectives relating to why you're homeschooling in the first place, and how you hope your children will turn out as adults. With this approach, you choose the outcome you're looking for, and then find the means to get there.

Founder: Educational psychologist Benjamin Bloom (1914–1999) is responsible for a very specific subset of Objectives-Based education: objectives relating to high-level thinking.

Methods: Objectives are written statements about the kinds of outcomes you desire at the conclusion of the lesson. Normally these objectives are stated in concrete terms. For example, you might describe a behavior, an observable activity, or a skill the child should be able to demonstrate so that you know the knowledge has been acquired. Use objectives in planning lessons. If you were, for example, teaching your children to publish their essays on the Internet, your lesson plan might say "Gina will be able to build a Web page independently and FTP it to the host server."

When it comes to academic subjects, you might want to consider the work of Benjamin Bloom, who proposes that those objectives be written in terms of *thinking* behavior. Bloom is the author of *Bloom's Taxonomy* (see sidebar), the well known six-level model of thinking. His research suggests that more than 95 percent of the questions test takers encounter require them to think at only the lowest level of thought. When a child reads a work of literature and is then quizzed on trivia (such as "What was Laura's nickname?" or "What breed of dog was Jack?"), the teaching parent loses the opportunity to instill in the child the capacity for higher levels of thinking. Learning has a higher, more diverse purpose than the simple accumulation of facts. Children who can think at a high level learn for pleasure; the acquisition of knowledge becomes a resource, rather than a chore. Bloom's taxonomy develops in children the capacity for wisdom.

Bloom's Taxonomy

Bloom's Taxonomy is widely available in educational literature and on the Internet. One of the best explanations of Bloom is provided by the Reading Services Center of the Omaha Public Schools, which applies the model to the story of *Goldilocks and the Three Bears*. A sample of the questions asked at each level:

* **Knowledge:** the recall of specific information (Who was Goldilocks?)
* **Comprehension:** an understanding of what was read (Why didn't her mother want her to go into the woods?)
* **Application:** the converting of abstract content to concrete situations (How were the bears like real people?)
* **Analysis:** the comparison and contrast of the content to personal experiences (How would you react in the bears' position?)
* **Synthesis:** the organization of thoughts, ideas, and information from the content (Do you know any other stories about children who escaped from danger?)
* **Evaluation:** the judgment and evaluation of characters, actions, outcome, etc., for personal reflection and understanding (Why would an adult tell this story to children?)

Adapted from "Comprehension: Bloom's Taxonomy," Omaha Public Schools, <www.ops.org/reading/blooms_taxonomy.html>.

Related Strategies: Evaluations, Lesson Planning, Literature-Based Learning, Logic and Rhetoric, Scope-and-Sequence, Traditional Curriculum

Ages and Stages of Bloom's Taxonomy of Questioning		
A	I	Ω
The lowest levels: Knowledge, Comprehension	**The intermediate levels:** Application, Analysis	**The highest levels:** Synthesis, Evaluation

School-at-Home

The School-at-Home approach is an attempt to replicate the public-school classroom at home.

Founder: Although many of the American founding fathers expressed a belief in free public education, only Thomas Jefferson (1743–1826) attempted to translate his conviction into reality, drafting legislation for a plan of public education, designing study plans for his family and acquaintances, and establishing the University of Virginia. He believed that democracy could be effective only in the hands of an enlightened people, but at the same time opposed compulsory education.[3] Horace Mann (1796–1859), the first secretary of the Massachusetts State Board of Education, supported an extended school year, increased school appropriations, increased teaching parent wages, and professional supervision. And proponent John Dewey believed society should be interpreted to the child through daily living in the classroom, which can act as a miniature society.

Methods: School-at-homers tend to be highly scheduled and highly disciplined. They may adhere to the calendar and schedule of the local public schools. They may use a full written curriculum—either commercially purchased or custom built—and follow the standards of learning of the public-school system. The most radical school-at-homers have school in a separate room from the living quarters of the home. Their children sit at standard school desks during school hours, and the room is equipped with all the conventional trappings of a classroom. It's not uncommon for new homeschoolers to begin with this approach because of its familiarity, later to discard it in favor of approaches more suited to their children's individual learning preferences.

Related Strategies: Build-It-Yourself, Correspondence Courses, Critical Reading, Evaluations, Learning Environments, Lesson Planning, Listening Skills, Memorization, Online Classes, Outlining and Note-Taking, Placement Testing, Rubrics, Scope-and-Sequence, Traditional Curriculum, Umbrella Programs, Worksheets

Unit Studies

This holistic approach to education involves taking a theme or topic and delving into it deeply over a period of time, integrating language arts, science, math, social studies, and the arts, under the theory that children learn better when their learning takes place in context. Unit Studies can be a fun, effective way to teach across the curriculum by blending disparate subjects under one main topic or theme. You can tailor Unit Studies to your family, teaching several ages at one time, as described under Layered Curriculum, above. The term "Unit Studies" covers a continuum of related approaches: Themes (mini units), to Web Quests (a sort of do-it-yourself theme, where the learner researches the topic on the Internet), to full-blown Unit Studies.

Founders: Homeschoolers Jessica Hulcy and Amanda Bennett are well known developers of commercial unit studies. Valerie Bendt has written several books on creating your own unit studies.

Methods: Units usually consist of preplanned lessons and activities on topics the teaching parent considers important for the children to understand. These topics tend to be very broad: marine life, for example, or weather, African history, native plant life, or the Byzantine empire. Typically, a unit study involves four to six weeks of in-depth study; themes might take only a week. If you're writing your own unit studies, or modifying someone else's, decide in advance how extensively you want to delve into the topic. Is it a brief introduction (theme) or a full-blown in-depth experience? Larger homeschooling families find success in having intermediate and older children participate in developing unit studies for the entire family—a practice that teaches older children valuable research skills while giving them a basic introduction to the subject of the unit study. In developing a unit study, research the topic using library materials and the Internet. You may want to use a chapter out of a textbook as a base. Supplement the chapter with learning activities, workbooks and worksheets, vocabulary words, reference resources, photographs, videos, field trips, and a list of topical readings—typically fiction, but sometimes classics—that can be read for enjoyment. (Reading can take place over the duration of the unit study.) You'll also want to consider a variety of assessment tools: dramatic presentations, speeches, reports, compositions, artwork, and more. Create an outline that includes important points to be covered and questions to be answered. Divide your finished outline into weekly segments.

Related Strategies: After-Schooling, Broadcasting, Case Studies, Copywork, Dictation, Discussions, Evaluations, Expert Resources, Field Trips, Interviewing, Journaling, Labs and Demos, Library Skills, Media-Supported Learning, Memorization, Nature Diaries, Notebooking, Presentations, Research Techniques, Rubrics, Scrapbooking, Self-Publishing, Traditional Curriculum

Faith-Based Values Approaches

Perhaps the most frequently cited factor in the decision to homeschool is a desire to teach children to live religious lives of holiness and devotion. It's not surprising, then, that homeschooling families have been at the forefront of efforts to define and categorize religious approaches to education.

Most of the eight Faith-Based Values approaches in this section originated with Christian homeschoolers, and so they are imbued with Christian understanding of religious truth. Interestingly, though, the basic principles apply just as well to families of any faith-based religious tradition. As far as possible, we describe each of these approaches in terms of principles and vocabulary shared by most religious people.

The first three approaches under this heading progress from the Alpha to the Omega of the Ages-and-Stages model. Faith-Based education begins with the concrete building block: Scripture Study. As children mature, they begin to apply that concrete knowledge to their personal mission, and their learning progresses to the Purpose-Based approach. Eventually, they grow beyond this introspective stage, and begin to look outward. At this point, their education becomes Religion-Based—in other words, focused outwardly on service within a community of faith.

Ages and Stages of the Faith-Based Values Approaches		
A	I	Ω
Scripture Study	Purpose-Based	Religion-Based

Scripture Study

Whatever your religious faith, you undoubtedly have written scriptures guiding your theology. The Scripture Study approach involves reading the Bible or other scriptures as a central part of your educational program.

Methods: Scripture study can be approached from two directions, either chronologically or topically by subject matter. Scripture study involves a variety of study methods, including discussion, copying and narrating verses, analyzing authoritative commentaries, memorizing verses, maintaining an extensive study notebook, creating historical timelines, and integrating scripture study with other academic subjects. Whether you take the chronological approach or the topical approach, scripture study lends itself to years of unit studies that incorporate the study of ancient languages, writing, research, evaluation, basic math, reading, history, and much more. The strategy of Concept Mapping is ideal for scripture study because it enmeshes the learner with the reading material.

Related Strategies: After-Schooling, Copywork, Critical Reading, Discussions, Evaluations, Expert Resources, Family Nights, Field Trips, Forums, Graphic Organizers, Interviewing, Journaling, Lectures, Lesson Planning, Library Skills, Listening Skills, Logic and Rhetoric, Memorization, Metaphors, Narration, Notebooking, Online Classes, Outlining and Note-Taking, Presentations, Research Techniques, Self-Publishing, Socratic Questioning, Theses and Dissertations, Timelining, Worksheets

Purpose-Based Learning

The second level of faith-based approaches, Purpose-Based Learning is grounded in a belief that a child is on placed on earth for a God-given purpose and, consequently, that each individual is bound to discover his or her purpose and fulfill "the measure of their creation."

Methods: Parents using this approach help their children find a purpose and mission in life, and teach to that purpose. Purpose-Based Learning says each child is endowed with unique gifts and talents, and that child should be allowed to follow God's plan for his or her life, rather than trying to fit into a mold created by parents or other people. To find a purpose involves scripture study, prayer, and exposure to a wide range of learning opportunities.

Related Strategies: Build-It-Yourself, Field Trips, Interviewing, Journaling, Online Classes, Research Techniques, Scientific Method

On Religion in Education

"For centuries it was never discovered that education was a function of the State, and the State never attempted to educate. But when modern absolutism arose, it laid claim to everything on behalf of the sovereign power. [When] Church and State found that they were educating for opposite ends and in a contradictory spirit, it became necessary to remove children entirely from the influence of religion."

—Lord Acton (1834–1902)

Religion-Based

The Religion-Based approach focuses on developing character and spiritual maturity. This approach suggests that education shouldn't be viewed as an end in itself. Nor should it be viewed in terms of mere academic or social preparation for life. Understood in its broadest terms, education is character training.

Methods: Curriculum is based around a religious approach to homeschooling. Specific methods might involve a study of comparative religions, in-depth study of the doctrines and scriptures of your own faith, and integration of a religious worldview with your academic studies.

Related Strategies: Case Studies, College Prep, Critical Reading, Field Trips, Journaling, Listening Skills, Online Classes, Outlining and Note-Taking, Presentations, Research Techniques, Scope-and-Sequence, Self-Publishing, Socratic Questioning, Theses and Dissertations, Timelining

Classical Christian

Despite the fact that classical schooling was intimately bound with Christianity, its modern secular application leaves many Christian homeschoolers uneasy. One classical Christian homeschooler responds to that uneasiness with this reminder: "Just as a mop can be used to clean a floor both by a Christian and by a non-Christian, so believers and [non-believers] alike can make use of the tools of learning."

Founders: Authors Harvey and Laurie Bluedorn are prominent proponents of the classical Christian approach.

Methods: The Bluedorns divide the Trivium into what they call "Biblical categories." The Knowledge category teaches facts. Historical dates, scientific data, and musical notes all fall into this category. The Understanding category organizes the facts into logical order. It teaches the reasons behind history or the theory of music. Finally, the Wisdom category applies knowledge and understanding in practical ways. The Bluedorns rely largely on the Book of Proverbs to present the Trivium from a Christian worldview.

Related Strategies: See the Classical approach.

Discipleship

Discipleship—another word for evangelism—is homeschooling with the goal of creating disciples—adults trained to go out into the world and share a religious message. Discipleship is, at its root, a missionary training program. Academics are incorporated in this training as a means of showing God's hand in all disciplines.

On Character Education

"Knowledge has outstripped character development, and the young today are given an education rather than an upbringing."

—Ilya Ehrenburg

Founder: Homeschooling father Jonathan Lindvall has written widely on the Discipleship approach.

Methods: Under the Discipleship approach, there's no set curriculum and no learning activities. Instead, parents direct their children as the family works together on meaningful, productive tasks that improve the family economy. This process knits together the hearts of the family, while children acquire important life skills such as time management, homemaking, goal setting, praying, and interpersonal skills. In preparation for eventual missionary service or entrance to a seminary or theology degree program, a child being taught under this approach might undertake religious study, including the study of comparative religion. Such a child might tour the religious sites of other faiths, perform charitable works, undertake projects to resolve social problems or influence political change, or conduct in-depth research related to the history of the church.

Related Strategies: Critical Reading, Evaluations, Field Trips, Logic and Rhetoric, Notebooking, Research Techniques

Heart of Wisdom

An eclectic mix of several methods, the Heart of Wisdom approach involves Bible-centered Internet-linked unit studies using the Charlotte Mason method, described later in this chapter.

Founder: Author Marilyn Howshall, extrapolating from a number of complementary approaches

Methods: The Heart of Wisdom approach focuses first on reading the Bible in one year and creating an extensive Bible portfolio. The second focus is on developing writing skills using Notebooking or Scrapbooking strategies as a learning tool. The model expands on the Classical Christian approach by comparing each of the Christian Trivium elements to "gates." The Knowledge Gate roughly corresponds to traditional elementary grades (kindergarten through fourth). Emphasis is on rote learning and exposure to a wide range of experiences. The Understanding Gate roughly corresponds to traditional middle-school grades. Learners compare, contrast, make connections, and learn to discern. The Wisdom Gate roughly corresponds to traditional high-school grates. This is where knowledge and understanding are put to use. The learners evaluate situations and arguments. They are directed toward holiness, right relationships, fruitfulness, and productivity. They take their place in the lifetime pursuit of more wisdom. This approach integrates several philosophies, including Hebrew language studies, unit studies, building a timeline, and various other approaches described elsewhere in this chapter.

Related Strategies: Journaling, Logic and Rhetoric, Notebooking, Scrapbooking, Timelining, Writing to Learn

Ages and Stages of the Heart of Wisdom Approach		
A	I	Ω
The Knowledge Gate (roughly kindergarten through fourth grade)	**The Understanding Gate** (roughly fifth through eighth grades)	**The Wisdom Gate** (roughly ninth through twelfth grades)

Identity-Directed

Very much like the Purpose-Based approach described earlier in this section, the Identity-Directed approach urges parents to find their children's unique spiritual identity. In this approach, though, parents are encouraged to accept their teenagers' unique talents and growing independence, and use those talents to encourage the child's intellectual specialization. "Too many parents dislike and fear adolescence," the founder says, "but if they understood the dynamics of the teen years, they would look forward to them with real excitement."

Founder: Homeschooling dad Chris Davis, from curriculum supplier The Elijah Company, has written and spoken widely in support of this approach.

Methods: Accept that each child is different. Use the elementary years to build a general academic foundation. As a child grows, continually narrow the focus of educational and practical experiences to be more and more specific to who this child was created to be. Davis advises parents to pray for insight to know who each child is destined to be, and then seek growing-up experiences tailored to the child's specific needs. He also advises parents to give their teenagers the large blocks of time they need to become good at whatever it is they need to master. Davis suggests that parents learn to speak "words of positive identification" to their children, such as "I notice you are really good at . . ." This technique imprints positive feelings about their individual identities.

Related Strategies: Interviewing, Journaling (and any other strategy that encourages introspection), as well as Field Trips and other activities that enable broad exposure.

Ages and Stages of the Identify-Directed Approach		
A	I	Ω
Broad academic exposure	Narrowing focus	Focus entirely on building child's strengths and identity

Principle-Based

Premised on the principle that God guided the founding of democratic government and the U.S. Constitution, the Principle-Based approach seeks to understand history through the perspective of fulfillment of scriptural prophecy. Every academic subject is taught with a view toward how it correlates with the written word of God.

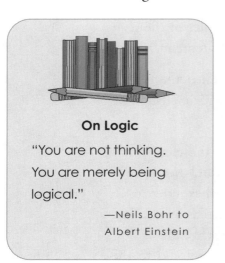

On Logic

"You are not thinking. You are merely being logical."

—Neils Bohr to Albert Einstein

Founders: Verna M. Hall (1912–1987), and author, educator, and Christian historian Rosalie Slater

Methods: This approach teaches children to reason from the scriptures and apply those lessons to themselves and to the academic subjects they study. It uses the "Four R's" model: Researching God's Word, Reasoning truth from the research, Relating (applying) reasoned truth to the learner and to the subject, and Recording the applied truth. This recording step is accomplished through the use of Journaling and Notebooking. The Principle-Based approach uses Webster's 1828 Dictionary to provide the "vocabulary of liberty"—usage that will familiarize children with the language used in the founding documents of the United States. In this model, teaching parents become the "living textbook," as they guide their children's character formation, reasoning, and scholarship.

Related Strategies: Critical Reading, Journaling, Logic and Rhetoric, Notebooking, Research Techniques, Scope-and-Sequence, Socratic Questioning, Writing to Learn

Ages and Stages of the Principle-Based Approach		
A	I	Ω
Researching	**Reasoning**	**Relating and Recording**
recognizing the elemental facts—the knowledge or grammar—of God's Providence	looking for the theory—the understanding or logic—of self-government	the practical application and the wisdom or rhetoric of the responsible use and extension of God's government to all of life

Secular Values Approaches

The Secular Values approaches that follow are practical, time-tested approaches to character education and moral development. Each of these approaches is compatible with faith-based education, but they all originate from reasoned theories about how best to imbue children with morality. The first three of these five approaches (Moral Development, Aesthetic Realism, and Values-Based Eclecticism) move from Alpha to Omega in the Ages and Stages model. The final two approaches—Maslow's Hierarchy of Needs and Frankl's Logotherapy—are wildly popular complex worldviews and stand alone as models of Ages and Stages.

Ages and Stages of Three Secular Values Approaches		
A	I	Ω
Moral dDevelopment	Aesthetic Realism	Values-Based Eclecticism

Moral Development

The theory of Moral Development is based on the belief that at birth children are blank slates—devoid of morals, ethics, or honesty. The founder of the approach identified the family as the first source of values and moral development for an individual. He believed that people progress in their moral reasoning. Interestingly, the model has been criticized as anti-feminist because it ignores the moral value of caring, while focusing on justice. It's a Constructivist approach.

Founder: Lawrence Kohlberg

Methods: Kohlberg's three-level, six-stage model of Moral Development is diagrammed in the chart on page 147. Each of the stages is a motivation for moral behavior. Kohlberg argues that each stage is progressive and that there's no functioning on a higher level until a lower level is mastered. Teaching involves introducing the next stage of development through discussion, narration, and age-appropriate experiences.

Related Strategies: After-Schooling, Case Studies, Concept Mapping, Discussions, Family Nights, Interviewing, Lesson Planning, Scope-and-Sequence

Ages and Stages of Kohlberg's Theory of Moral Development		
A	I	Ω
Pre-conventional (obedience and punishment, individualism, instrumentalism, and exchange)	**Conventional** ("good boy/girl," law and order)	**Post-conventional** (social contract, principled conscience)

Aesthetic Realism

Aesthetic Realism has been compared with a cult, and its adherents have published a number of leftist anti-government screeds. Despite those concerns, the approach itself is of interest to the homeschooling community. The philosophical foundation of Aesthetic Realism is comparable to the gentle Charlotte Mason approach to education. The purpose of education, founder Eli Siegel believed, is "to like the world through knowing it." Learners taught with the Aesthetic Realism approach learn to see beauty in the world, other people, art, and even themselves by finding harmony in opposites. (Ironically, practitioners of this avowedly "kind" philosophy are highly politicized and frequently engage in vitriolic attacks on government and the press.)

Founder: Poet and lecturer Eli Siegel (1902–1978)

Methods: Siegel advocated a philosophy of teaching that involves finding a positive opposite to every negative and relating all of nature's lessons to oneself. A teaching parent using the Aesthetic Realism approach teaches by helping learners to discover and appreciate opposites in every facet of education.

Related Strategies: Discussions, Forums, Literature-Based Learning, Journaling, Nature Diaries, Notebooking, Self-Publishing

Values-Based Eclecticism

A teaching approach focused on values, ethics, and morals, with or without a religious foundation, most Values-Based theory operates on the premise of teaching ethics without suggesting values. A worrying trend in public education is the practice of dividing children into peer groups and requiring individuals to comply with an arbitrary, consensual values set that the group itself creates. Homeschooling parents, freed from the constraints of value-neutral education, are free to teach their own values.

Methods: As with Religious-Based teaching, in Values-Based Eclecticism all academic information is "filtered" through a screen of ethics. Individual families vary in how much input children have in the development of the values set of the family. Once a family's values set has been defined, though, children are trained in ethical behavior with techniques such as storytelling, theater, discussion, copywork, and narration. Ethics are also taught through service and through interaction with organizations and groups sharing the family's values. Families taking this approach are involved in service organizations such as Habitat for Humanity, homeless shelters, food banks, CASA advocacy, fostering, adopt a highway, or raising guide dogs.

Related Strategies: Case Studies, Field Trips, Interviewing

Hierarchy of Needs

Unlike behavioral scientists, who studied animals and concluded that people can be similarly trained, or Freud, who studied the mentally ill and extrapolated his pessimistic determinism to healthy, functional people, the creator of the Hierarchy of Needs model took a different tack. He studied exemplary people such as Einstein, Eleanor Roosevelt, and Frederick Douglas and concluded that "A musician must make music, an artist must paint, a poet must write, if he is to be ultimately at peace with himself. What a man can be, he must be."

Founder: Psychologist Abraham Maslow (1908–1970)

Methods: Maslow advanced a model called the Hierarchy of Human Needs (see Figure 4.2). This popular theory suggests that people have various levels of "needs," and that they can't seek fulfillment of the higher needs until the lower ones are substantially satisfied. A hungry child can't be affectionate, for example, and a lonely child can't compose classical music. When families meet their children's basic needs, those children are freed to seek "self-actualization" to become the very best people they can be. A teaching parent using this model would attempt to inspire children to reach the pinnacle of their human potential: creativity, philanthropy, invention, or whatever else drives an individual child. Maslow proposed that education should involve teaching and living the following principles:

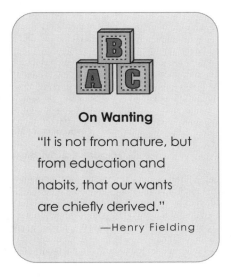

On Wanting

"It is not from nature, but from education and habits, that our wants are chiefly derived."

—Henry Fielding

- ✳ Authenticity (heeding advice from the inner voice)

- ✳ Cultural transcendence (becoming a citizen of the whole world)

- ✳ Vocation (discovering one's calling, fate, or destiny and becoming equipped to choose a compatible career and spouse)

- ✳ Appreciation (life is precious; find the good in every situation)

- ✳ Acceptance (accepting the limitations and aptitudes of ourselves and others is key to discovering both inner nature and potential)

- ✳ Satisfaction of basic needs

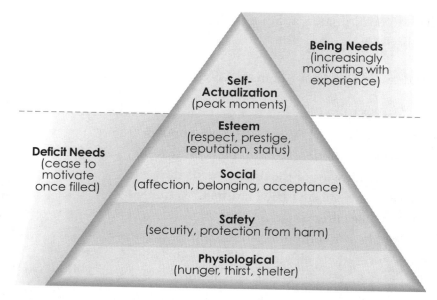

Figure 4.2 *Maslow's Hierarchy of Needs*

Adapted from the Maslow, *Toward a Psychology of Being* (1970)

* Refreshing consciousness (appreciation of beauty and the good things in nature and life)

* Control (Abandon is bad, Maslow wrote. Control improves the quality of life.)

* Transcendence of trifling problems (Everyone has problems, Maslow would say. Get past the trifling and grapple with the serious problems of life: injustice, suffering, poverty.)

* Choosing well

Related Strategies: Case Studies, Creativity, Interviewing, Metaphors

Ages and Stages of Maslow's Hierarchy of Needs		
A	I	Ω
Physiological, Safety and Security	Love and Belonging, Esteem	Self-Actualization

Logotherapy

Also known as "Existential Analysis" or "Man's Search for Meaning," this philosophy regards the search for meaning as the focus and purpose of human life. The founder, an Auschwitz survivor who lost his beloved wife, parents, and only brother in the Holocaust, said that even in the degradation and abject misery of a concentration camp, not even a sadistic Nazi SS guard could take away the final freedom: the freedom to choose one's own attitude and spiritual well being. No one can take away from another control over the inner life of the soul.

Founder: Viktor E. Frankl (1905–1997). Logotherapy is the "Third Viennese School of Psychotherapy," after Sigmund Freud (1856–1939) and Alfred Adler (1870–1937).

Methods: The work of the teaching parent is to help children find real and deep meaning in life. Teach by strengthening their trust in the unconditional meaningfulness of life and the dignity of the individual. Children—and adults—can find meaning "by creating a work or doing a deed; by experiencing something or encountering someone; and by the attitude we take toward unavoidable suffering." Center the curriculum around biographies and inspirational stories of heroes: philanthropists, religious leaders, inventors, humanitarians, and other people whose lives inspire emulation and awe. Also teach children that they are capable of deciding their own attitudes and responses and that they are responsible for their decisions. A human being is not a mere puppet of biological, hereditary, and environmental forces, but is always free to choose inner conditions.

Related Strategies: Awards, Case Studies, College Prep, Creativity, Critical Reading, Discussions, Expert Resources, Field Trips, Forums, Graphic Organizers, Interviewing, Journaling, Lectures, Listening Skills, Literature-Based Learning, Media-Supported Learning, Metaphors, Self-Publishing, Writing to Learn

Ages and Stages of the Psychotherapy Model		
A	I	Ω
Freudian: Dominion of the Unconscious	**Adlerian:** Dominion of the Community	**Frankl:** Search for Meaning

Informal Approaches

The six approaches in this section share a relatively unstructured, casual way of educating. Parents may direct the approach, but children are deeply involved in its implementation.

Charlotte Mason

Based on the writings of a nineteenth-century educator who believed children should learn from "living" books and not from textbooks. The method is characterized by no homework, no grades, short lessons, and few lectures.

Founders: Charlotte Mason (1842–1923). Karen Andreola, Penny Gardner, and Catherine Levinson have all written important books interpreting the method for homeschoolers.

Methods: Factors that comprise a Charlotte Mason education:

* No twaddle ("dumbed down" literature)
* "Living" books (classic, timeless stories)
* Whole books (no anthologies)
* Narration
* Short lessons (fifteen minutes for younger children)
* Weekly nature walks (observation, not conversation)

* Daily walks (for fun and fresh air)

* Nature notebooks

* Art appreciation (Study one artist at a time; six paintings per artist, one painting per week.)

* Journaling

* Copywork

* Dictation

* Book of the centuries (timeline in a notebook, two pages per century)

* Free-time handicrafts (afternoon hours for free time to pursue crafts and other leisure activities or areas of personal interest)

* Habits training (focus on correcting or developing one habit at a time for four to six weeks)

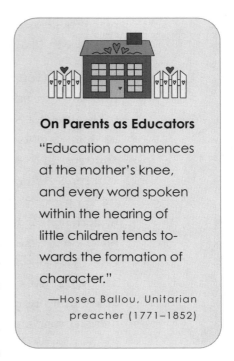

On Parents as Educators

"Education commences at the mother's knee, and every word spoken within the hearing of little children tends towards the formation of character."

—Hosea Ballou, Unitarian preacher (1771–1852)

Related Strategies: Copywork, Dictation, Journaling, Literature-Based Learning, Narration, Nature Diaries, Timelining

Contract Learning

The Contract Learning approach enables children to "contract" for their own education. When people learn by their own initiative, proponents say, they learn more deeply and more permanently than when they learn through traditional techniques. Moreover, when taught under the Contract Learning approach, children learn at their own pace—fast or slow.

Founders: Carleton Washburne (1889–1968), professor of education at Brooklyn College and architect of the 1919 "Winnetka Plan"

of contract learning; Helen Parkhurst (1886–1973), proponent of the Dalton Plan of self-paced learning.

Methods: Contract Learning is readily adaptable to home education and can involve virtually any "input" strategy, from textbooks, to Online Classes, to Literature-Based Learning. Under this approach, parents and children work together to develop a learning contract. The contract doesn't demand completion of a task by a certain time. Rather, it eliminates all time considerations and focuses instead on expectations that must be fulfilled before a new project is undertaken. Having agreed to a contract, children are free to complete the program at their own pace. No new contracts are permitted, though, until the current one is satisfactorily completed. The contact can be agreed to at any frequency, depending on the nature of the task. A family might agree, for example, that when the child completes three chapters in a math book, the child will be rewarded with a sleepover at Grandma's. Or on a larger scale, a child might contract to produce an in-depth research project on the Civil War, after which the family takes a vacation tour of various Civil War historical sites. The contract doesn't necessarily involve a "reward" (although it might). Rather, it is an agreement that a child pursue a chosen task and see it through to completion before starting on a new project. Parent and child work together to design the parameters of the project, after which the parent serves primarily as a resource. The child undertakes the responsibility for learning, from initial note-taking, to record-keeping, all the way through to an outcome, which should involve a demonstration of competency.

Related Strategies: Case Studies, Creativity, Critical Reading, Evaluations, Expert Resources, Field Trips, Interviewing, Library Skills, Literature-Based Learning, Online Classes, Outlining and Note-Taking, Research Techniques, Road School, Rubrics, Scientific Method, Scope-and-Sequence, Traditional Curriculum, Writing to Learn

Eclectic

An Eclectic homeschooler is one who looks at the different approaches and methods of homeschooling and takes from each according to the family's own unique philosophy.

Methods: Mix-and-match from approaches listed here to fit your family's personal educational beliefs.

Related Strategies: Awards, Build-It-Yourself, College Prep, Competitions, Road School, Scope-and-Sequence, Traditional Curriculum, Umbrella Programs

Hybrid

A combination of public or private school and home education, Hybrid is more than a practical approach; some homeschoolers dream of a "golden age" for education where anyone, of any age, can use public schools the same way they presently use public libraries, museums, and community centers. Wander in and out at will, and learn what you want to learn at an age when it seems particularly interesting or useful.

Methods: Until the future arrives, homeschoolers who want to supplement homeschooling with resources located in public schools are subject to a variety of regulations and restrictions. (See Chapter 2 and Appendix A for details about access laws.)

Many homeschooling families who would not otherwise be interested in public-school programs might be interested in having their children participate in extracurricular activities such as drama, music, and sports programs, or in certain specialized courses, such as advanced biology.

Some parents supplement homeschooling with public school in order to get assistance with a special needs child. (We discuss the issue of special learning needs in Chapter 9.)

Some families combine homeschooling with school-operated alternative-education programs designed for homeschooled children. When those programs are flexible and open, and the family retains primary responsibility for tracking and providing education, many homeschoolers would still consider AEP students to be homeschooled. There's quite a bit of controversy among homeschoolers, though, about how AEPs should operate. Some homeschooling families want fairly structured programs, with conventional records for their children. Others would like access to school resources, but with considerable latitude allowed in how they may use those resources.

Almost all homeschooling families enrolled in public school programs expect to have a significant role in determining the course and content of their child's program, and prefer that any required record keeping be both simple and relevant to the work being done.

Related Strategies: After-Schooling, Collaborative Learning, Placement Testing, Scope-and-Sequence, Traditional Curriculum

New Media

The New Media approach involves a curriculum supplemented by, or based on, various electronic media.

Founder: Sidney Leavitt Pressey (1888–1979), an educational-psychology professor at Ohio State University

Methods: In the early 1920s, Pressey created a crude teaching machine for rote-and-drill learning. B. F. Skinner, in a 1954 article called "The Science of Learning and the Art of Teaching," claimed the deficiencies of traditional teaching could be alleviated through the use of teaching machines. Home educators using this approach take advantage of the following tools: educational software (commercial and shareware), educational television, prerecorded media, online classes, online teaching resources, research, and online experts.

Related Strategies: Awards, Expert Resources, Field Trips (online), Forums, Media-Supported Learning, Online Classes, Outlining and Note-Taking, Research Techniques, Scope-and-Sequence, Self-Publishing, Web-Based Education

Peer Tutoring

Humans remember best what they teach someone else, goes the theory. Homeschooling families that incorporate Peer Tutoring as a teaching approach discover that their children take responsibility both for their own learning and for one another's education.

Methods: This approach is effective in large families, as well as in homeschooling cooperatives. The traditional methods are peer-to-peer, where a same- or similarly-aged child teaches a peer, and cross-age tutoring, where an older child tutors a younger child. A variation: Within a family, each child prepares a unit study for the entire family, with or without parental assistance, depending on the child's age. The presenter then becomes a "project manager" for the duration of the unit study. Families with younger children find success asking the child to lead a simple discussion or demonstration or introduce a single concept. When peer tutoring is insufficient, consider commercial tutorial services, private tutors, and tutoring exchanges. If you're in the market for a tutor, consider hiring a college student, a neighbor whose strengths complement your child's weaker areas, a family member, a retired neighbor, or a fellow congregant at your place of worship. Visit our Tutoring Web page at *<www.home schoolsteps.com/seealso/tutoring>* for listings of commercial tutoring services.

Related Strategies: Awards, Discussions, Expert Resources, Evaluations, Family Nights, Labs and Demos, Lectures, Lesson Planning, Memorization, Socratic Questioning, Traditional Curriculum

Scouting

Arrange your curriculum around the program of an established youth organization. In addition to the Boy Scouts and Girl Scouts, the Scouting Approach covers organizations such as religious youth group programs, 4-H, American Heritage Girls, Campfire, Civil Air Patrol, various debate programs, Keepers of the Faith, Outward Bound, Voices Across America, and Young Astronauts. It also includes youth programs offered through the YMCA such as Model United Nations, Youth and Government (a program in most U.S. states that emulates the state political process), youth camps, leadership conferences, and Earth Service Corps.

Founder: The original Boy Scout, Sir Robert Stephenson Smyth Baden-Powell, Baron of Gilwell (1857–1941)

Methods: Families using the Scouting approach organize their curriculum around the merit badge requirements of the Scouting program. Learners work through rigorous standards for advancements and maintain accurate records and extensive notebooks related to their studies. Other youth organizations—the YMCA's Youth and Government program, for example—have demanding and rigorous academic expectations for youth participants, making those programs ideal launch pads for a homeschool curriculum. These programs are also useful as a basis for homeschooling cooperatives, where several families meet together to charter a youth group under the auspices of a national organization.

Related Strategies: After-Schooling, Awards, Build-It-Yourself, Competitions, Discussions, Evaluations, Expert Resources, Family Nights, Field Trips, Forums, Interviewing, Kitchen Science, Library Skills, Memorization, Outlining and Note-Taking, Research Techniques, Scientific Method, Web-Based Education, Writing to Learn

Questioned Learning

The five approaches under this heading all share an approach that involves asking and answering questions. Children taught with any of these approaches get involved in posing questions and taking the initiative for investigation of a topic.

Ages and Stages of Three Questioned-Learning Approaches		
A	I	Ω
Project-Based	Inquiry-Based	Problem-Based

Project-Based Learning

The introductory phase of Questioned Learning, Project-Based Learning involves an in-depth investigation of a parent-assigned topic, undertaken by one child or a small group of children. Unlike themes and units, a project involves the study of real phenomena that learners can investigate directly, rather than through library research. Project-Based Learning attempts to captivate learners by encouraging them to think critically and to take responsibility for their own learning.

Founder: Heard Kilpatrick, a one-time student of John Dewey, introduced the project approach around 1916.

Methods: Parents using this approach design projects that encourage a child to acquire knowledge, problem-solving skills, self-directed learning strategies, and—when you can arrange group work—team participation skills. Children respond to topical questions such as "What do people do when . . . ?" "How does . . . work?" "What tools do are required to . . . ?" Project-Based Learning demands research, reading, recording observations, interviewing experts, and analysis.

As children gather information, they summarize it in the form of written reports and oral presentations. An important component of a project for young learners is dramatic play, in which children express new understanding and use new vocabulary. Dramatic play is discussed under the Learning Centers strategy in Chapter 3.

Related Strategies: Case Studies, Critical Reading, Field Trips, Graphic Organizers, Interviewing, Journaling, Kitchen Science, Labs and Demos, Learning Centers, Narration, Notebooking, Outlining and Note-Taking, Portfolio Building, Presentations, Research Techniques, Scrapbooking, Self-Publishing, Socratic Questioning, Theses and Dissertations, Timelining

Ages and Stages of the Project-Based Approach		
A	I	Ω
Select and refine topic for investigation	Conduct fieldwork	Complete culminating and debriefing events

Inquiry-Based

The middle level of Questioned Learning, Inquiry-Based teaching encourages learners to design their own activities, conduct theoretical research, and share authority for answers.

Founder: Related to the Functional Pedagogy of Edouard Claparède and the genetic psychology of Jean Piaget, who proposed the notion of learning through experience.

Methods: Parent and child work together to develop inquiries that are based largely on the academic interests of the child. As self-directed learners, children process information; interpret, explain, hypothesize; design their own activities; and prepare a bibliography and citation list for their research.

Related Strategies: Project-Based Learning, Research Techniques, Scope-and-Sequence, Writing to Learn

Problem-Based

Problem-Based learning is the highest, most scientific level of Questioned Learning. Learners engage in scientific investigations to satisfy their own curiosities, and to construct mental frameworks that explain their experiences.

Founder: Originated with a curriculum reform by the medical faculty at Case Western Reserve University in the late 1950s. The approach later spread to more than fifty medical schools and diffused into many other professional fields including law, economics, architecture, and mechanical and civil engineering. It's founded primarily on the work of Max Wertheimer (1880–1943), a leading proponent of Gestalt theory.

Methods: Gestalt theory, the basis of Problem-Based learning, involves three principles:

1. **Discovery.** Encourage the learner to discover the underlying nature of a topic or problem (i.e., the relationship among the elements).

2. **Understanding.** Understand that gaps, incongruities, or disturbances are an important stimulus for learning.

3. **Organization.** Base instruction on the Gestalt laws of organization—the four rules that explain how individuals mentally group raw sensory input into larger, more abstract entities. This grouping process is nearly subconscious, and people are almost never aware of explicitly joining small points together to form lines, or combining lines to form objects. Those four laws are:

   * **Proximity.** Learners tend to group elements together according to their physical nearness to one another.

* **Similarity.** Items similar in some respect tend to be grouped together.

* **Closure.** Items are grouped together if they tend to complete some entity.

* **Simplicity.** Items are organized into simple figures according to symmetry, regularity, and smoothness.

Learners using this approach would conduct in-depth research using the scientific method.

Related Strategies: Inquiry-Based strategies, plus Scientific Method

Foxfire

This approach was developed in 1966 by a teacher who was trying to develop a method for teaching basic English skills. His project became the Foxfire approach, in which students interviewed community members who had special expertise or historical perspectives and then wrote about what they learned. This project led to the publication of the *Foxfire* magazine and a series of books on Appalachian life and folkways.

Founder: Eliot Wigginton (1942–), author and high-school English teacher

Methods: This approach encourages children to go out into their community and interview real people about real life. To prepare for these interviews, they may conduct preliminary research. They then compile, analyze, and publish those findings.

Related Strategies: Broadcasting, Case Studies, Expert Resources, Field Trips, Interviewing, Listening Skills, Logic and Rhetoric, Notebooking, Outlining and Note-Taking, Research Techniques, Self-Publishing, Timelining, Writing to Learn

Mediated

Mediated Learning describes a special quality of interaction between a learner and a mediator—in our discussion, a parent. The mediator is not concerned with solving the problem at hand; rather she is concerned with how the learner approaches solving the problem. This approach places great faith in a child's ability to learn.

Founder: Cognitive psychologist Professor Reuven Feuerstein (1921–)

Methods: The role of the mediator is significantly different from the traditional role of a teacher. A mediating parent does not help a child to solve a problem. Instead, the mediator helps the child think through the problem and come up with a solution. Specifically, the mediator teaches a child to think by using lessons from previous experiences to adapt to new situations. The mediator doesn't correct or judge the child's response. Instead, she reflects back to the child the nature of his response so that he can understand how it would appear to someone else.

Related Strategies: Creativity, Critical Reading, Graphic Organizers, Listening Skills, Logic and Rhetoric, Scientific Method, Socratic Questioning, Writing to Learn

Undirected Approaches

"You can lead a child to fodder, but you can't make him think." Each of these three Undirected approaches to teaching strongly considers the child's desires in developing a curriculum.

Ages and Stages of the Undirected Approaches		
A	I	Ω
Waldorf	Reggio Emilia	Freinet

Waldorf

The Waldorf philosophy proposes that man is a threefold being of body, spirit, and soul, whose capacities unfold in three developmental stages (see chart below).

Founder: Austrian philosopher, scientist, and artist Rudolf Steiner (1861–1925)

Methods: Education proceeds in three major steps as the child "incarnates." The first step, Hands, symbolizes the body, or physical development. In this step, the child develops pictorial and imaginative consciousness. Work with the child's imagination, proceeding from fairy tales, legends, and fables through Bible stories and ancient mythology. The second step, Heart, represents feelings or emotional development. Focus on artistic and spiritual development. Around the age of twelve, add the element of reason. Begin to make the transition to actual history and science. The third step, Head, represents thinking and intellectual development. Without losing imaginative and artistic elements, present curriculum in a more scientific manner, increasingly relying on direct observation, objective description, and reflection in all subjects. Throughout this process, the child's consciousness develops. The approach strongly discourages use of electronic media. Children taught by the Waldorf method learn to play a stringed instrument. They create extensive notebooks, and they are introduced to academic subjects through artistic media. The method de-emphasizes early academics in favor of art, music, gardening, and foreign languages.

Related Strategies: Creativity, Logic and Rhetoric, Notebooking, Scientific Method

Ages and Stages of the Waldorf Approach		
A	I	Ω
Hands (Body)	**Heart** (Feelings)	**Head** (Thinking)

Reggio Emilia

This Undirected project-oriented approach developed in the municipal preschools of Reggio Emilia, Italy. One of the interesting features of the Reggio Emilia approach is the concept of teachers as learners, in other words, observers of children.

Founder: Italian educator Loris Malaguzzi (1920–1994) strongly influenced the program.

Methods: A major element of this approach is to purposefully allow for mistakes to happen, or to begin a project with no clear sense of where it might end. Projects may be designed by the parent, but more often they move in unanticipated directions as a result of problems children identify. In this approach, teaching parents find opportunities for children to engage in what Malaguzzi called the hundred "symbolic languages" of children: drawing, sculpture, gesture, drama, play, writing, conflict, negotiation, imagination, generosity, logic, and many more. Another primary role of the teaching parent is to arrange the environment so that the child constantly discovers, explores, and creates meaning. In an ideal environment, learning areas open to a center piazza, the kitchen is open to view, and access to the surrounding community is assured through wall-size windows, courtyards, and doors to the outside in each learning area. Entryways use photographs, children's work accompanied by transcriptions of their discussions, and mirrors on the walls, floors, and ceilings. Interiors are filled with displays of project work interspersed with arrays of found objects and learning materials. The ideal environment includes ample space for supplies, frequently arranged to draw attention to their aesthetic features. The learning area includes studio space in the form of a large, centrally located atelier.

Related Strategies: Learning Centers, Learning Environments, Logic and Rhetoric

Frienet

The Frienet approach involves naturist, cooperative education. This child-centered model focuses on projects or activities based on children's genuine interests.

Founder: French educator Célestin Freinet (1896–1966)

Methods: This approach has lots of unique teaching methods, easily adaptable to homeschooling. These include:

* **Productive work.** All education is work-based.

* **No rigid curriculum.** Instead, parents sit down each Monday with each child to lay out the week's work in the form of learner-chosen schedules. These weekly schedules are flexible, yet never lose sight of a larger scheme that the parent establishes in advance.

* **Varied schedules.** Schedules cover not only academic subjects (spelling, grammar, math), but also presentations, scientific enquiry, letters to pen pals, and printing and illustration of the family newsletter.

* **Research and field investigations (*sortie-enquête*).** Children regularly leave the classroom in order to observe and to study both their natural environment and their local community. When they return home, they present their results, print out texts, and produce a journal.

* **Experimental learning.** Children are allowed to learn through trial and error. Freinet believed children learn when they are invited to face real situations that present a problem to them and work out ways of solving it. It's important to allow them to make mistakes and to learn from these mistakes.

* **Self-correcting worksheets.** Permit children to build up their basic skills in an ordered but flexible way.

* **No textbook teaching.** But textbooks are freely available on bookshelves. Learning resources (classes, the Internet, and other media) aren't imposed, but are made available for self-study.

* **Free writing.** Writing only when you've got something to say, when you feel a burning need to set down in writing or in pictures something bubbling up inside you.

* **Group revision.** When children do elect to write, the writing is "corrected" by the entire family. "Elected" pieces of free writing are revised, both for accuracy of content and for grammar and spelling. The draft is copied or written on a board, and the entire family works with the author to improve the text and to make it clearer for other readers. Spelling errors are first corrected and then grammar, style, and substance.

* **Publication.** Once revised, the text is ready to be printed up for the family newsletter, produced by the children themselves to give the text permanent life and make it their own.

* **Exchange of work.** Parcels and collective letters can be exchanged with other Freinet learners. Individual letters can be sent from one family to another when each child has a pen pal. Exchange journeys are often organized to meet one another. Today, new technologies are also used in pen pal correspondence: video, fax, and the Internet all play a role.

* **Formal presentations.** Children voluntarily prepare a topic they choose and present it to the family.

On Conceptual Learning

"By the time the child can draw more than scribble, an already well formed body of conceptual knowledge formulated in language dominates his memory and controls his graphic work. Drawings are graphic accounts of essentially verbal processes. As an essentially verbal education gains control, the child abandons his graphic efforts and relies almost entirely on words. Language has first spoilt drawing and then swallowed it up completely."

—Karl Buhler, psychologist (1879–1963)

* **Diplomas.** Progress is rewarded with "diplomas" (*brevets*). For example, a diploma can certify each main topic in the math curriculum. Children also get diplomas by passing tests. Some diplomas are required, such as reading diplomas, spelling and grammar diplomas, writing diplomas, and math diplomas. Additionally, there can be *brevets* in cookery, electricity, music, chemistry, printing, engraving, pottery, carpentry, or anything else the family chooses.

* **Wall journal.** Freinet believed children should be allowed to freely air their grievances. Those grievances are written on what he called a Wall Journal. Each Monday a large sheet of paper is posted on a the "writing wall." The sheet contains four columns labeled Criticisms, Congratulations, Wishes, and Accomplishments. A pencil is attached to the panel so that children can at any time freely write what they have to say. Erasing is forbidden. All written remarks must be signed, to stop any imputation of tattling. The criticism column is used to air grievances about life, education, and behaviors of family members, but also to confess one's own errors and bad choices. Younger children are encouraged to dictate their comments as a parent writes them on the Wall Journal.

* **Cooperative meeting.** At the conclusion of each week, the family gathers to review its progress, discuss the information on the Wall Journal, and find solutions to grievances. The cooperative meeting always ends on a positive note, ensuring children that they've been heard and that they're valued, treasured members of the family.

Related Strategies: Awards, Correspondence Courses, Evaluations, Logic and Rhetoric, Media-Supported Learning, Notebooking, Online Classes, Rubrics, Self-Publishing, Web-Based Education, Worksheets

Unschooling

Unschooling covers any of nine related approaches, all of which share a philosophy of deliberately unstructured schooling. These approaches give children the responsibility for their own education, in the belief that children are inherently curious and that left to their own preferences, will prefer learning. The term "Unschooling," coined by educator John Holt, loosely describes any approach that rejects the School-at-Home model of a teacher lecturing a captive audience.

The nine approaches can be divided into two categories:

Directed Unschooling

Undirected Unschooling

Directed Unschooling

This approach involves at least a little parental guidance and facilitation of learning, combined with a basic goal-oriented approach to schooling. These directed approaches comprise Delayed Learning (and the related Moore Method), Natural Learning, Integrated Learning, and Relaxed Schooling. Three of these approaches (see chart) can be seen as progressive stages of Directed Unschooling.

Ages and Stages of the Directed Unschooling Approaches		
A	I	Ω
Delayed	Natural	Integrated

Delayed Schooling

Delayed Schooling can be considered the Alpha stage of Directed Unschooling. Under this approach, children's formal academics are delayed until the children are ready for them (about eight or ten years of age). By this time, the children, now developmentally ready, quickly learn and become proficient in their studies.

Methods: This approach is founded on fascinating research that compares three groups of children: Those who entered kindergarten at the usual age and then repeated their kindergarten year; those who entered kindergarten at the usual age and then continued on in their school as usual; and those who were held out of kindergarten for one year, and allowed to continue their childhood for an extra year. When these children were studied in subsequent years these findings emerged:

* Those who had the *worst* academic performance were those who went to kindergarten twice.

* Those who had average academic performance were those who went to kindergarten once.

* Those who had the *best* academic performance were those who didn't go to school at all during the traditional kindergarten year.

The conclusion is inescapable: Overall, kindergarten attendance may actually harm school performance! And the ideal teaching method? Just keep doing whatever you were doing before your child reached kindergarten age. Apparently, it works! Continue to spend the early years reading to your children, doing projects together, cleaning the house, and serving others.

For more information about research supporting delayed school entry, see the Delayed page of our companion Web site, *<www .homeschoolsteps.com/seealso/delayed.htm>*.

Related Strategies: Creativity, Learning Environments, Listening Skills, Placement Testing

Moore

The Moore approach to Delayed Schooling is a more work-oriented and more structured variation of the Delayed approach, described earlier.

Founders: Dr. Raymond Moore and his wife, Dorothy Moore

Methods: Dorothy Moore described her approach as "Study, with a balance of Work and Service, meaning about as much or more work and service as study." The Moores advocate informal study prior to the age of ten. Informal study means learning games, life experiences, and true books on a variety of subjects including language arts, the Bible, nature, biographies and travelogues. Reading instruction, if any, should be strictly phonics based. Formal schooling, once begun, takes place at an accelerated pace. The Moore approach involves structured bedtimes and mealtimes to accommodate a child's natural circadian rhythms.

Related Strategies: Creativity, Field Trips, Interviewing, Kitchen Science, Labs and Demos, Learning Centers, Learning Environments, Listening Skills

Natural Learning

The middle stage of Directed Unschooling, Natural Learning—also known as "holistic" or "organic" learning—means finding educational experiences in everyday occurrences. This approach is more family-centric than child-centric. Life happens, goes the theory, kids participate, and it's all naturally educational. Natural Learning builds upon a belief that learning unfolds naturally from within the individual and grows to include social settings such as family, close friends, community, and society in general.

Founder: In 1908, William Wirt instituted the Gary Plan in Gary, Indiana, by creating an exemplary all-round education embracing work, study, and play. The complete school was comprised of a playground, garden, workshop, social center, and traditional school under one management. This format maximized the use of the school's facilities day and night, twelve months a year.

Methods: In a homeschool setting, Natural Learning should continue the rhythms already existing in daily life, says Australian homeschooler Beverly Paine, whose writing inspires this approach. Above all, don't focus on your child's life as the center in the family.

Remember that everyone in your family is a learner, with unique needs and experiences. No single member is more important to the family's social structure than any other. Paine recommends welcoming children into the world of adults in "apprenticeship" roles. Naturally Unschooled children become intimately involved in all aspects of family life, including family working life, where their contributions are greatly valued. Where skills and knowledge are needed, Paine says, "within these rich social contexts, resources are always found." Within the framework of the family, Natural homeschoolers build a rich and comprehensive educational experience by allowing children to choose what, when, and how to learn things on their own. Paine warns against leaving children to be responsible for themselves. Instead, "encourage them to explore responsibility, and to gradually accept self-responsibility according to their overall development." Finally, Paine warns against overscheduling unnatural learning experiences. Learn to let go of what you don't need—unhelpful attitudes, experiences, and materials—and focus on what you really want out of each experience. Stay rooted in the real world of everyday existence and don't offer unrelated fragments of "learning experience" simply for the sake of learning.

Read more about Paine's—and other people's—approach to Natural Learning at the Natural page of our companion Web site, <*www.homeschoolsteps.com/seealso/natural.htm*>.

Related Strategies: Creativity, Learning Environments, Listening Skills

Integrated

The advanced, radical form of Natural Learning, the Integrated approach rejects formal education in all forms and instead proposes that children learn by actually taking part in life—including the world of work. While it doesn't reject the principle of parental supervision, the Integrated approach does reject child labor laws, regulations that would prevent competent children from having bank accounts or establishing contracts, and any other government-mandated form of isolating children from real life. It decries "the government-imposed separation of education from work, travel, leisure, housekeeping and other daily-life activities." By isolating children from adult society, say proponents, formal schooling destroys essential ingredients for learning—ingredients such as building up practical experience; developing interest in matters from personal preferences; and having an open-minded, creative, and independent personality.

Founder: Ben Mettes, Australian political activist who supports autonomy for families

Methods: Instead of memorizing formulas, facts, and details, solving artificial problems, or working within unnaturally appointed teams of people with no common goal, children should learn how to cope with life in a rapidly changing world. Integrated learning encourages children to participate in society, under the supervision of their parents. Schools create social misfits and nurture violence and mental paralysis, Mettes says, because "school keeps children away from real-life situations, from the world outside school, from that world with all its practical examples, its incentives and opportunities, from a world in which events are not scheduled in rosters as predefined routines and where situations are not artificially set up like acts in a play."[4] The Integrated approach involves a combination of naturally occurring work activities such as housekeeping, caring for children, and conducting a home-based business.

Related Strategies: Creativity, Learning Environments

Relaxed

Primarily a backlash against the secular humanist approach of Unschooling founder John Holt, Relaxed homeschooling takes essentially the same philosophies as the undirected approaches, below, while adhering to conservative Christian beliefs in authoritative parenting and the transcendence of God. Some practitioners call themselves "relaxed" as a euphemism for "Christian, anti-secular-humanist unschooler."

Founder: Mary Hood, author of *The Relaxed Home School,* is touted by some as "the Christian John Holt."

Methods: The Relaxed philosophy: You are a family, not a school; a mother, not a teacher; a father and the head of your household, not a principal. You have relationships with your individual children, not with a "class." And above all, God is in control. Hood says of her own family, "We have a Christian family structure in our household, and our kids know that there are limits to their behavior." The Relaxed approach requires prayerfully setting long-range goals and letting those goals drive education, rather than being driven by someone else's ideas about what should be done in a particular grade.

Related Strategies: Creativity, Learning Environments

On Education

"Curiosity about life in all of its aspects, I think, is still the secret of great creative people."

—Leo Burnett, quoted in *100 LEO's* (1995)

Undirected Unschooling

The even more progressive (some say "radical") category of Unschooling, where there is virtually no formal teaching, and all learning arises out of the natural lessons of daily living. These four approaches comprise Play, Child-Led Learning, Self-Directed Learning and Christian Unschooling.

Ages and Stages of the Undirected Unschooling Approach		
A	I	Ω
Play	Child-Led	Self-Directed

Play

This approach calls for noncompetitive, unstructured play in an environment that invites exploration. Advocates of Play theory say society has forgotten that play is a critically important factor in the normal development of children. We've neglected enjoyable, self-motivated, nonlinear play, they say, and we've substituted parent-purchased educational games, competitive toys that demand memorization of academic concepts, puzzles requiring matching skills, pre-drawn coloring books, realistic dolls, and other preformatted products that deprive children of creativity and the simple joy of playing in a box or banging pot lids together.

Founder: Ironically, the theory arises from the progressive ideas of John Dewey (1859–1952), the American philosopher and educator whose writings and teachings profoundly influenced the current state of public education in the United States. Dewey's philosophy of education, instrumentalism (also called pragmatism), focused on learning-by-doing rather than rote learning and dogmatic instruction, the current practice of his day.

Methods: Children learn best when they play for love of the game and the experience; when they don't fear being corrected or directed; and when they become completely involved in their play activities. Families adopting the Play approach should allow children to play freely without measuring or censoring their choices or their results. Provide unstructured toys—shoeboxes, paint, sticks, clothing, and the like—so that children have the opportunity to engage in creative, original play. Parents should avoid directing their children's natural games or suggesting alternatives focused on winning. And children should not be involved in organized competitive sports before the age of twelve.

Related Strategies: Creativity, Learning Environments

Child-Led

The Child-Led approach—also called interest-led learning, "delight-directed" learning, or invited teaching—follows the interests of the child to create knowledge. Under this approach, parents are responsible for leading kids (generally by setting their own example as delight-directed learners), rather than driving them. Proponents of this approach believe that when students are given good instructional materials, they can teach themselves and they will eventually learn to locate their own resources.

Methods: The most basic premise of the Child-Led approach is "no uninvited learning." Parents trust in the intrinsic curiosity of children and wait until the child invites mom, dad, or other experts (what one writer calls "the docents in the museum of life") to share knowledge. Learning is never forced on a child, although parents needn't be entirely passive. As learners in their own right, parents might schedule family activities that are inherently educational and invite children to join them in their personal learning adventure. Under the Child-Led approach, children initiate and direct their own learning and are free to use self-paced commercial curricula, to conduct independent research, or to simply sit and think. One advocate of Child-Led learning urges reluctant parents to try it as a one-year experiment. No homework. Just follow your educational interests and have fun. "At the end of the year," she says, "evaluate what you feel you missed out on by not enforcing a schedule or a curriculum (besides the arguing)."

On Liberty

"Liberty is the prevention of control by others. This requires self-control and, therefore, religious and spiritual influences; education, knowledge, well being."

—Lord Acton (1834–1902)

Related Strategies: Creativity, Learning Environments

Self-Directed

The Self-Directed approach is the most radical form of Unschooling. Older than Child-Led learning, this approach opens the way for older children to attain independence. The goal of Self-Directed learning is emancipation and the habit of lifelong learning, where teenagers plan their own schedules, earn their own way, pursue their own education, and eventually take complete responsibility for their own lives.

Founders: Self-study played an important part in the lives of such Greek philosophers as Socrates, Plato, and Aristotle. Other historical examples of self-directed learners included Alexander the Great, Caesar, Erasmus, and Descartes. Social conditions in Colonial America and a corresponding lack of formal educational institutions necessitated that many people learn on their own.

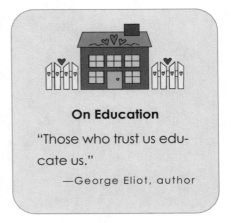

On Education

"Those who trust us educate us."

—George Eliot, author

Methods: In the Self-Directed approach, the role of parents is to guide Omega-level unschoolers to locate their own learning resources and become fully engaged in the larger community. To create lifelong self-directed learners, support self-directed activities such as online classes, independent study, internships, participation in study groups, self-guided reading, online discussions, and reflective writing. Restrict television viewing, computer and video games, and other forms of mindless entertainment. Talk often. Discuss goals and priorities. Involve teenagers in adult decisions, and model self-directed learning.

Related Strategies: Build-It-Yourself, Case Studies, College Prep, Competitions, Critical Reading, Field Trips, Graphic Organizers, Interviewing, Learning Environments, Kitchen Science, Labs and Demos, Library Skills, Online Classes, Portfolio Building, Research Techniques, Socratic Questioning, Writing to Learn

For More Information

For more information on any of the homeschooling approaches and philosophies described in this chapter, visit the Approaches section of the Homeschool Steps Web site <www.home schoolsteps.com/see also/approaches.htm>.

Christian Unschooling

Christian unschoolers choose to place their faith in God, and not in curriculum. Proponents call Christian Unschooling "God-led" learning.

Methods: In addition to setting an example of self-motivated learning, advocates of Christian Unschooling urge parents to be sensitive to where God leads, to pray for guidance, and to follow the example of Christ in their teaching and parenting. God instilled in children individual interests and a desire for knowledge. Stand back and let them follow those God-given interests.

Related Strategies: Creativity, Learning Environments

Self-Test

On each of the following scales, circle the number that is most representative of your beliefs about family life:

I am most comfortable in a home that is more:

Authoritative ← → Democratic
1   2   3   4   5

Disciplined ← → Undisciplined
1   2   3   4   5

Organized ← → Chaotic
1   2   3   4   5

Structured ← → Unstructured
1   2   3   4   5

Strict ← → Lax
1   2   3   4   5

Neat ← → Cluttered
1   2   3   4   5

Scheduled ← → Spontaneous
1   2   3   4   5

I am more concerned with:

Responsibilities ← → Rights
1   2   3   4   5

Factual Information ← → Theories
1   2   3   4   5

Destinations ← → Journeys
1   2   3   4   5

Sciences ← → Arts
1   2   3   4   5

(continues)

In my children, I most value the qualities of:

Obedience ←——————————————————————→ Originality
1   2   3   4   5

Organization ←——————————————————————→ Spontaneity
1   2   3   4   5

Intelligence ←——————————————————————→ Kindness
1   2   3   4   5

Hard Work ←——————————————————————→ Sense of Humor
1   2   3   4   5

Ideal Family Structure

Parent	Child
1. Leader	Follower
2. Teacher	Learner
3. Expert	Seeker
4. Guide	Explorer
5. Partner	Partner
6. Audience	Actor
7. Shadow	Leader

Scoring

Total of all circled numbers: _____

65+ An unstructured approach (Unschooling or Undirected Learning) is most compatible with your beliefs about family life.

50–64 Your easy-going beliefs about family life are most compatible with the relaxed (Informal Learning or Questioned Learning) approaches to homeschooling. 30–49 You are of two minds about how structured your family life should be. Eclectic approaches to home education allow you to blend your desire for structure with your beliefs about exploration. Values-Based approaches will provide a strong theoretical framework, while giving you freedom to customize your approach.

29 or less Your success-oriented, structured approach to family life works well with the formal approaches to homeschooling. Consider adopting a Directed or a Psychological approach for your family.

Curriculum and Materials

How Do I Obtain Teaching Materials?

Microscopes, flannel boards, textbooks, maps . . . In this chapter we'll help you locate or create all the educational materials you need to teach your children at home. We'll introduce both commercial and noncommercial resources, so that you can customize your teaching to fit your family's resources and needs.

What Will I Need to Get Started?

If you have the money, you can outfit your home with every kind of reference book, textbook, and audio/visual device available in the largest government-funded school.

Most homeschoolers educate quite effectively, though, on a much smaller scale. The typical homeschooling family manages to teach its children with just a home computer, some basic educational materials, and a lot of creativity.

Double Your Money

The book you're holding would be three or four times its size if it weren't for the Internet. As you read this text, you'll find dozens and dozens of references to supplementary pages at our companion Web site, Homeschool Steps <*www.home schoolsteps.com*>. Your investment in this book will be much more valuable if you're able to get online to access the supplemental material over the Internet.

Do I Really Need a Computer?

You could spend scads of money on commercial products. You could set up a temporary home at a well stocked public library. Or you could do the smart thing and get a home computer and an Internet connection. With all the free educational resources available over the Internet, and the invaluable access it provides to homeschooling support resources, you'll find that the computer will pay for itself many times over.

But, like most homeschoolers, you're probably on a budget, so if you're shopping for an inexpensive home computer with an Internet connection, you might want to start with an entry-level product such as WebTV or a similar Internet appliance.[1] This device provides you with the equipment to get onto the Internet for less than $100, plus a monthly access fee of around $22.

If you already own a computer and a modem, your Internet connection can be completely free. Companies such as Juno, NetZero, and DotNow offer free or very inexpensive Internet connections from most well populated locations in the United States and Canada.[2]

The average homeschooling family will want to own one or two full-scale desktop or notebook computers—one for parents, who are compiling and researching teaching materials, preparing lessons, and searching for homeschooling support; and a second machine for adolescent children, who will use it for research, online classes, writing papers, and much more.

If you can't establish an Internet connection at home, you might want to inquire at your church or local public library, community center, college, public school, educational alternative center, YMCA, CYO, or other community organization to see whether you can use their equipment to get online. The Net is a valuable tool. Take advantage of it to improve your children's educational opportunities!

What Other Teaching Aids Do I Need?

Basic educational materials fall into three categories:

1. **Supplies.** There's no such thing as a paperless school. To learn, your children must have paper, art supplies, science supplies, music supplies, visual aids, software, workbooks, journals, and writing implements. Later in this chapter we'll discuss ways to obtain, or create, many of these materials inexpensively.

2. **Equipment.** The list grows as technology improves. A chalkboard, microscope, and protractor might be enough to get by on, but don't be surprised to find yourself drooling over graphing calculators, electronic white boards, e-books, and specialized audio and video equipment. Don't forget the basics, though: In the hands of an enthusiastic homeschooler, a frying pan and a water balloon can be as educational as sophisticated scientific test equipment.

3. **Books.** Over the years, your home library will grow to include books on homeschooling, parenting books, reference books, and academic books (i.e., textbooks, study guides, and workbooks). We review hundreds of the best homeschooling and parenting books

Online Safety

Many homeschooling families we talk to about computers and education have serious reservations about online safety. They've heard frightening tales of child abductions, and they worry about the threat of pornography, enticements for gambling, and other influences they don't want in their homes.

The online industry not only acknowledges your fear; it has created fairly effective mechanisms for addressing it. Filtered Internet service providers screen everything that comes across your Internet connection for compliance with strict standards of decency. AOL and several other commercial providers allow parents to set parental controls for their children's Internet accounts, blocking out uninvited email, chats, and other problematic features.

We discuss these and several other measures for keeping your children safe on the Internet on the Safety page of the Homeschool Steps Web site, *<www.homeschoolsteps.com/seealso/safety.htm>*.

on the Reading page of our Web site at *<www.homeschoolsteps.com/seealso/reading.htm>*.

Which Reference Materials Should I Have?

Sometimes parents worry that they can't give their children as many resources as the public schools can provide. But the truth is, you can do even better. Homeschooled children aren't forced to work within ten- or twenty-minute allotments designed to accommodate classes of thirty children. If your children want to curl up in an armchair and read the dictionary for two hours, homeschooling is flexible enough to accommodate them.

Here are the basic materials you'll need for your home reference library:[3]

A Dictionary. Our family has more than a dozen cheap dictionaries stuffed in bookshelves around the house, and we use them all the time. Inexpensive pocket dictionaries are sufficient for most situations, but we also make frequent use of a serious hardback dictionary we've affectionately nicknamed "Big Blue." Inexpensive used dictionaries are available at thrift shops and used-book stores. We also consult regularly with free online dictionaries. Our favorites are Merriam Webster *<www.m-w.com>* and Dictionary.com *<www.dictionary.com>*.

An Encyclopedia. A handful of homeschooling moms have told us that their children's favorite educational activity is lying on the floor reading the encyclopedia. Many families haunt thrift stores for great bargains on used sets of encyclopedias. They're a fun resource, if you can afford them, but at $750 for a new set, full-scale encyclopedias are outside the budget of the average family. If you're not able to locate an affordable print edition, try a CD-ROM encyclopedia such as Comptons, Encyclopedia Britannica, Grolier, IBM Worldbook, or Microsoft Encarta. These products cost an average of about $20 from retailers such as DirectDeals *<www.directdeals.com>*, but may be bundled at no charge with your PC. Alternatively, you might consider any of the dozens of encyclopedias available online. Britannica *<www.britannica.com>* was our former favorite, but it recently began charging a subscription fee. The next best thing: Bartleby *<www.bartleby.com>*, which provides free access to Columbia encyclopedia, as well as to dozens of other reference books.

> **On Learning**
>
> "Education should include knowledge of what to do with it."
>
> —Unknown

Geography Materials. Whether your children are studying politics, history, current events, or geography, they need to know where in the world events take place. Pricey electronic **globes** are available for around $100 at discount retailers, but your kids will get along just fine with a $25 model on a table stand. (If you have trouble finding an inexpensive model locally, Amazon.com sells a wide variety of globes.) Your very young children might even prefer cheap inflatable, plush-toy, or jigsaw-puzzle globes, which cost $10 or less. Nice laminated wall **maps** are available from many retailers, including Elijah Company <*www.elijah co.com*>, for around $12. A large-sized **atlas,** from retailers such as Costco or Wal-Mart, is a useful portable substitute for a wall map, and can be had for about the same price.

Beyond those basics, the world of reference materials is unlimited. If you're on a budget, you might want to "store" your secondary reference materials at the public library. They'll be used infrequently enough, and require updating so often, that it's probably not worth spending the money.

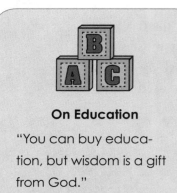

On Education

"You can buy education, but wisdom is a gift from God."

—Unknown

Should I Buy a Commercial Curriculum?

If you're planning to homeschool in a highly structured, school-at-home format, it's tough to beat a full-scale commercial curriculum package. They tend to be highly regimented and provide lots of handholding for parents who are apprehensive about teaching on their own. The downside? Well, they're highly regimented—a major drawback, in the opinion of many homeschoolers—and they're also pricey. Nevertheless, commercial curricula continue to be a very popular option for large numbers of homeschooling families.

Curriculum Review Project

Wondering which curriculum package to choose? We had the same question and so in late 2000 we organized a massive undertaking: A curriculum review project with more than seventy-five board members—homeschoolers who volunteered to read and review commercial educational materials with their own children in their own homes. By mid-2002, the board had reviewed products from more than 1,500 education companies. This ongoing project will continue to review new materials as they become available.

The Curriculum Review Board's recommendations are available on the Web to readers of *Homeschooling Step by Step*. The Curriculum Review Project's online home is at *<www.homeschoolsteps.com/curriculumproject>*. In addition to curriculum reviews, you'll find company names, links to Web sites, complete contact information, and more.

Commercial curricula (and curriculum services) are available in several broad categories.

Traditional. In this category are curricula that cover every subject—or at least, most subjects—for an entire school year.[4] Families purchase a packet of materials—books, audiotapes, videotapes, software, workbooks, tests—and the child works through the material under the tutelage of the parent. There is no "reporting back" to a central organization, and the family is entirely responsible for determining the child's progress.

Correspondence. This category is similar to the traditional curriculum method, but the student reports back to a central organization.[5]

In a correspondence program, the child submits papers, tests, or other materials, which an educator from the correspondence school then reviews and grades. Correspondence schools are increasingly tied into the Internet, meaning that children who participate in correspondence classes are encouraged or required to submit their work and take examinations online.

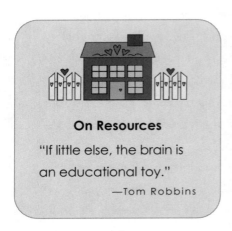

On Resources

"If little else, the brain is an educational toy."

—Tom Robbins

You might enroll your children in a full-time, yearlong correspondence program that covers the entire curriculum, or you could choose to enroll them in only one or two classes. Some correspondence schools adhere to a strict calendar; others allow homeschoolers to work at their own pace and submit work as it's completed.

Partial Curriculum. Several curriculum publishers specialize in a single educational category and provide in-depth curriculum for that particular subject, but no others. These classes tend to be similar to a traditional curriculum, in that the family purchases the materials but doesn't report back to a correspondence school. Subcategories under this heading would include unit study products, stand-alone workbooks, educational software, and other media products such as video- and audiotapes.[6]

Umbrella School. Some families choose to educate under the guidance or jurisdiction of an umbrella school.[7] These schools have varying degrees of interaction with the homeschooling family, and offer a variety of benefits. Umbrella schools can provide very loose supervision (the parent might, for example, write a note once a year describing what the child has or will accomplish), or it can provide very tight supervision (some schools might require students to spend two or three days per week on campus and report in every day they're not on campus). Most umbrella schools fall between those two extremes.

Families who affiliate with an umbrella school might receive, in return for their affiliation, any of these benefits: accreditation, curriculum guidance, diplomas, school credit, transcripts, evaluations, testing, legal protection, commencement exercises, and college admissions assistance.

Other Commercial and Community Education Services. This is the catchall category that defines "curriculum" as any product that teaches. Under this heading you'll find several services provided by business and government—services that offer a way to supplement homeschooling with a structured program. These programs include commercial tutorial services, classes offered through community centers and commercial providers, hybrid public/homeschool programs, alternative education programs, and early college admission programs.

Commercial tutorial services[8] offer an interesting way to augment homeschooling. Several national companies offer to teach children one-on-one, either face-to-face or through a correspondence or online system. Some academic tutors operate nationwide, and children are required to attend individual or small-group classes in a learning center. Other tutors work as individuals on a local level. You might, for example, find specialized tutors through your local university, or you might even hire an older homeschooled child to tutor your child in a particular academic subject.

A popular way to supplement homeschooling is through specialized classes and lessons: karate, ballet, art, horseback riding, pet grooming, and hundreds of others. These classes are available online, through correspondence programs, and—of course—through local programs offered by private teachers, local businesses, and community recreation programs. Contact your town's parks and recreation department, your local community college, the public library, the YMCA or CYO, 4H Club, and other organizations that sponsor adult education and youth classes, and ask to be put on their mailing list for catalogs and flyers. When you visit your local craft store, home center, and bookstore, ask to be notified when classes are organized. And contact the youth leader at your place of worship to be notified when children's classes and activities are scheduled.

The other three subcategories—hybrid public/homeschool programs, alternative education programs, and early college admission programs—are somewhat related. Hybrid programs involve supplementing your homeschooling by enrolling your child in one or more classes at a local public or private school. Alternative education programs require that your child be enrolled in a formal program administered by the local school district. The program receives funding, and your child is required to adhere to laws regarding testing, attendance, and similar requirements. But while AEP students are not, technically, homeschoolers, they are educated outside of the traditional classroom, often in a setting that allows parents to be intimately involved in their children's education. Early college admission programs—commonly operated under the title "Running Start"—allow mature teenagers to test into college. The cost of tuition is borne by the local public-school system, but the child actually attends college classes and earns college credit. Information about all three alternatives is available through your local public-school administrator.

Without a Commercial Curriculum, How Will I Know What to Teach?

Parents who are comfortable with the premise of the Unschooling movement don't even ask this question. Unschoolers believe that natural curiosity and a rich environment will naturally stimulate children to learn everything they need to become fully functioning adults.

But families that want more structure look to several sources for quantifiable academic guidelines. Every U.S. state has developed a comprehensive set of "learning standards" for public-school students. These standards describe, for example, when a child should have mastered academic subjects such as spelling, algebra, biology, and critical thinking. State learning standards are available on the Internet,[9] and copies can be obtained from cooperative school administrators.

As a practical matter, even the most adamant unschooling family will want to be familiar with the standards of learning taught in their own state. This knowledge will, at the very least, guide you in choosing the resources you keep in your home so that your independent learners have access to age-appropriate materials.

Another resource for planning your home-school program is the Internet, home to dozens of scope-and-sequence plans that aid in deciding which subject material should be taught at which age.

One of our favorite sites, Home2School *<www.home2school.com>*, actually builds a custom scope-and-sequence for your child based on his or her age and geographic location. As your child learns each skill or principle, you check it off the list and begin teaching another concept. Enter the first names of several children, and the site accommodates them all. Home2School con-

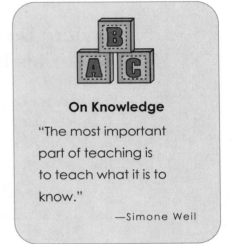

On Knowledge

"The most important part of teaching is to teach what it is to know."

—Simone Weil

sists of hundreds of essential learning objectives correlated to each of the fifty states' academic requirements. The site includes parental tutorials so that you can refresh your memory as you teach. And the resource is completely free.

We also cover scope-and-sequence questions, provide a sample scope-and-sequence, and review numerous free planning resources, in our first homeschooling book, *Homeschool Your Child for Free* *<www.hsfree.com>*.

The third option is to use one of the many scope-and-sequence books[10] on the market. The most prominent of these books are those in the series *What Your X-Grader Needs to Know,* edited by E. D. Hirsch. The Core Knowledge Foundation, which arose out of the popular series, operates a free Web site at *<www.coreknowledge .com>* to compile lesson plans that correspond with the series.

The final option is to simply sit down and develop your own educational plan. Counsel with your children, decide together how they can best accomplish their personal educational goals, and write down those goals and your basic educational plan to serve as a guide throughout your school year.

Where Do I Find Inexpensive, Quality Materials to Build a Curriculum?

Thousands of quality resources are available to homeschoolers on a budget. Creative families will develop custom-made curricula with books, supplies, equipment, and ideas obtained inexpensively—or free—from these resources:

School Surplus. Contact local school districts to find out what they do with discarded textbooks, equipment, and supplies.

Purchasing Cooperatives. Work with an established homeschooling group to buy new or used materials at a group discount. Some groups also purchase single items—a videotape, a math book, and so on—for a traveling library that is housed in the homes of group members.

Gleaning. Gleaning groups make arrangements with libraries, bookstores, educational suppliers, office-supply stores, department stores, large businesses, and other commercial and government organizations to regularly collect all their discarded usable materials for redistribution. A large percentage of the gleaned materials are donated to charitable organizations (they might be repackaged and given to a homeless shelter or an international children's charity, for example), and the remainder is divided among members of the gleaning group.

Book Sales. Contact public libraries, churches, and other organizations that periodically discard older or less-than-pristine books.

Used-Book Stores. Often found in the low-rent district around colleges and universities, used-book stores are stuffed with educational treasures at a reasonable price.

College Bookstores. Remember the mad rush to buy used books from your own college bookstore? You don't have to be enrolled to buy used books at university and college bookstores. Time your shopping for about two weeks before the beginning of a new term, when used books are still plentiful and the books in good condition haven't all been snapped up.

Thrift Stores. Culling through the book section of thrift stores can be a great way to build the "classics" section of your home library. There's always some recent college graduate who celebrates his first job by giving away all his no-longer-useful textbooks. Stock up!

Crafting. Consider using materials found around the home, as well as inexpensive crafting supplies from craft stores, hardware stores, thrift stores, and electronics stores. Utilize these supplies to create anything from timelines to sock puppets to soap bubbles. Ideas for hundreds of do-it-yourself educational aids are found on the Tools page of the Literate Folk Web site at <*www.literatefolk.com/tools*>.

On Creating

"Children have a natural antipathy to books—handicraft should be the basis of education. Boys and girls should be taught to use their hands to make something, and they would be less apt to destroy and be mischievous."

—Oscar Wilde (1854–1900)

The Internet. For homeschoolers looking for cheap or free curriculum, the Internet has two major offerings: used curriculum exchanges and online teaching materials.

What Are Curriculum Exchanges?

Homeschoolers swap, buy, and sell used curricula from various locations on the Internet, as well as within large local homeschooling groups. If you're looking to buy or sell curricula, you could try your hand on E-Bay *<www.ebay.com>*, but you'll probably be more successful at a homeschool-specific site. The most active of the dozens of homeschooling curriculum exchanges online is the Homeschool Talk and Swap at VegSource *<www.vegsource.com/homeschool>*. We review this, and many other curriculum exchanges, on the Used page of the Homeschool Steps Web site at *<www.homeschoolsteps.com/seealso/used.htm>*.

What Teaching Materials Are Available Online?

In addition to the commercial materials described earlier in this chapter, you'll find an amazing selection of free materials to support your efforts to build your own curriculum. There are tens of thousands of resources for every conceivable academic subject, and you'll find a vast array of materials to assist you in lesson planning, unit studies, and worksheet development. You'll also find hundreds of "freebie" sites for teachers, free educational software, and a wealth of noncommercial online classes.

Our earlier book, *Homeschool Your Child for Free* *<www.hsfree.com>*, reviews hundreds of academic and teaching resources for homeschoolers and gives access to thousands of additional sites via the companion Web site. Materials are arranged by subject, subtopic, and age grouping. We also give advice about how—and why—to teach each academic subject. What follows is a sampling of some of our favorites.

Unit Studies

Unit studies provide across-the-curriculum study of a specific subject that might take a month or two of study. Here are some of the best resources for free, ready-made unit studies:

Mr. Donn's Pages *<members.aol.com/donnandlee/SiteIndex.html>* A huge collection of unit studies and resources for creating unit studies. Covers history, social studies, geography, language arts, and literature for K through grade 12.

Unit Study 101 *<www.andwhatabout.com/articles/unit_study_101.htm>* Amanda Bennett, a commercial unit-study developer, wrote this article to guide parents in the use and preparation of unit studies in a homeschooling program.

Unit Study Directory *<homeschooling.about.com/library/weekly/aa051601a.htm>* About.com's links to hundreds of online unit studies. Topics are categorized alphabetically and by grade level.

Lesson Plans

Lesson plans are one- or two-day lessons on a single topic. Some of our favorites are:

Baltimore Curriculum Project *<www.cstone.net/~bcp/BCP Intro2.htm>* K through grade 5 lesson plans that follow the Core Knowledge Sequence.

LessonPlanz *<www.LessonPlanz.com>* A free searchable directory of online lesson plans and lesson plan resources for all grades and subjects. You'll find some 4,000 online lesson plans for preschool to grade 12.

Microsoft Lesson Connection *<k12.msn.com/LessonConnection /Teacher.asp>* A searchable database of lesson plans from sources across the Web. Search by subject area and grade.

Worksheets

Also called reproducibles and printables, worksheets provide a tangible project for your kids to work on. Here are some of the best collections of worksheets:

Free Teaching Ideas *<www.evan-moor.com/freeidea.htm>* From Evan-Moor Educational Publishers, free worksheets for grades K through 6. Each month the subject matter changes. Worth revisiting.

Free Worksheets for Elementary Grades *<www.ezschool.com /example/EZTrack2?Name=index>* English and math worksheets for K through grade 5. Browse by grade or by subject. You can use the worksheets online or on paper—a very nice option.

Learning Page *<www.learningpage.com>* A collection of about 1,500 worksheets for grades K through 3. You must register, but it's free. The worksheets are very well done and cover a range of subjects: alphabet, calendar, money, senses, time, measurement, and numbers. Numerous theme worksheets are available for older children on oceans, zoo animals, dinosaurs, reptiles, and insects. You'll also find links to lesson plans, clip art, e-books, and much more.

Freebies

Before you start signing up for freebies, we recommend that you open a "junk email" account at a free service such as Hotmail.com.

Most freebies are offered only in exchange for your email address. Here are some fun sites for acquiring lots of educational freebies:

Free Things for Educators *<www.geocities.com/Heartland/Oaks /9122/subject.html>* This is a don't-miss site for homeschooling on the cheap with a massive collection of educational freebies.

Homeschooler Freebies *<www.geocities.com/tolerance_diversity /HomeschoolerFreebies.html>* An extensive collection of freebies in several subject categories. Includes a good link to free worksheets.

Weekly Freebie Compilation *<www.weeklyfreebie.com>* Not education specific, but it's regularly updated, and the Miscellaneous category is stuffed with free educational products.

Free Software

No need to go shop for software when the free stuff can be downloaded from the Internet. The following sites offer freeware (software available at no cost), shareware (software available for free trial, after which you are asked to pay for it), and demos (software demonstrations of full commercial products):

ZDNet Downloads *<www.zdnet.com/downloads/home.html>* Visit the Home and Education category of C|Net, with thousands of free software downloads. This category covers home management software, as well as straight educational software for teaching health, language, math, music, and more. May require free registration.

PCWorld **Downloads** *<www.pcworld.com/downloads/browse /0,cat,546,sortIdx,1,00.asp>* *PCWorld*'s education category has more than two dozen fun freeware, shareware, and demo packages not available anywhere else.

Freeware Filz *<www.freewarefilz.com/Educational>* Really interesting educational freeware categorized by language, literature, math, science, teaching tools, kids, and miscellaneous. Fun stuff.

Classes

Adult education classes abound online, but so do terrific online classes for kids. Classes are offered by school districts, commercial enterprises, educational Web sites, and generous people who just want to share their expertise in some area. Check these sites for a taste of what's available online:

Barnes and Noble University *<www.barnesandnobleuniversity .com>* Take free classes on a huge variety of topics at this Web site. Current course offerings cover everything from Shakespeare to C++ programming to yoga.

Free-Ed *<www.free-ed.net>* Free education on the Internet. It's that simple. More than 120 vocational and academic courses, including GED Preparation, offered entirely free, online.

Mental Edge *<www.learningshortcuts.com>* You study the material, then you take the test. Right? Not with the Mental Edge. Although this site is designed to help students reviewing for exams, it also works as an interesting, challenging alternative to learning from textbooks. A child takes a test, and the answer—right or wrong—is displayed, alongside an explanation of the correct response. The Mental Edge includes "tests" for virtually every academic subject for grades 3 through 12, along with reviews for college entrance exams and national standardized tests such as the Iowa Tests of Basic Skills, Stanford 8 & 9, and CTB/McGraw-Hill. All told this site offers nearly 2,000 subject reviews, coordinated with all major textbooks.

Are There Other Sources for Noncommercial Curricula?

Two biggies: Start by checking with suppliers to and local organizers of youth-oriented organizations such as the Boy Scouts, Girl Scouts, Campfire Girls, and 4H. All offer inexpensive educational materials that can be used to supplement or direct your educational efforts.

The second, and most important, source of noncommercial curricula is the public library. There are more than 16,000 public libraries in the United States—an average of more than 320 per state—but fewer than two-thirds of Americans have visited a library in the past year.[11] That leaves lots of elbow room for your family, especially during the hours that public-school students are in class.

Think about the library as more than a repository of books. You'll find books, of course, but also take advantage of the library's collection of reference materials, periodicals, educational videotapes, audiotapes, CDs, DVDs, pamphlets, and computers. And don't forget the library as a resource for free lectures, plays, story hour, demonstrations, poetry and book readings, discussions, political meetings, and other functions that will help your children expand their educational horizons.

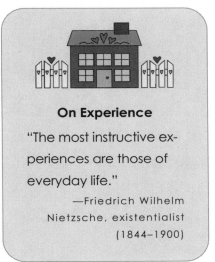

On Experience

"The most instructive experiences are those of everyday life."

—Friedrich Wilhelm Nietzsche, existentialist (1844–1900)

6

Gaining
Confidence

How Do I Teach My Child?

As you've read through this book, you've decided why you're homeschooling, learned how to comply with local laws, chosen a homeschooling philosophy, and found your materials.

Now it's time to get in there and teach. This chapter explains how to
find the confidence you need to educate your children at home. We begin
with an introduction to home education, and then explain how you can
teach your children effectively.

Where Do I Start?

You won't be truly successful at educating your family until you develop a
moral foundation. Over time, you will get discouraged, you will flounder,
you will burn out. But if you have a deep and abiding belief that you're
doing what is right—if you believe that teaching your children is truly

On Religious Education

"Education ought everywhere to be religious education. Parents are bound to employ instructors who will instruct their children religiously. To commit children to the care of irreligious persons is to commit lambs to the superintendency of wolves."

—Timothy Dwight, President of Yale University (1752–1817)

moral, good, and honorable—then you'll have the strength and determination to get through the most difficult days.

If you are a religious person, make homeschooling a matter of deep and thoughtful prayer and study. Your long-term success will depend on knowing that you have divine approval and support in your efforts to educate your charges.

If religious belief is not a part of your life, it's just as important that you develop a moral foundation for education. Rather than jumping in and hoping for the best, spend time contemplating your beliefs about what your ethical duty is as a parent. Consider what makes the world a good and virtuous place, and ponder how you—as a parent—can improve the world through teaching and influencing your own children.

We strongly urge parents who don't yet have a moral framework for homeschooling to consider the articles on the Inspire page of the Homeschool Steps Web site at *<www.homeschoolsteps .com/seealso/inspire.htm>*. It's filled with inspiring stories, descriptions of people's decision to homeschool, and specific arguments for the morality of homeschooling.

If I Don't Have a Teaching Certificate, Am I Qualified to Teach?

Do the children of schoolteachers tie their shoelaces better than the children of "amateurs" do? Did you need a teaching certificate to teach your children to walk? Did your parents require a college degree to teach you to talk?

Should Religious Families Homeschool?

It's a controversial subject. Many people of faith believe they have an obligation to keep their children in public school to act as leaven, and to serve as witnesses. Some adherents feel duty-bound to enroll their children in private religious schools operated by their church or synagogue.

We address these issues, list resources related to religion and homeschooling, and provide scriptural study resources supporting home education at the Religion page of the Homeschool Steps Web site at <www.homeschoolsteps.com/seealso/religion.htm>. People of every religious faith will benefit from the support material on this page.

Teaching is intuitive. Families throughout history have taught their children how to get along in the world without any "teacher training" at all. The fact that you know—and love—your own child better than anyone else makes you the *best* teacher for that child. You recognize when your own children understand. You know immediately when they don't understand. You know, intuitively and through a lifetime of experience, how best to reach your own child. An example: Suppose you wanted to teach your son to load the dishwasher. You might tell him "the dishes need to face the center." When he stares back at you, slack-jawed and wide-eyed, you know he doesn't have a clue. So you demonstrate. You point to the center. You show him the device that sprays the water. You load a few dishes properly. Then you ask him to try it himself.

You don't go to college to learn these techniques. You learn them by trial and error, observation, and contemplation. The dishwasher principle applies to every academic subject. Suppose you know your oldest son has a low tolerance for lectures. He might want to know how to add three and two. Rather than explain the principle of addition, you know, intuitively, to grab five apples from the refrigerator and help him manipulate them until he understands the principle.

You might have a daughter who is bored by games and who wants to wrap her mind around the theoretical application of addition. So you sit down knee-to-knee, with a notebook or a small whiteboard, and sketch it out for her, while watching her face to see whether she comprehends the principle.

These teaching principles are skills you've applied since the time you taught your baby sister to sing, or taught your best friend to duck when you hit the tetherball. Now you're the parent—not a professional stranger. You know when your own child "gets it," and you know, intuitively, to change your teaching method—several times in the same lesson, if necessary—until you hit on the one that works.

Still worried that you lack the training of a "professional" teacher? Relax. Unlike college professors, public-school teachers don't get hired to teach because they've mastered an academic subject at an advanced level or because they've conducted groundbreaking scientific research. To the contrary. Teacher certification requires only a minimal level of expertise in academic subjects, if that.[1] A degree in education provides skills that don't have any relevance in a homeschool setting. Teacher training helps adults manage a classroom of thirty unrelated, unfamiliar children. It teaches them how to operate expensive audiovisual equipment. It teaches college students—inexperienced non-parents, for the most part—how children learn. It teaches them the latest pedagogical

On True Education

"The supreme end of education is expert discernment in all things— the power to tell the good from the bad, the genuine from the counterfeit, and to prefer the good and the genuine to the bad and the counterfeit."

—Samuel Johnson, English essayist (1709–1784)

theories—theories that are still in the experimentation stage and that haven't yet withstood the test of time. It teaches them how to interact with a principal and faculty. It teaches them how to comply with laws and regulations related to discrimination, sexual harassment, and occupational safety. It teaches them how to deal with violence, drug and alcohol use, and overt sexual behavior.

None of these group-management skills would make you a better homeschool educator. In fact, say several former schoolteachers who are now homeschooling moms, if anything, teacher training convinces you to stay home and teach your own children, no matter what the cost.

How Will I Teach Difficult Academic Subjects I Didn't Study in College?

Suppose I sat you down and began lecturing you on the arcane details of English jurisprudence—one of my own law-school specialties. I'm betting you wouldn't learn it even if you were strapped to a chair and denied food and water. Like most people, you simply don't care about the philosophical development of the British legal system.

Learning arises out of interest. It can never be forced. Your children learned to walk, talk, and tie their shoelaces not because you demanded that they learn, but because you facilitated their ability to master something they genuinely wanted to know. They had a natural, internal, intrinsic motivation to learn. You simply made it easier to acquire the knowledge.

That's good news for homeschooling parents because it puts the responsibility for learning squarely on the shoulders of the student. Your job, as a parent, is to facilitate education by providing

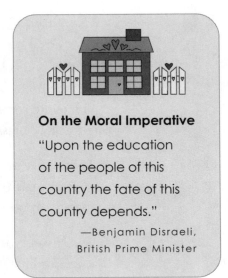

On the Moral Imperative

"Upon the education of the people of this country the fate of this country depends."

—Benjamin Disraeli, British Prime Minister

Still Lacking Confidence?

There are entire books and magazines on the subject of gaining confidence to homeschool. We list several of them, along with dozens of confidence-building online articles, at the Confidence page of the Homeschool Steps Web site at <www.home schoolsteps.com/see also/confidence.htm>.

access to resources and encouraging your child's desire to learn and understand. The bottom line is that no matter what you "teach," your children's interests will determine what they actually learn.

No matter how many college degrees they've earned, nobody is an expert at everything. Even parents who hold advanced degrees in multiple subject areas are lacking when it comes to teaching—say, anthrax prevention or Visual C++ programming—subjects that didn't even exist when they were college age. Can they still teach these subjects? Absolutely. When you are faced with a child who is fascinated by Greek or brain surgery or telecommunications, you, too, can be an effective teacher.

If your older or academically advanced children are looking for help on a difficult subject, your role might be to simply direct them to some helpful resources and encourage them to study the subject independently. If you have a younger child learning advanced material, you might choose to learn the material thoroughly and attempt to teach it yourself, or you might learn alongside your child so that you can explain your own understanding of the material you're studying together.

Here are some of the resources you or your older or gifted child might use to master an advanced subject:

"Cheat." Commercial curricula come with teacher's manuals and other materials that help the parent teach anything from biology to trigonometry to Latin.

Take Private Instruction. Piano teachers, algebra tutors, soccer coaches, and karate masters are all private instructors. Private instruction is still homeschooling—even if it takes place outside the home—because of the supervision and personal involvement of parents.

Consult Experts. Consider how large your network of experts might be: your dentist, your doctor, the owner of a local plant nursery, local merchants, operator of a nearby nursing home, the local newspaper, a fish hatchery, park rangers, and anyone else in your area who might be willing to work with or mentor a child in learning a particular academic skill. (See the Experts Resources strategy in Chapter 3 for tips on finding helpful people with specific knowledge.)

Intern. Investigate the possibility of doing an apprenticeship or internship. There's no better preparation for a career than getting some hands-on experience.

Network. Find opportunities to meet people. The more people you know, the more likely it is that you'll be able to find someone with answers to your questions. Take advantage of the talents of friends, relatives, and neighbors. Include in your support network scoutmasters, youth leaders, and people who share your religious faith.

On Childhood

"You are told a lot about your education, but some beautiful, sacred memory, preserved since childhood, is perhaps the best education of all. If a man carries many such memories into life with him, he is saved for the rest of his days."

—Fyodor Dostoyevsky, author

Read Widely. Don't just read a textbook on, for example, psychology. Read original research, essays, and monographs that changed the way people think about the subject. Read popular magazines related to psychology. Read biographies on leading thinkers in the psychology field. Read books written for lay people.

Enroll. Enroll in a class at a community college, an independent-study class through a university, or a single advanced-level class at the local public school or a private school. It's a good way to begin earning inexpensive college credit, and instills confidence about taking on the whole college experience. (The Correspondence Courses and College Prep strategies in Chapter 3 have related tips.)

Get Wired. Take an online, televised, or video course. (See the New Media approach in Chapter 4 for additional suggestions.) Televised instruction is available from colleges and universities that offer classes over the public airwaves. Your children may not earn college credit for watching television, but they can certainly get a college-level education.

Study. Teach yourself with self-instructional textbooks and tapes.

Visit the Library. Use the resources your tax dollars pay for. Take advantage of the inter-library loan system, tapes, and other instructional materials. If you live in a college town, ask about using the campus library as well.

Collaborate. Get involved with a homeschooling co-op where someone can teach the course, or trade teaching with another family.

Volunteer. Offer to work for an organization related to the subject you want to study.

Use a Tutor. If you don't know someone with a particular expertise, contact a local college to find a student who might be willing to tutor.

Need More Advice?

Educating gifted children and teenagers is a challenge. You'll find a treasure trove of resources and recommendations for teaching advanced subjects on the Advanced page of the Homeschool Steps Web site at <www.home schoolsteps.com/seealso /advanced.htm>.

How Will I Teach Laboratory Sciences?

Learning from a book is great for studying history, but some subjects require hands-on learning. Science instruction doesn't require a full-blown (pardon the pun) laboratory. Your children need to have a thorough understanding of the scientific method,[2] but those principles can be taught without resorting to the laboratory sciences. Earth sciences and oceanography are best learned in the field, for example. And your child can conduct observations and test hypotheses in the social sciences by sitting in a shopping mall and watching people.

If you still have your heart set on the idea of a lab, the following resources will assist in teaching science without requiring a government grant:

*   "Kitchen" experiments. Most principles of chemistry and physics can be taught using common household items.[3]

*   Commercial laboratory products for homeschoolers.[4]

*   Learning cooperatives

*   Apprenticeships, internships, and volunteer work.

*   Internet lab experiments

*   Science classes in schools or colleges

On Humility

"Every act of conscious learning requires the willingness to suffer an injury to one's self-esteem. That is why young children, before they are aware of their own self-importance, learn so easily; and why older persons, especially if vain or important, cannot learn at all."

—Thomas Szasz

How Do I Manage Such an Enormous Undertaking?

You could make the same mistakes most new homeschoolers make: You could sit your children around the kitchen table and hand out dry textbooks. Or you could line the kids up on the sofa and lecture them about eighteenth-century geopolitical systems. (Are you asleep yet?)

If you've caught the vision of home education, though, you'll be thinking in much broader terms. And that's great! The best home-schooling arises out of the grandest vision. Why focus on two-digit addition when you could be researching and writing a twenty-generation family history? Why study the gross national product of Surinam when you could be solving world hunger?

Our family has found the greatest success using an approach we call PROJECT Management (see Figure 6.1). The PROJECT Management system gives your whole family the framework to spin out your dreams and achieve them together as a working unit. Once you've read over how this approach works, we recommend that you sit down as a family and spend a couple of fun hours developing your own family and individual PROJECTs. If you like, you can use the copies of the worksheet provided at the end of this chapter.

On an ongoing basis, your family should plan weekly family nights where you talk about your progress on your PROJECTs, spend fun family time together, and support one another in your dreams.

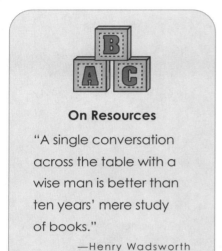

On Resources

"A single conversation across the table with a wise man is better than ten years' mere study of books."

—Henry Wadsworth Longfellow

The PROJECT system works with any homeschooling approach—or with none at all. If your entire homeschooling year is spent preparing for your family's dream of a winter in Hong Kong, for example, you and your children might learn Cantonese, introduce a unit study on Chinese history, learn the geography of Southeast Asia, work an extra job to save money, sell your house, read the online classified ads in the *South China Morning Post*, apply for jobs, get credentials to teach English as a Second Language, learn the differences between British and American spelling, find Chinese pen pals for your children, price airplane tickets, practice converting your local currency to Hong Kong dollars, and sew baby quilts for a Mainland orphanage. Without intending to, in your preparation you've studied languages,

Figure 6.1 *The PROJECT Management Approach to Homeschooling*

The PROJECT Management approach to homeschooling works like this:

Picture it. Dream about the wildest, most interesting things you can imagine doing. Your daughter wants to become the Prime Minister of England? Your son wants to build an underwater city? You want to harness clouds to meet the world's energy needs? Why not? If anyone's going to do it, why not you and your family?

Record it. Write down your ideas so you can see them begin to take shape. Keep a family PROJECT journal where you write down your family's goals and dreams. Update it from time to time with a record of your progress. Keep an individual journal of your personal PROJECTs so that you may monitor your own successes.

Order it. Prioritize the goals that appeal to you most, and determine where you'd most like to put your energy. With limited time, and limited money, you're going to have to choose either the flying lessons or the horse farm—this year. If your PROJECTs are sufficiently grand in scope and ambition, they'll require all of your focus.

Judge it. Consider what specific outcomes you'd like to achieve. In other words, rather than "I'd like to be a really good athlete," you might decide "I'd like to complete a marathon, improve my body-mass index by four percent, and bike across America."

Explain it. Talk with your family about your goals. Share your dreams. Seek support.

Chop it up. Divide your goal into its component parts. Like eating the proverbial elephant, consider how you can break down your goal into bite-sized chunks. The Boston Marathon is an elephant; a two-mile fun run next Saturday is edible.

Take it on. Accomplish something toward your goal every single day.

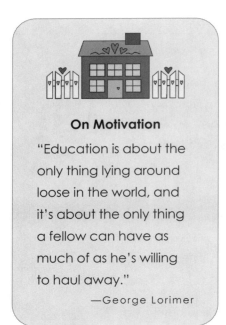

On Motivation

"Education is about the only thing lying around loose in the world, and it's about the only thing a fellow can have as much of as he's willing to haul away."

—George Lorimer

history, geography, economics, English, writing, personal finance, and intermediate mathematics.

Suppose your family dreams of climbing a mountain. You and your children will comparison shop for affordable gear, you'll train for high altitudes, you'll study rocks and land formations, you'll practice at lower elevations, and you'll learn first aid and climbing techniques. And quite by accident you'll find yourself more knowledgeable about math, finance, anatomy, health, geology, earth sciences, medicine, and safety.

Although it easily accommodates any of the homeschooling approaches described in Chapter 4, PROJECT Management is far more than Unit Studies, School-at-Home, Charlotte Mason, or any other single philosophy. It's education with a purpose and an application, and it means that lessons learned will be remembered throughout life.

We discuss PROJECT Management, and goal setting in general, on the PROJECT page at the Literate Folk Web site at *<www.literate folk.com/project>*.

Will the PROJECT System Work for Younger Children?

The PROJECT system works beautifully for younger children. You'll find that children who still believe in magic and Santa Claus and infinite possibilities actually *inspire* their parents and their older siblings. Typically, a child over the age of four will be able to think in very concrete terms about, say, earning money for a bicycle for a family bike trip, but will also think of wild possibilities such as turning the bike into a rocket ship and flying to grandma's house. The best approach with a younger child is to write down every crazy idea, no matter how unlikely. Let your children illustrate the words they've dictated to their parental scribe. You want to encourage this creativity and imagination.

Later, in the ordering and judging stages, you'll be amazed to see your young child turn flights of fancy into practical goals that can be accomplished in a day or a week.

Will the System Work with Traditional School-at-Home Approaches?

It'll work better than anything else you'll try. Once you realize that you and your children are solely responsible for the quality of your family's education, you'll be freed to choose traditional curriculum to suit your interests, rather than suffering through the usual process of trying to force yourselves into the procrustean bed of commercial curriculum.

If your child wants, more than anything, to quickly master all the traditional academic subjects in order to enroll in college before her twelfth birthday, by all means, give her a full-blown commercial curriculum and let her loose. If she enjoys learning by reading, taking tests, and completing worksheets, facilitate her wishes.

The key is that you view curriculum as a tool, and not as a goal.

Any Cautions Before I Pull My Child Out of School?

Be sure you've read and understood the legal guidelines in Chapter 2 and Appendix A. Of

On Dreaming

"Let us think of education as the means of developing our greatest abilities, because in each of us there is a private hope and dream which, fulfilled, can be translated into benefit for everyone and greater strength for our nation."

—John F. Kennedy, former U.S. President (1917–1963)

course, no matter how progressive the homeschooling laws are in your state, once you're "in the system," it's a good idea to inform the school in writing that you're going to be teaching your children at home. Withdrawing your children without any notice could result in a visit from your state's child protective services workers.

Then be ready for some acclimatization. There will be an adjustment period that could last anywhere from an hour to a year or even more. Some writers have described this time as "deschooling." Others call it decompression.[5]

No matter what you call it, there'll be a learning curve as you and your children all learn a whole better way of living. For most families, this adjustment period seems to last about a tithe of the time your child was in public school. There are several reasons this adjustment period is so difficult.

First, you and your children have become strangers while they were in public school. They were gone all day and were under the extended control of homework-assigning teachers all night. If your children were in school for a prolonged time, you may not even like one another all that much. Don't worry. This will pass. As you and your children learn again what it means to be a family unit—a group of people who actually live and eat and play and work and learn together—you'll soon find yourself enjoying their company, discovering their personalities, and learning to like them all over again.

Second, your children may not trust or like you. They've been "sent away" to strangers where they were taught habits and beliefs and mannerisms that just don't sit well with mom and dad. It takes time and trust for them to unlearn bad habits, to learn to interact with adults, and to appreciate your commitment to teaching them.

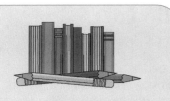

On Public Education

"We who are engaged in the sacred cause of education are entitled to look upon all parents as having given hostages to our cause."

—Horace Mann, father of common (government) school movement (1796–1859)

Give it a chance. Those strong ties that existed when they were young are still there, and they'll spring back into place given sufficient love and nurturing.

Third, your children may have become so "burnt out" on the whole education "thing" that they want only to collapse in front of the television and rot. That's okay. After a day or two, tear out the television cord, and help your children rekindle their innate desire to learn by showing them the wonders and joy of the world.

Finally, it takes time to discover who and where your child is academically. You'll learn more about your children as you explore their learning styles, determine placement levels, create appropriate learning environments, and work through other transitional issues we'll cover in the next chapter. So take a deep breath, relax, and let's ease into education.

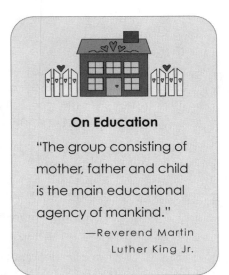

On Education

"The group consisting of mother, father and child is the main educational agency of mankind."

—Reverend Martin Luther King Jr.

Self-Test

The following test is an assessment of your own confidence in your ability to teach your children at home.

Circle the correct response.

T   F   I have a strong, loving relationship with my children and believe we can work together.

T   F   I honestly enjoy seeing my children learn.

T   F   My children are motivated by the idea that their parents are watching. I can envision my children shouting with pride "See Mom? No hands!"

T   F   I am confident that if I don't know the answer to a question, my child and I can find the answer together using a variety of resources.

T   F   I feel confident that my network of supportive friends, family, acquaintances, and community is broad enough to fill in the gaps when my own knowledge about a subject is lacking.

T   F   I recognize that there will be times of discouragement, but my belief in the principle of home education is strong enough to carry us through.

T   F   I recognize that there may be times when I resent the sacrifice of time, money, and leisure, but I'm committed to work through these issues for the sake of my children.

T   F   Even if I harbor a few fears, overall I am excited about teaching my own children and look forward to the experience.

Calculate your score by recording the number of True and False responses you gave.

T ____   F____

If you answered true to five or more questions, you'll be a committed, strong home educator and will likely enjoy your teaching experience.

If you answered true to four or fewer questions, you may need to spend more time reading about homeschooling and resolving your apprehensions. You may want to begin by reading some of the inspirational stories and testimonials to homeschooling found on the Confidence page of the Homeschool Steps Web site at <www.homeschoolsteps.com/seealso/confidence.htm>.

Worksheet

This is the worksheet for the PROJECT Management system of goal setting. Photocopy this worksheet for each member of your family, and make an extra copy for the entire family. You may also print out additional copies from the PROJECT Management Web site at <www.literatefolk.com/project>.

The PROJECT Management Worksheet

NAME_____   DATE _____

Picture it. Dream about the wildest, most interesting things that you can imagine doing. What could you imagine doing that might change the world? Thought of a few things?

❑ COMPLETION DATE: _____, 20___

Record it. Write down your ideas so you can see them begin to take shape. Use a blank journal, a notebook, or a composition book to manage and track your PROJECTs. Finished recording?

❑ COMPLETION DATE: _____, 20___

Order it. Prioritize the goals that appeal to you most, and determine where you'd most like to put your energy. Have you put your goals in order?

❑ COMPLETION DATE: _____, 20___

Judge it. Consider what specific outcomes you'd like to achieve. Rather than words like "better" or "more," use specific, measurable outcomes. Are your outcomes written down?

❑ COMPLETION DATE: _____, 20___

Explain it. Talk with your family about your goals. Share your dreams. Seek support. Finished sharing?

❑ COMPLETION DATE: _____, 20___

Chop it up. Divide your goal into its component parts. The components may be sequential or simultaneous. Is your PROJECT broken out?

❑ COMPLETION DATE: _____, 20___

Take it on. Accomplish something toward your goal every single day. Have you recorded your goals for the upcoming week?

❑ COMPLETION DATE: _____, 20___

A Learning Environment

What Is a Learning Environment?

Children learn best in a rich environment that supports education. In this chapter we explain learning styles, environmental factors, and other issues that impact learning.

What Are Learning Styles?

The term "learning styles" describes thinking skills, behaviors, abilities, and preferences that determine how a child learns. One group of educators described learning styles as "the composite of characteristic cognitive, affective, and physiological factors that serve as relatively stable indicators of how a learner perceives, interacts with, and responds to the learning environment."[1]

At present, there are more than four dozen competing models of learning styles, ranging from Gardner's Multiple Intelligences model, to the Myers-Briggs Personality Sorter, to equally plausible theories put forth by

On Learning Styles

"I hear, I know. I see,
I remember. I do,
I understand."

—Confucius (551–479 B.C.)

thoughtful homeschooling parents. Some models divide learners into sixteen or more categories; others divide learners into just two groups. And there are dozens of popular models with numbers in between.

The bottom line on learning styles is this: There is no agreement about how children, or adults, learn. However, solid research demonstrates that children learn better when they are able to learn in ways that are familiar and comfortable to them, and when they can get at information in a variety of ways.

It's easy to get lost in all the competing models of learning, but most theories are derived from the basic model of Visual, Auditory, and Kinesthetic learning styles—what we will call the VAK model.

* Visual learners prefer to learn through pictures, the written word, graphs, and diagrams. Some models further divide this category into Visual and Reading styles.

* Auditory learners are most comfortable hearing information and learn best through discussions, lectures, tapes, and spoken instruction.

* Kinesthetic (or Tactile) learners learn through touch and movement and prefer to "do" a task, rather than read about it or hear about it.

In addition, there are several somewhat-more-complex models that teaching parents ought to be familiar with. These models include:

* Felder's four-dimension model of learning styles (Learners are categorized according to their preference from each of the four dyads: Active/Reflective, Sensing/Intuitive, Visual/Verbal, and Sequential/Global.)

* Gardner's Multiple Intelligences model (The original model sorts learners into seven categories: Linguistic, Logical/

Mathematical, Spatial, Musical, Bodily/Kinesthetic, Interpersonal, and Intrapersonal. Gardner's model has recently acquired an eighth element: Naturalist.)

* Gregorc's Abstract/Concrete, Random/Sequential model

* Kolb's layered model (Abstract/Concrete, Active/Reflective styles, layered over Diverging, Assimilating, Converging, and Accommodating types)

* McCarthy's 4Mat model (Innovative, Analytic, Common Sense, and Dynamic)

* Sternberg's addition to Gardner (Contextual and Experiential intelligences)

It's also important to know about the two leading psychological models, both of which arise from the work of Jung.

* Myers-Briggs Personality Sorter (Extraversion/Introversion, Sensing/Intuition, Thinking/Feeling, and Judging/Perceiving)

* Keirsey's Character Sorter (Guardian, Artisan, Idealist, and Rational)

You'll find in-depth information about each of these learning-style models, and numerous other models, in the Styles page of the Homeschool Steps Web site at <www.homeschoolsteps.com/seealso/styles.htm>.

How Can I Know My Child's Learning Style?

Here's a simple test you can administer at home with your own child. This self-test of Visual/Auditory/Kinesthetic preferences is diagrammed in Figure 7.1.

First, sit your child across from you at a table supplied with scratch paper and writing instruments. Without giving any clues about how the child should communicate, ask the child to give you

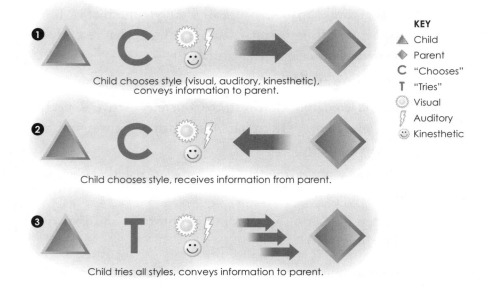

Figure 7.1 *The V-A-K Self-Test*

instructions about how to get to a place that's some distance away. For a younger child, the place might be the bathroom, the corner store, or the home of a nearby neighbor. For a pre-adolescent, it might be a location one to two miles away. And for a teenager, it might be a location ten or more miles away. The answer should require from five to fifteen steps, depending on the age of your child.

Observe whether your child's impulse is to explain with gestures and movement (Kinesthetic), with drawings or written instructions (Visual), or with simple step-by-step verbal instructions involving no bodily movement (Auditory).

The second step is to reverse the test. Tell your child you're going to give directions to, say, a neighboring state or some other fairly complex location. Ask the child how he or she would prefer to receive those instructions. Should you go outside and point the way (Kinesthetic), draw a map or write the steps down (Visual), or just explain the steps while sitting down at the table (Auditory)?

The third element of this test involves a little more preparation. Consider some tasks that are unfamiliar to your child (reading a story, finding a hidden object, threading a needle, hanging pants, making a pie crust, parallel parking). Think of three unfamiliar tasks that are of approximately equal difficulty.

Spend some time teaching the three tasks, using a different approach with each task. The Visual approach might involve written instructions, a diagram, or a photograph. It might also involve a demonstration where the child watches, rather than participates. The Auditory approach will involve simple spoken instructions. (Be as precise as possible when giving oral direction.) The Kinesthetic approach involves giving the child the tools to perform the task, and actually holding the child's hands or arms while he or she does the task for the first time.

When you've taught all three tasks, conduct an assessment. Ask the child to repeat each of the three tasks, describe how to do the tasks, or write down what he or she learned. (The assessment step of teaching involves learning styles every bit as much as the teaching step does.) It will become apparent rather early on which of the three basic styles your child prefers.

Inward Forces

"Human nature is not a machine to be built after a model, and set to do exactly the work prescribed for it, but a tree, which requires to grow and develop itself on all sides, according to the tendency of inward forces which make it a living thing."

—John Stuart Mill,
On Liberty

Some cautions, when it comes to learning styles. And these cautions apply regardless of the learning-style model you choose.

Learning Styles Are *Preferences*, Not Straightjackets. Your auditory child is not doomed to a lifetime of sitting quietly. No matter what their *preference,* all children are capable of learning through multiple approaches.

Learning Styles Can Be Extended. Learners face many situations that won't be adapted to their own preferences. While it's important

Inventory Time

Want to test your child (or yourself) for learning-style preferences? Inventories of various learning styles are available from commercial suppliers, and a large number of free tests are available on the Internet. We provide links to more than two dozen free online tests at the Inventory page of the Homeschool Steps Web site at <www.homeschoolsteps.com/seealso/inventory.htm>. You'll also find contact information for several commercial suppliers. These online tests use a variety of learning-style models, and most include strategies for teaching children according to their learning strengths.

to teach to a child's strengths, it's also important that your child learn how to acquire knowledge, regardless of the style in which it's being offered. To take full advantage of all learning opportunities, your child must become a flexible learner. A visual child should learn the skill of listening, a kinesthetic child should learn the skill of reading comprehension, and an auditory child should get involved in hands-on learning.

Don't Keep It a Secret.   In earlier times, information about children's learning abilities was a state secret—literally. It sometimes took a court order or a legislative act to view your own school records. And even then, your IQ score would probably be blacked out. New research demonstrates that children who know about their own learning styles, and who are invested in their own education, are better able to choose appropriate strategies for various learning situations. Researchers say children who understand their learning styles develop flexibility and adaptability in their thinking, set realistic goals, and minimize learning weaknesses while maximizing strengths.[2]

Over Time, Preferences Change. Young children are naturally more kinesthetic—wiggly—and their preferences change as their bodies mature. Other factors contribute to changing preferences. A child might, for example, get corrective lenses and become more visually attuned. An adult loses visual acuity and learns to acquire knowledge through other means. A child figures out how to listen, and discovers a whole new way of learning.

Preferences Change as Knowledge Is Acquired. After an adult visits a foreign country for the first time, her interest in reading about that country rises dramatically. She's developed a context for her knowledge and can feed it in different ways. Likewise, the first time a new concept is introduced to a child, he might learn best by doing. But as he builds his knowledge base, he might add new knowledge most efficiently by viewing pictures, reading, or listening.

Preferences Change with Practice. Each learning style is a learned skill. As children learn to perceive information visually, aurally, or tactilely, they become more adept, and discover new skills.

Learning Styles Don't Compensate for Bad Teaching. A writer tells the story of one of his college professors who, when questioned by a confused student, would either repeat his words in a louder voice, or write the same words on the board using various colors of chalk—"as if the reason we could not understand him was that we were either deaf or color blind."[3] If one style isn't working, be flexible enough to change approaches until your child comprehends.

Styles Don't Make Substance. Your children's ability to make cognitive connections, their problem-solving skills, and their fundamental motivation will have a much greater influence on their education than will their learning styles.

On Kinesthetics

"The doer alone learneth."

—Friedrich Wilhelm Nietzsche

Preferences Don't Equal Skills. Learning *preferences* don't matter nearly as much as the learning *skill* of "transfer." The ability to transfer learning from one situation to a variety of other settings is the heart of education. It's pointless, for example, to focus on how your children can best learn world history if they don't learn something more than a list of facts. History becomes valuable if learners are able to use it to see patterns in human behavior and to develop generalized beliefs about right and wrong, wisdom about politics and war, and personal convictions about moral conduct.

How Can Learning Styles Help Me Be a Better Teacher?

Suppose you discover that your child is a kinesthetic learner. How successful will you be sitting that child down at a desk and lecturing her about ancient Egyptian funerary practices? Clearly, your approach with a tactile child will be more hands-on and active. Instead of lecturing, you're going to be most successful helping that child find Egypt on a globe, drawing hieroglyphs together, visiting a funeral home, and mummifying an exanimate mouse.

Classroom teaching favors children with very specific learning skills. Nonstandard kinds of learning simply aren't a part of traditional curriculum, instruction, or assessment. Homeschooling parents who know their children well have a huge advantage over classroom teachers. They're able to focus on skills such as creativity, sensing, intuition, and imagination, as well as the valuable academic skills of reasoning, logic, analysis, and sequential problem solving.

As you learn more about other learning models—Multiple Intelligences, for example—you'll find yourself teaching to learning preferences that make sense for your family. You'll be sensitive to opportunities to expand your children's ability to reflect, to conceptualize, and to experiment. You'll employ a variety of techniques in your teaching. You'll introduce movement, music, drama, graphics, and games. You'll find holistic, complex learning opportunities that teach to your children's strengths, while strengthening their weaknesses.

Your teaching methods are only part of the story. It's also good parenting to teach your children strategies for better learning. After your kids understand their preferred learning styles, help them use the following techniques for increasing understanding.

Strategies for Visual learners

* Turn on the closed captioning when watching television or movies.

* Diagram the ideas presented in a lecture or a discussion.

* Watch a video that supplements the material you're learning.

* Attempt to visualize whatever you're listening to or reading.

* In lectures and meetings, sit close enough to the speaker to read lips. Facial expressions and mouth movements are an aid to understanding for people who don't process auditory communication efficiently.

* Read along in the text, the script, or the book as you listen to tapes.

* If you don't understand a principle, ask a parent or a tutor to map it for you. Drawings, graphics, text, charts, maps, and pictures will help you grasp unfamiliar concepts.

Strategies for Auditory learners

* Listen to tapes while reading. Books on tape are valuable not just to quell boredom in the car; they're also valuable as a way to work through books. Read while the voice in your ear reads to you.

∗ Use mnemonics. "Every Good Boy Deserves Fudge" is an easy, auditory way to remember the lines of a musical staff.

∗ Set information to a music. It's easier to memorize the names of the states if you can sing them to a familiar tune.

∗ Record lectures and discussions so you can review the taped information.

∗ Close your eyes while listening. It helps to shut out visual distractions.

Strategies for Kinesthetic learners

∗ Take notes. While you're listening to a lecture or a discussion, the physical act of note-taking can act as a kinesthetic prompt to learning.

∗ Use an exercise bike. Rather than forcing yourself to sit at a desk or in a chair while listening, watching, or reading, try sitting in a rowing machine or working out on an Exercycle. It'll give your body something to do while your mind is trying to absorb information.

∗ Walk around, lie down, put your feet up over your head. Get physically comfortable while reading, writing, and listening.

∗ Doodle. Keep your hands engaged while you're thinking.

∗ Walk and think. If you're struggling with new information, walk around, wave your arms, and point and gesture while you mentally process what you've learned.

∗ Lecture. Real audience or pretend, it helps if you stand up and *tell* someone what you're learning.

∗ If you're easily distracted by noise or movement, try wearing earplugs or working in an area away from other people.

How Can I Know My Child's IQ?

Tests of so-called Intelligence Quotients have always been controversial. At one time, the controversy surrounded issues such as racism and gender bias. Now that we understand more about learning-style preferences, the debate centers on whether IQ tests are even a valid measure of cognitive abilities. They tend to measure a very limited array of academic skills and completely ignore other, equally important skills. An IQ test cannot, for example, measure a child's social acumen, sense of humor, or innate determination. Nor can it measure a child's musical talent, mastery of esoteric sports trivia, or ability to use outside resources to find answers to difficult questions. In short, IQ tests fail to measure all the individual interests, abilities, and characteristics that make us unique and interesting and human.

Nevertheless, they do have some value, in that the reputable ones (the Stanford Binet and the Wechsler, for example) tend to be replicable, and they are somewhat effective in discerning factors such as mathematical reasoning, spatial relationship skills, and language acquisition.

They're also valuable—if the results aren't taken too seriously—in teaching a child to take tests. For example, the "a:b as x:?" question form is ubiquitous on college-entrance exams, and a child can learn to master the form with practice. Moreover, informal IQ tests have a secondary value in exposing test takers to the same questions they might actually encounter on a more critical test. And the tests have some value in exposing children to logic and critical thinking.

On Parents

"Those in society who are in charge of schools must never forget that the parents have been appointed by God himself as the first and principal educators of their children and that their right is completely inalienable."

—Pope John Paul II

You can have your child's IQ tested by various bodies such as the counseling office at a public school, psychologists, or commercial test providers. If you're interested in administering your own tests—which will, of course, be less reliable—consider the vast number of free online IQ tests available on the Internet. We provide links to a large number of these tests at the IQ page of the Homeschool Steps Web site at *<www.homeschoolsteps.com/seealso/iq.htm>.*

Is My Child Ready for School?

Both formal and informal education demand that a child master some basic developmental skills. Children can't ride bikes, for example, before they're capable of balancing themselves while walking, or before they can turn the pedals and steer.

Likewise, children can't read books until they learn how to hold a book right side up, turn the pages, distinguish the letters from the pictures, learn the alphabet, and understand the basic relationship between letters and sounds.

If you are concerned about developmental issues, you can assess your own children's readiness for formal education by comparing their skills with a set of standard guidelines. These guidelines will assist you in choosing learning areas that require more development.

Even if you're a committed unschooler, you can encourage learning readiness by focusing your family's educational experience around building the skills your child is lacking. For example, if you discover that your five-year-old child falls short in the area of counting, you might want to incorporate more counting experiences in your day-to-day activities. You could:

* Play a game of counting all the red cars as you're driving down the street.

* Count all the books you find out of place as you're cleaning the house.

* Ask your child to set the table with five place settings one night and six place settings the following night.

* Count out coins while you're in line at the drive-through window at a fast-food restaurant.

Once you become aware of areas where your child needs development, you'll find countless opportunities to teach those academic skills as you go through your regular day.

You'll find more than fifteen resources for assessing development and learning-readiness skills on the Readiness page of the Homeschool Steps Web site at <*www.homeschoolsteps.com/seealso/readiness.htm*>.

What's My Child's Grade Level?

Many homeschoolers reject the entire grade-level paradigm. They believe that different children progress at different rates and that it's meaningless to try to categorize them by some external standard. An individual homeschooled child could be working at a ninth-grade level in math, a fourth-grade level in art, and a college level in reading. For most homeschooling families, children are at whatever level they're at, and grade levels are irrelevant.

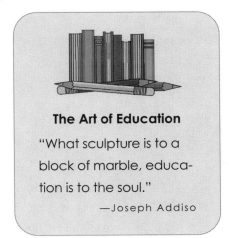

The Art of Education

"What sculpture is to a block of marble, education is to the soul."

—Joseph Addiso

But in states where homeschoolers are subject to grade-level testing, and in families that use grade-level curriculum, the question is very relevant. How do you know which math book to buy if you don't know what level of math your child has mastered?

To resolve questions about grade levels, homeschooled children can take a variety of placement tests. Placement tests are different from the assessment tests described in Chapter 2 in that they are used only as a basic guideline for curriculum planning and never as a legally required assessment of a child's progress. They tend to assess only a single subject area and are more qualitative—squishy—than objective. (Placement testing is discussed further in Chapter 3.) We provide links to a number of free online placement tests on the Placement page of the Homeschool Steps Web site at *<www.homeschoolsteps.com/seealso /placement.htm>*.

How Do I Create Lesson Plans?

Whether you're committed to a philosophy of Child-Led Learning, or attached to the idea of School-at-Home, you'll want to be able to teach formal lessons when it's appropriate for your educational format. An unschooled child might, for example, ask a question about human reproduction, religious doctrine, or fractions. While it's helpful to watch puppies being born, read Genesis, or divide a recipe into thirds, you might choose to reinforce and expand that child's learning by teaching a formal lesson or unit study on the subject.

On Testing

"I think animal testing is a terrible idea; they get all nervous and give the wrong answers."

—"A Bit of Fry and Laurie" (BBC comedy)

Pre-written lesson plans and unit studies are available from a variety of commercial resources. We discuss resources for free and commercial prewritten lesson plans in Chapter 5. Also, our first homeschooling book, *Homeschool Your Child for Free* *<www.hsfree.com>*, contains information about hundreds of resources for free lesson plans, themes, and unit studies.

The most useful lesson plans, however, are going to be the ones you customize or create for your own children, taking into account their learning-style preferences and addressing academic areas they need to strengthen.

Following are the basic steps to creating your own lesson plans. While you may not want to create a formal plan for every lesson, consider starting out with formal plans until you master the format. You'll find a worksheet for lesson planning at the end of this chapter, as well as an online version on the Planning page of the Homeschool Steps Web site at *<www.homeschoolsteps.com/seealso/planning.htm>*.

Steps to Creating a Lesson Plan

Lesson plan creation is a ten-step process

1. Describe learning concepts.

2. Determine learning objectives.

3. Consider learning-style preferences and learning gaps.

4. Find your children's motivators.

5. List new vocabulary.

6. Gather materials and equipment.

7. Review your resources.

8. Plan the introduction.

9. Determine your procedures.

10. Decide on the assessment.

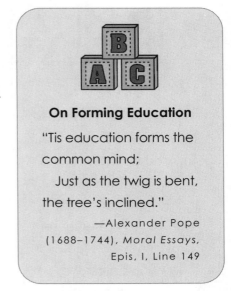

On Forming Education

"Tis education forms the common mind;
    Just as the twig is bent, the tree's inclined."

—Alexander Pope
(1688–1744), *Moral Essays,*
Epis, I, Line 149

Describe Learning concepts. Learning concepts are written as a two- to ten-word description of the focus of your lesson. Learning concepts can be very narrow or very broad. They can be covered in a single lesson, or they could involve a yearlong unit study. "Long division," "Chinese history," and "The significance of sacrifice in the Old Testament" are examples of learning concepts.

Determine Learning Objectives. Learning objectives are positive statements of skills to be mastered or knowledge to be demonstrated. The learning objective is typically written in the form "Anna will be able to count to 100 by fives," or "Jason will be able to parallel park," or "Lynn will be able to name three lessons to be learned from Germany's invasion of France."

Consider Learning-Style Preferences and Learning Gaps. This is where all the testing you conducted earlier in this chapter begins to pay off. Once you know your child is, for instance, an auditory learner with a deficiency in reading comprehension, you can customize your lessons to address her individual needs.

Find Your Children's Motivators. This may be the most important step in lesson planning. Ask yourself why it's important that your children learn what you're about to teach. Will it help them balance a checkbook and avoid financial ruin? Get into college? Distinguish right from wrong? Build a stable marriage and family? Keep a job? Understand higher mathematical concepts? Broaden their exposure? Hold their own in a social setting? Appreciate literature? Avoid embarrassment?

Whatever the reason for your lesson, it'll motivate your children to know how they'll benefit from what they're being taught, and your belief that the subject matter is relevant and useful will animate your teaching.

List New Vocabulary. What words will your children need to understand to learn from this lesson? Typically, a lesson introduces no more than about five new words. If you're introducing fifteen or more new words in a fairly brief lesson, you're probably teaching beyond your children's ability.

Gather Materials and Equipment. Whether you're teaching a lesson on pet grooming, public speaking, or personal finance, you'll

On Hope

"It is because modern education is so seldom inspired by a great hope that it so seldom achieves great results. The wish to preserve the past rather than the hope of creating the future dominates the minds of those who control the teaching of the young."

—Bertrand Russell (1872–1970)

need the proper tools. Create a materials list before you teach so that you're sure to have everything on hand. Don't neglect visual aids, auditory supplements, or materials for hands-on learning. See Chapter 5 for additional ideas.

Review Your Resources. Where will you find background information about this subject? Consider library resources, local experts, textbooks, and Internet searches. And don't forget our favorite resource, *Homeschool Your Child for Free <www.hsfree.com>,* which provides links to thousands of free resources for every academic subject from AIDS Education, Algebra, and American History, to Yiddish, Young Adult Literature, and Zoology.

Plan the Introduction. How will you introduce your lesson? Will you quiz your children to find out what they already know? Will you show a video? Discuss the history of your subject? Play a game? Offer a challenge? Ask a question? Send them on a Web quest?

Determine Your Procedures. What information will you teach? Considering your child's learning preferences and deficiencies, what steps will you take to convey information? Number your steps.

Decide on the Assessment. How will you know your children have learned what you intended to teach? Here are some ways your children might demonstrate understanding or mastery of a subject:

* oral summary of the lesson
* timeline
* display
* written summary
* dramatization of the lesson
* repetition of the task the lesson taught
* follow-up questions
* written or oral examination
* research project

* essay

* notes or outline

* art project

* multimedia presentation

* Web page about the lesson

There are hundreds of other ways children can demonstrate what they've learned. Be creative in coming up with possibilities that work for your family. Remember, your assessment needn't be onerous. Its primary purpose is to provide feedback so that you, the teaching parent, can know whether you've taught what you intended to teach.

How Do I Motivate My Child to Learn?

Your child is already motivated to learn. Witness any twelve-year-old boy who wants to master a video game or his fourteen-year-old sister who wants to French-braid her hair. Children are highly motivated when they believe the knowledge will give them pleasure or happiness.

Your task as a teaching parent, then, is to help your children experience the pleasure of learning and the power of knowledge, so that they are motivated to devour information.

There are many motivations for learning. When children believe that knowledge itself is valuable and brings intrinsic joy, spiritual strength, popularity, wealth, or power, they are highly motivated.

Interestingly, the strongest motivation for learning—among both younger children and adolescents and teenagers—is parental approval. Every parent has heard a toddler call "Watch me, mommy!" That urge to be admired by mom and dad doesn't go away with age; it only matures. A teenager who can intelligently debate politics and history with dad, or religion and literature with mom, gets the pleasure of feeling respected, listened to, and admired. That's a stronger incentive for learning than virtually any other motivator.

Are My Lessons Effective?

If you're looking for a more formal way of assessing your children's understanding—either because you're required to legally, or because you simply think it's a good idea—consider developing an assessment rubric. In education-ese, a rubric is a guideline for assessing or judging the quality of a person's work. Find an in-depth discussion of this strategy in Chapter 3. We provide examples of rubrics, as well as links to dozens of resources for developing your own lesson rubrics, on the Rubric page of the Homeschool Steps Web site at <www.homeschoolsteps .com/seealso/rubrics.htm>.

As children mature, they are also motivated by a desire for their *own* approval. They want to be proud of themselves and to feel good about their own accomplishments.

So how do you help your children get motivated to learn? Homeschooling families have found the following ideas very helpful in encouraging thinking and education:

Games. Logic games, puzzles, board games, and brain teasers. These activities are especially rewarding when children challenge—and beat—mom and dad.

Family events. If your family holds weekly family nights, your children might take turns preparing lessons, giving talks, planning refreshments and activities, and conducting discussions. Your children might also plan holiday parties for your extended family, prepare a family history, or arrange a family vacation.

Competitions. In recent years, homeschooled children have won or placed highly in several high-profile academic competitions, including the National Spelling Bee and the National Geography Bee. You'll find a database of national academic competitions that welcome homeschoolers on the Competition page of the Homeschool Steps Web site at *<www.homeschoolsteps.com/seealso/competition.htm>*.

Recitals, exhibitions, and talent shows. Arrange family or support-group events to showcase your children's progress in music, dance, public speaking, and art.

Be open with your praise of your child's academic achievements. Use family nights to formally award significant academic progress, hard work, memorization, goal attainment, and the completion of difficult projects.

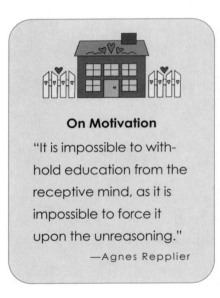

On Motivation

"It is impossible to withhold education from the receptive mind, as it is impossible to force it upon the unreasoning."

—Agnes Repplier

In addition, you might want to create actual awards for noteworthy achievements. You can obtain attractive award certificates, inexpensive trophies, and ribbons from office supply and craft stores. Or print out certificates from your computer's word processor. The Internet is rife with resources for creating award certificates, diplomas, and other motivational documents. See the Motivators section of *Homeschool Your Child for Free* *<www.hsfree.com>* for information on hundreds of free educational games, brain teasers, resources for motivating children, awards, and much more. You'll find additional advice for motivating your homeschooled child with the Motivational Strategies discussed in Chapter 3.

How Should We Schedule Our School Year?

A major advantage of homeschooling is flexibility. Unless you're legally obligated to follow a particular school calendar, you have the freedom to homeschool according to any calendar that suits your family. We discuss legal requirements for scheduling in Chapter 2 and Appendix A. Beyond that, you might want to try any of several approaches.

Daily Scheduling

Your day-to-day approach to scheduling can range from the highly organized to the completely relaxed.

Formal Structure. A significant number of homeschooling families choose a highly structured approach to scheduling. These families use complex hour-by-hour programs that have each child studying specific subjects and doing particular chores at scheduled times throughout the day. This approach is effective for highly organized families, and for children who prefer a non-kinesthetic approach to learning.

Semiformal Structure. Many families find success with days that are only partially structured. They might, for example, have family reading time before breakfast, followed by individual math instruction for an hour. Children might then be required to write a certain number of lines in their journals at any time during the day. The remainder of the time consists of a variety of educational and homemaking activities that change from day to day.

Informal Structure. Using the Unschooling, Child-Led, or Eclectic approach? You might choose to have completely unstructured school days. With this approach, you could spend Monday doing research at the library, Tuesday exploring the woods and writing a nature journal, Wednesday cleaning the house and volunteering at a retirement home, Thursday studying history and science with formal lessons, and Friday reading classic literature. The following week you might have an entirely different format, where you spend the week planting a garden or making a quilt and canning peaches.

Long-Term Scheduling

From week to week and year to year, your homeschooling calendar can take several different forms.

Traditional School Year. There are several reasons that most home-schooling families follow a traditional school year: legal requirements, summer camp, vacation plans with extended family, summer jobs, or simple habit. Not infrequently, homeschooled children ask to follow a traditional school calendar in order to spend non-school time with schooled neighbors and friends.

Off/On. Some families follow a two-weeks-on/two-weeks-off schedule, or some variation thereof. Under the daily off/on schedule they might, for example, study formally two or three days per week, and spend the off days working, traveling, taking field trips, or relaxing.

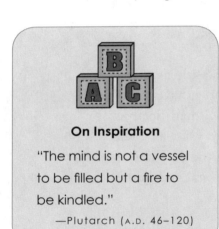

On Inspiration

"The mind is not a vessel to be filled but a fire to be kindled."

—Plutarch (A.D. 46–120)

Year-Round Schooling. Other families—particularly those with a less formal approach to education—educate year round without regard to calendars or schedules.

Part-Time Schooling. Every good parent home-schools—even if the homeschooling is only part-time. A significant portion of people who call themselves homeschoolers teach their children at home only during school holidays, vacations, and after school hours. These families may send some children to public or private school while they homeschool other children full-time. Some enroll their children in school for as few as one or two classes. Some enroll their children in school full-time, but are genuinely committed to teaching in the home outside of school hours and get involved with homeschooling cooperatives and support groups during summer breaks and holidays. And other good parents—people who take education and parenting seriously, and who are deeply involved in their children's education—homeschool without ever knowing or using the word.

Fortunately, the word "homeschooling" is broad enough to encompass any serious approach to education in the home. And committed homeschoolers can broaden their base of support—politically and educationally—by reminding other parents that any time they're teaching their own children, they're homeschooling.

Practical Habits for Homeschoolers

No matter which basic schedule you choose, you'll want to establish some practical habits for your school days. Successful homeschoolers suggest:

Establish a Strict Morning Routine. Wake up at the same time every school day. Straighten the house. Have family breakfast. Throw in a load of laundry. Read together. You'll feel successful before lunch even rolls around.

Limit Distractions. Let the answering machine pick up, don't answer the doorbell, don't make appointments during school hours, and limit your online time to certain days of the week or certain hours of the day.

Take Breaks. Take everyone out for a mid-morning walk. Put on an aerobics tape while lunch is warming. Have a beanbag toss.

Keep It Short. Homeschooling does not require six hours a day. Even if you're trying to replicate the public-school experience, keep in mind that schooled children average only a few minutes a day of actual teacher contact time. Not only are they competing with thirty other kids for the teacher's attention; beyond that, a major portion of the public-school day is taken up with recess, attendance, announcements, seat work, pep rallies, lunch, study hall, assemblies, bathroom breaks, distributing and collecting papers, and just plain standing around.

Watch for Peak Learning Times. Retention is affected, dramatically, by a number of factors: fatigue, hunger, physical discomfort, and excitement. (You'll never teach an eight-year-old long division on the morning of his birthday party, for example). Everything else being equal, though, children have individual circadian rhythms and learn best at different times of the day. Three of our sons like to stay awake into the wee hours to study, but stumble into doorways and walls before 10 A.M. Two other sons get up at the crack of dawn to study and fade out in the afternoons. Our oldest daughter is most efficient around mid-morning, but loses her focus after lunch. And our three-year-old wants to cuddle up to read every evening just before dinner. Fortunately, homeschooling accommodates all their individual preferences.

Take It Easy. The mind can absorb and use only a finite amount of new information each day. If your child comes away from an hour-long study period with one or two new ideas, you've been successful. No child is capable of processing or keeping a permanent memory of thirty or forty new ideas in a day.

Scheduling Advice

Looking for more ideas on homeschool scheduling? You'll find dozens of online forms and articles about setting up a schedule on the Schedule page of the Homeschool Steps Web site at <www.homeschoolsteps.com/seealso/schedule.htm>.

Have a Weekly Field Day. Volunteer, sightsee, visit museums, go people watching. Homeschooling's more rewarding when you take advantage of the flexibility and let your kids experience the world without having to stand in line.

If Necessary, Night School. Hey, it worked for Abraham Lincoln. Some families have such full days with lessons and volunteering and chores that education never seems to fit in. If that's your family, turn off that television and spend your evenings reading, talking, and listening.

Say "No." Don't allow other people to take advantage of you or your kids. You're *homeschooling*. No you won't do daycare. No, your teenagers can't baby-sit. No, you can't pick up the neighbor kids from school. No, your house isn't a good place for latchkey kids to spend their afternoons. And no, you won't homeschool other people's kids who are doing poorly in public school. Don't enable other people to be uninvolved parents. Encourage them to make the same sacrifices you're making, by staying home and parenting their own children. It'll be the kindest thing you ever do.

How Does Our Home Environment Influence Learning?

You've been in homes that were sterile and unwelcoming. You've probably also been in homes that were so chaotic you wondered whether the inhabitants even knew one another's names.

In a home that invites learning, children feel inspired to read, to think, and to acquire knowledge. You can take positive steps toward creating an education-friendly home.

Build Bookshelves. When it comes to creating an environment for education, the single most important thing you can do to encourage learning is to fill your home with books. Like most homeschooling families, we've lined the walls of our home with bookshelves. We have roughly 200 feet of bookshelf space in our home, and the shelves are filled to overflowing. Not only do we store our own books; we also shelve the kids' books, library books, journals, scrapbooks, and photo albums.

The cheapest way to create bookshelves is the bricks-and-boards system you probably used in college. Unfortunately, bricks and boards aren't very stable, and they present a safety hazard around climbing toddlers. Sturdier—and still inexpensive—shelving is available from discount department stores such as Kmart, Wal-Mart, Target, and Fred Meyer, as well as at discount furniture stores. Ikea sells attractive, moderately priced shelving and lighting that can fill walls up to eight feet high. Be sure to stabilize shelves by bracketing or cabling them securely to walls.

On Goals

"The principle goal of education is to create men who are capable of doing new things, not simply of repeating what other generations have done—men who are creative, inventive and discoverers."

—Jean Piaget

Prevent Distractions. Especially for children who are easily distracted, it's critical that you provide quiet, visually calming study space. Quiet bedrooms can be a refuge from noisy siblings, but if they're equipped with radios, televisions, CD-players, telephones, toys, comic books, and computers, it'll take superhuman strength for a child to resist the distractions. Our children's bedrooms are relatively spartan, because the rest of our home is noisy and distracting. The bedrooms enable each child to have a quiet, peaceful place to read and write and think.

If your children's bedrooms double as play areas, it's important that you designate another room or area of the house to quiet, undistracted study and reading. In temperate regions, that area could even be outdoors or in a well lit garage.

Create Comfort. Children do not learn better pinned under tiny one-size-fits-all school desks or tied to hard kitchen chairs. Fidgeting to get comfortable is a distraction to learning. Instead, consider permitting your kids to read sprawled on couches and in beanbag chairs. Equip them with clipboards or lap pads for writing, and be certain that wherever they're reading is well lit.

Pay Attention. Keep the computer and the television in a location that's visible from the kitchen or from wherever you spend most of your day. Turn the computer monitor so that it can be seen from high-traffic areas of the home. Eat together. Play together. If you're cheerfully involved with your kids, they'll learn—regardless of the approach, their learning styles, or the curriculum choices you make.

How Can I Create the Best Possible Learning Environment?

Research suggests that early and regular exposure to large quantities of information has a beneficial effect on intellectual development.[4] The bottom line: When children are nurtured in homes filled with brain food—books, paintings, and enthusiastic intellectual debates—they grow up smarter than children who grow up in sterile institutions and vacuous homes.

On Environment

"The most effective kind of education is that a child should play amongst lovely things."

—Plato (427–347 B.C.)

Maximilian Berlitz, the founder of Berlitz International language training centers, was raised in a multilingual home where every family member spoke a different tongue. He grew up fluent in eight different languages. When asked by an interviewer whether it had been confusing growing up that way, Berlitz responded that no, he had simply assumed from infancy that every person had a different language. Educator Tom Rogers (whose own multilingual children were guinea pigs for his "high-powered learning environment" method) argues persuasively for filling the walls and surfaces of your home with high-content information—maps, periodic tables, and the like—so that children grow accustomed to the information and view it as part of everyday living.

Filling your home with "brain food" doesn't require a large investment of money. In Chapter 5 you'll find suggestions for obtaining materials inexpensively. Below we discuss materials you might want to incorporate in your home, organized by learning style. Remember, too, that learning styles are acquired through practice, so don't neglect an area simply because your child hasn't yet developed a preference for it.

These learning aids are high content—meaning that they contain a lot of dense information. Don't worry if a particular item doesn't immediately appeal to your children. They might ignore a particular wall hanging for years and then suddenly discover that they know the information from that item without ever having consciously studied it.

High-Content Visual Aids

Hang information-rich graphics and text on every wall. Consider placing these items in high-use areas such as the kids' bathroom, or laminated and taped to the kitchen table.

* Wall maps. You might also consider wallpapering an entire room with a single map or with multiple smaller maps.
* Topical timelines. Consider isolated timelines that describe important events in, say, art, American history, or music.
* Table of chemical elements
* Handwriting charts
* Multiplication tables
* Literary quotations
* Prints of famous paintings
* Poetry
* Scriptural quotations
* Chart of mathematical symbols
* Chart of proofreading symbols

* Word strips naming objects they're taped to. Try foreign words.
* Glow-in-the-dark globe
* Constellation chart

High-Content Auditory Aids

Challenging audio aids will help your children learn. Many families find success playing audio items during chore time, while driving in the car, and at bedtime.

* Music that teaches academic concepts. An ideal choice is *Schoolhouse Rock*, which teaches about grammar, math, politics, and more with catchy songs that appeal to children.[5]
* Educational tapes
* Classical music
* Familiar children's stories taped in foreign languages
* Hymns
* Children's songs
* Patriotic songs
* Books on tape
* Radio plays
* Scriptures on tape
* Educational television
* The foreign-language option on DVD. Once your children have seen *Shrek* in English, spend a week or more listening to it in French.

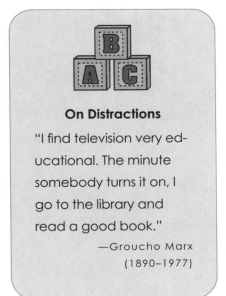

On Distractions

"I find television very educational. The minute somebody turns it on, I go to the library and read a good book."

—Groucho Marx
(1890–1977)

High-Content Kinesthetic Aids

These learning aids will keep the most distractible children involved as they move from place to place around their home.

* Challenges. Leave a quality chess set out in the open and challenge your child to beat Dad. Or challenge two children to beat one another over the course of several days, by moving a game piece once or twice a day in passing. Multi-dimensional tic-tac-toe, jigsaw puzzles, various board games, a Rubik's cube, and manipulative puzzles all lend themselves to once-or-twice-a-day attempts at solutions and will keep your children's interest over the course of days, weeks, or years.

* Manipulatives. Instruct with dowels, beans, beads, oranges, and other objects that teach scientific and mathematical principles.

* Blocks. Wooden and plastic alphabet, number, and building blocks.

* Relief maps

* Globes with raised surfaces

* Quilting or sewing projects. Set out a quilt frame, and invite your children to take a few stitches every time they pass the quilt.

* Art and craft projects

* Science projects

* Embossed word strips. Place a tag-board word strip with block letters on the ironing board, and rub the letters with an embossing tool or a spoon.

* Braille tags

* Pets

For More Information

You'll find hundreds of online teaching resources, as well as ideas for creating a rich learning environment, on the Teaching page of the Homeschool Steps Web site at <www.home schoolsteps.com/see also/teaching.htm>.

* Gym equipment

* Gardening projects

* Workshop projects

* Kid-friendly kitchen projects.

There you have it: A rich environment that will support education and motivate your children to learn. In the next chapter, we discuss practical ways to balance home, family, finances, and education.

Self-Test

How well does your home support learning?

T   F   1. I've read about learning styles and understand the theoretical basis behind them.

T   F   2. I've tested my children's learning styles and believe I understand their individual learning preferences.

T   F   3. I have administered IQ tests or believe I have a good grasp of my children's intellectual capacity.

T   F   4. I am familiar with the development skills typical for children of my child's age and understand where my child excels and where my child needs additional work.

T   F   5. If there are academic areas where I'm unsure of my child's level of knowledge, I've administered placement tests or taken other steps to assess my child's understanding.

T   F   6. I understand how to develop lesson plans and am confident in my ability to find the information and materials I need to teach the subjects my child is interested in.

T   F   7. I have lots of ideas for stimulating my children's interest in learning.

T   F   8. I have considered what kind of schedule will work best for our family and have a plan in place.

T   F   9. Our home has a place for books and other educational materials.

T   F   10. There are areas of our home available for quiet study and learning.

T   F   11. We have already begun filling our home with content-rich learning aids.

Scoring: Give yourself one point for each True response.

0 to 3 You've got some work to do. Share the information in this chapter with other family members to get their support in improving the learning environment in your home.

4 to 7 You're well on your way to creating a strong learning environment. A few more wall posters and a bit more interaction, and you'll be there.

8 to 11 Congratulations! You've created a welcoming environment for learning. Good luck keeping the neighbor kids away!

Worksheet

See page 233 for an explanation of this worksheet.

LESSON TITLE_____ DATE: _____

Learning concepts. List one to three concepts your lesson will cover:

_____

_____

Learning objectives. What skills will be mastered or demonstrated at the completion of your lesson?

_____

_____

_____

_____

Learning styles. What learning preferences and learning gaps must you consider in developing this lesson?

_____

_____

_____

_____

Motivators. Why is it important that your children learn what you're about to teach?

_____

_____

_____

New vocabulary. What words will your children need to understand to learn from this lesson? (Try to limit new words to five or fewer.)

_____

_____

_____

(continues)

Materials and equipment. What materials (visual aids, auditory supplements, or manipulatives) will you use in this lesson?

_____

_____

_____

Resources. Where will you find background information about this subject? (Consider library resources, local experts, textbooks, and Internet searches.)

_____

_____

_____

Introduction. How will you introduce your lesson? (Consider quizzes, videos, discussions, games, challenges, questions, and Web quests.)

_____

_____

_____

Procedures. What information will you teach? Considering your child's learning preferences and deficiencies, what steps will you take to convey information?

1. _____

2. _____

3. _____

4. _____

5. _____

Assessment. How will you know your children have learned what you intended to teach?

_____

_____

_____

The Balancing Act

How Do I Balance So Many Obligations?

Keeping a home and educating a family requires determination and organizational skills. In this chapter we look at practical ways to stay well organized and financially fit—without losing patience with your children or burning out on homeschooling.

Should We Name Our Homeschool?

Naming your homeschool is a wonderful idea for several reasons. Your family will feel unified and your homeschooling venture official, plus you'll qualify for free products and discounts. Get your kids involved. Design business cards, letterhead, a logo, and laminated student ID cards. The ID cards will be helpful if your children are ever asked for school identification. And a document on your school letterhead will qualify you for discounts at most bookstores and educational product supply stores.

Free Stuff

We list links to several free products—free business cards, videotapes, and other goodies—for your homeschool on the Freebies page of the Homeschool Steps Web site at *<www.home schoolsteps.com/see also/freebies.htm>*. We discuss other resources for free educational products in Chapter 5.

You'll find more advice about how and why to name your homeschool at the Naming page of the Homeschool Steps Web site at *<www.home schoolsteps.com/seealso/naming.htm>*.

How Can I Get Organized?

Every family has its favorite organizational tricks. Here are some that have worked for our family, and for some of the most successful homeschooling families we know.

Use Plastic Boxes

Plastic storage boxes are stackable, sealable, and sturdy. They're available in sizes from shoeboxes to Christmas trees. They resist moisture and keep even the most cluttered home looking neat. We purchased about forty-five large boxes for our last big move, and have made good use of them in the two years since. We've donated several to other families who were moving, and the rest have had various uses.

We use 28-gallon plastic boxes for craft supplies, genealogical records, sewing projects, photographs, scrapbooks, rubber stamping supplies, electric cords, and holiday decorations. We have boxes for office supplies, picnic items, and toys for our homeschooling co-op. We use some of our boxes for recycling and others for storage in the kids' closets. Plastic boxes hold nonperishable food on family vacations, and they're also a good way to transport muddy shoes and wet coats while we're travelling.

Each of our kids has a portable plastic box containing school materials—journals, mechanical pencils and replacement lead, pens, projects, books, worksheets, and so on. When we are in the car, the school boxes come with us so the kids have something intelligent to keep themselves occupied.

We've found the transparent boxes to be most useful for frequently accessed items. The opaque boxes are sturdier and work best for items such as holiday decorations, which spend more time in storage.

Declutter

There's an old story about a fellow who came into a thrift store every day and bought a white shirt. One day the clerk asked what he did with so many shirts. He blushed and confessed, "Oh, no. I have only three white shirts. But you see, the dry cleaner next door wants four dollars to clean an article of clothing. So I donate one of my shirts to you each day, you guys wash it for me, and I buy my shirt back the following day for two bucks."

It's more economical to "store" all your knick-knacks, wobbly furniture, and out-of-season clothing at the local thrift store than it is to pay rent on a storage area, or to live in an overly large home with entire rooms dedicated to hiding junk. I gave away my old shoes, empty milk cartons, shoeboxes, disassembled toys, outdated jeans, and all the rest of my clutter when I discovered that replacing items as they were required was less expensive than buying the shelves it would require to store them.

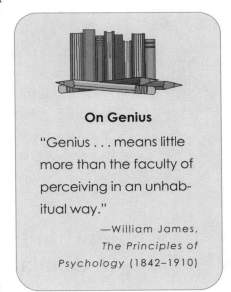

On Genius

"Genius . . . means little more than the faculty of perceiving in an unhabitual way."

—William James,
*The Principles of
Psychology* (1842–1910)

It's easy to get rid of clutter when you view Sears and the Goodwill as your personal storage units. And what a bargain! You don't pay a penny in storage fees until you actually take items out of your "storage" area!

Set Up Your Own Office Space

Most homeschoolers spend their entire educational budget on their children's needs. If you're feeling disorganized, though, we highly recommend diverting some of that money to furnish parental office space. If your own life is in control, you're better equipped to help your children handle their challenges.

At a minimum, getting your paperwork under control requires desk space, an easily accessed filing system, and drawers for stamps, mail, checkbooks, and filing materials.

We set up office space on an open wall in our dining area (see Figure 8.1) The office consists of a tall bookcase unit with doors to hide reference books and office supplies, a three-drawer unit under a long, narrow table, a small printer stand that also fits under the table, and a two-drawer lateral file.

The notebook computer and a telephone fit neatly on the printer stand, and the whole table/lateral file unit doubles as a buffet area when we entertain.

Since setting up a permanent headquarters for all incoming and outgoing correspondence, we have finally gotten the paperwork, computer work, and tax documentation in our home under control, and we have been much more organized about helping the kids with their own educational endeavors.

How Do We Get Our Documents Organized?

The home filing cabinet is critical to staying organized. We highly recommend a legal-sized cabinet rather than a letter- or A4-sized cabinet, because it holds items such as mortgage papers and other legal documents without mutilating them.

If you can afford the $200 or higher cost of sturdy, well made wooden cabinets, you'll get a lifetime of use out of them. Be on the

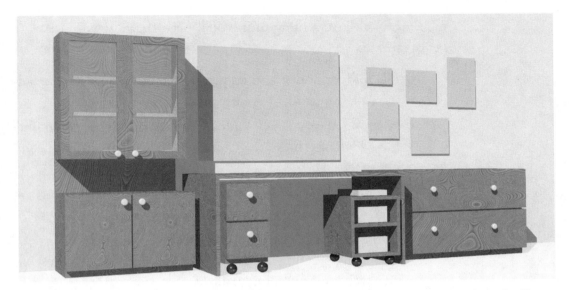

Figure 8.1 *A bookshelf with storage space, desk space, drawers, a printer stand, and a filing cabinet provides all you need for an efficient home office. An office chair fits between the drawer unit and the printer stand. Wall space becomes a display area for schoolwork.*

lookout for cabinets with ball-bearing rollers on suspended racks, racks for hanging files, and anti-tip mechanisms that don't allow more than one drawer at a time to be opened.

Inexpensive secondhand filing cabinets are available at thrift stores, yard sales, and going-out-of-business sales. You can buy new two-drawer polystyrene vertical cabinets for less than $20 at discount and office-supply stores. But if you don't have a four-drawer or two-drawer lateral filing cabinet, you can make do with cardboard or plastic filing boxes.

Before we could afford a filing cabinet, we had separate plastic boxes for taxes, bills, documents, correspondence, and homeschooling records. Now all those items fit nicely into one well made lateral filing cabinet. (Out in the corner of our garage we keep a second very cheap thrift-store-sourced filing cabinet for older documents. It gets opened twice a year or less, and nobody notices the large rust spots on the back.)

Once you have a filing unit, you'll need the following items to get organized:

* File folders: Some families prefer colored folders, and we admire their ingenuity. We use plain 1/3-cut manila files.

* Hanging files: We hang individual files within larger hanging files. Hanging files are generally sold with plastic tabs and perforated labels.

* File folder labels: The $2\frac{1}{2}$ inch labels work nicely. Labels are neater than handwritten tabs and allow you to reuse files.

* In/out basket: Ours is a three-drawer basket that we use for incoming, pending, and fileable documents. We have a separate basket for outgoing mail.

* Wastebasket: Keep a wastebasket next to your desk so that mail can be handled on the spot.

We disagree with the "handle it only once" maxim you've heard from office efficiency experts. Doing so at home would demand that whenever paperwork arrives, you drop whatever else you're doing and handle paper as a top priority. For homeschoolers, children are the top priority. Paperwork is way down the list of life's daily crises.

As you collect each day's mail, throw junk mail straight into the trash, put bills directly into the incoming drawer of your in/out basket, and put other items that need to be handled—rebate forms, insurance reimbursements, tax forms, et cetera—into the pending drawer. When you receive homeschooling catalogs or other freebies, throw them into a plastic box to share at your next homeschooling co-op meeting.

Twice a month, go through your pending drawer and your bill drawer. If you pay your bills online, set up payment dates. If you pay manually, write out checks, put them into stamped envelopes, and seal them. On the back of each envelope, write the date the envelope must go into the mailbox, and a reminder notation about the amount of the payment. (A payment of $203.68, for example, would be notated "204," without the dollar signs, decimals, or other information that would tell an outsider the meaning of the number.) On the bill stub itself, make a notation of the payment date, check number, and payment amount. If you pay bills online, record a confirmation number on the bill stub.

Then put the outgoing mail in its basket, and the bill stubs, receipts, and other material to be filed into the file-able drawer of your in/out basket. Don't actually put outgoing mail into the mailbox until the mail date you've recorded on the backs of the envelopes.

As you begin organizing your documents, you'll find yourself filing the following items.

Paid Bills. Create and label a separate file folder for each payee. You can put files for multiple payees in a single hanging file. File bill stubs and all other documents in reverse chronological order, with the newest information at the front. Some people throw bills out. We used to do so, but find this system much more efficient. We can easily compare bills from month to month (and have thereby uncovered an astonishing number of billing errors; computers are only as smart as the people who program them). We have simplified our taxes, improved our budgeting, eliminated late fees, and successfully argued away several hundred dollars of billing errors because we keep our bill stubs.

Homeschooling Records. Keep a separate hanging file for each child. Depending on the legal requirements in your state—and your family's

Need More Help?

If you're not naturally organized, there's help. On the Organize page of the Homeschool Steps Web site, we provide book reviews, software reviews, Web site addresses, and dozens of other resources for organizing your homeschool and your home. You'll also find hints for quick meals, information about cooking in bulk, and other homemaking tips for balancing home and family. Visit the Organize page at <www .homeschoolsteps.com /seealso/organize.htm>.

interest in tracking educational progress—you might want to maintain calendars, attendance records, grades, and transcripts. If you use record-keeping software, file hard copies of the documents in your children's files. Also be sure to maintain copies of your children's best work so that they can assemble a portfolio as an aid to their college admissions applications. If your children create projects that aren't easily filed—murals, sculpture, woodwork, service projects, and the like—file photographs, scrapbook pages, and journal entries describing the project. The last category of homeschooling records you'll want to maintain are lesson plans, unit studies, and other creations that you may want to share or reuse in the future.

General Paperwork. Insurance forms, policies, loan documents, and contracts all go in your filing cabinet.

Documents. File birth certificates, passports, marriage certificates, and immunization records in individual folders in a single hanging file. We know one family that wraps document files in a sheet of heavy-duty foil to afford some level of protection in the event of a fire.

Financial Records. Photocopy the contents of your wallet and the wallet of your spouse, so that you have documentation in the event of a loss. Photograph the valuable contents of your home, and keep a copy on file. Store a copy of your will, bank account numbers, investment records, and insurance documents. Keep copies of tax documents for at least seven years. It's wise to store a second copy of these documents off-site. (We suggest sending sealed backup photocopies of these documents to a reliable adult sibling or parent, so they'll be available in the event of a catastrophe.)

Receipts. The more complex your tax situation, the more critical it is to keep receipts. For our own situation, which is very complex, we store receipts in a small accordion file that sorts receipts by month. When life is too complicated to file, we just shove the receipts into a one-gallon plastic storage bag that's stashed in a desk drawer. And whenever we anticipate waiting in a doctor's office or another time-wasting place, we grab this year's accordion file and the plastic bag and use the time to sort receipts.

Product Documentation. Whenever you purchase a computer, a vacuum cleaner, or any other item that comes with instructions and serial numbers, place all the documents into a -gallon-sized locking storage bag (see "Plastic World"). Then use a file label to record the name, purchase date, and price of the item. If your home is peopled with electronics nuts, as ours is, you may want to store all this documentation in an entirely separate box. We file our bags of documentation alphabetically, by the name of the manufacturer. (Actually, this filing job is a task for kids. They enjoy digging through the box, and alphabetizing is a good cognitive task.)

Can We Keep a Clean Home While Homeschooling?

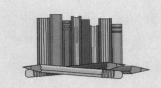

On Organization

"It is because the body is a machine that education is possible. Education is the formation of habits, a superinducing of an artificial organization upon the natural organization of the body."

—Thomas H. Huxley
(1825–1895)

Some homeschoolers have impeccable homes. Some live in comfortably cluttered surroundings. Others live in near chaos.

A tidy home makes for easier homeschooling. You know where things are, and you have the freedom to focus on what matters. Many of the homeschoolers we've talked with say they need clean homes as a matter of emotional health and marital accord. But the bottom line is that your house will be as clean as you decide it will be.

If you're feeling frustrated at the disarray in your own home, the following tips might help.

Counsel Together. Talk with your family and decide what level of clutter is acceptable in your home. Don't allow the discussion to

Plastic World

Our family buys and uses gallon-sized resealable plastic storage bags by the case—and fewer than 10 percent of the bags get used for food storage. We also use disposable plastic containers produced by the same manufacturers. These products can be pricey, but we stock up when they're on sale and when we run across coupons. Here are some of the hundreds of organizational uses for gallon-sized bags, as well as Ziploc resealable bags and GladWare disposable storage containers, and their generic counterparts:

Classroom. Store pens, pencils, erasers, replacement leads, tape dispensers, crayons, markers, paperclips, and glue sticks in individual bags. Keep protractors, math manipulatives, counters, beads, felt board pieces, and other educational products in bags and disposable boxes. And while you'd normally file worksheets and other papers, those that involve cutouts and small pieces are easily stored in plastic bags.

Toy room. Crayons, doll outfits and accessories, game pieces, miniature cars, plastic people, marbles, card games, building blocks, and puzzle pieces stay together—and out of your vacuum cleaner—when they're stored in plastic bags and stackable plastic containers.

Sewing room. Bag up quilt blocks, cross-stitch projects, yarn, patterns, seam rippers, cutters, and blades in gallon-sized bags. Store bobbins, buttons, elastic, ribbon, and other sewing notions in disposable plastic containers.

deteriorate into nit-picking over a toothpaste cap or an errant sock. This philosophical discussion is meant to get everyone on the same page and working toward the same goals.

It's not unusual for parental standards of hygiene to be higher than children's standards. Be prepared to explain why it's important

Warranties and product instructions. Keep the documents for your new washing machine (or any other major purchase) in a resealable bag. Letter-sized documents fit perfectly in a gallon-sized bag.

Art supplies. Keep all those watercolor palettes together. Store paints, clay, brushes, and other tools in containers that won't spill or mix.

Pet supplies. Grooming supplies, food for trips, medications, and documents stay clean and usable in plastic bags.

Travel. Keep plastic bags for maps, card games, quiet books, snack food, changes of clothing, first aid kit, and road flares, to keep your family safe and happy on the road. And store products that could leak or stain—medications, sippy cups, shampoos, and toothbrushes—in plastic bags to keep clothing and other items safe.

Bathroom. Makeup, hair bands, soaps, product samples, manicure equipment, nail polish, travel items, wet wipes, and all the other little items that never stay in one place can be kept clean and separated with plastic bags. We also use clear plastic shoeboxes from a discount store to store combs, manicure products, and other items that we buy in large quantities when they're on sale.

Scrapbooking. We are avid scrapbookers and rubber stampers. We use plastic storage bags to store inks and powders, glitter, rubber stamps, markers, papers, labels, templates, photographs, and tools.

to you to have a clean home, and seek at least reluctant agreement to the parental standard.

Clean as a Team. Many parents find themselves in a losing battle with children who'd rather hide clothes under the bed than hang them in a closet. If you struggle with slothful cleaners, try switching to the group cleaning method where children who need parental supervision start cleaning under Mom's watchful eye at one end of the house, while those who are more responsible are permitted to clean without supervision from the other end of the house. The goal, of course, is to meet in the middle.

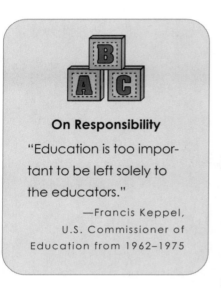

On Responsibility

"Education is too important to be left solely to the educators."

—Francis Keppel, U.S. Commissioner of Education from 1962–1975

The team method works just as well with just one parent and one child. Working together gives you time to talk while cleaning, and speeds up the work.

Do an Eight-Minute Clean. Chores used to be a source of contention in our home. Housecleaning sometimes dragged on all day, and even more often, didn't get done at all. But nobody argues over an eight-minute clean.

Our family cleans twice a day, for eight minutes each round. During the morning clean we get the beds made and make the house presentable. If we have a messy morning, we do an intermediate eight-minute clean before lunch. The late afternoon clean gets the floors vacuumed and all the surfaces picked up before Dad gets home from work. Deeper cleaning is saved for Mondays, our free day.

Any family member who works flat out for the full eight minutes is relieved of chores until the next round. Slackers, of course, get extra chores. We don't have a lot of slacking anymore.

Whistle While You Work. Cleaning time is a great time to turn on loud music, classical music, or books-on-tape. Fast music promotes fast cleaning.

Set Speed Goals. Yesterday it took 16 minutes to straighten the entire house. If it gets done today in 12 minutes or less, the kids get an hour of free computer time or a trip to the library.

Carry Your Cleaning Tools. Try an apron with pockets or an inexpensive plastic tote or bucket. Equip each family member with age-appropriate cleaning tools, so that everyone can be cleaning at the same time.

Enforce the Laundry Rules. Laundry doesn't pile up in our home, as long as we enforce our Family Laundry Rules. The Family Laundry Rules are:

1.   No dirty clothes in the laundry room. All dirty clothing stays in hampers in bedrooms and bathrooms until it's time to wash it. No exceptions.

2.   No unfolded clothing touches a surface. Nothing comes out of the dryer unless it's folded or hung on the spot. If you don't have time to fold it or hang it immediately, you don't have time to take it out of the dryer. Leave it there until you do have time.

3.   Everything with sleeves or legs goes on a hanger. We keep armfuls of empty hangers hung on a rack in the laundry room, so that clothing can go directly onto a hanger as it comes out of the dryer.

4.   All socks in the sock bucket. We don't try to put away socks any more. We just keep a round plastic laundry basket on a rack in the laundry room, and as we pull socks out of the dryer, they go directly to the bucket, matched or not. We also have a hat-and-glove bucket, where we throw ties, mittens, belts, and other items that get carried to the laundry room, but don't go through the washing machine. It's also useful to keep a small plastic box to hold found buttons, coins, and other pocket contents. In the evenings, while we're watching videos or doing something else mindless, we might match up socks and distribute the contents of the miscellaneous bucket to be put away in the owners' rooms. If not, no problem. Everyone knows where to go to find these items.

These four rules have solved our laundry problems. Before these rules, dirty clothes got mixed in with clean clothes, we were constantly rewashing clothing that hadn't even been worn, we had baskets of unclaimed clothing around the house, and we were buying socks on almost a weekly basis, because we could never find a clean pair.

Stick to It. Keep working until the job is done. Nothing is so frustrating to Mom's mental health as a half-swept floor, a partially unloaded dishwasher, and wet towels wadded over a towel rack. Regardless of your family's standard of cleaning, see that whatever tasks you and the kids set out to do get carried through to completion. It'll teach your children good work habits, and it'll improve your own emotional well being.

A Place for Everything. Often, people live with clutter because they simply can't decide what to do with the plaster handprint, the bronze baby shoe, and the plastic-grapes centerpiece. The easiest way to get a disorganized home under control is to simply box up everything that's out of place. That's right. Walk through a room and put every single out-of-place item into a box or a trash bag, then put the box or bag in the attic, out back, or in the garage. If you later discover you actually need a particular item—your toaster, for example—don't remove it from the box until you've created a permanent home for the item. Either throw away your unused popcorn popper to make room for the toaster or eat your bread cold until you find an appropriate place to store it. If you don't pull anything out of the box for six weeks, donate it. Don't look inside first. Just close your eyes and give it away.

How Should We Handle Chores?

Your mother told you two things that you ought to remember when it comes to requiring your own children do household chores:

First, "It's for your own good." Part of your goal as a parent is to teach each of your children to live as independent adults in a manner that won't involve complaints to the health department. Learning to cook, clean, and perform other household chores helps them become better adults.

Second, "I'm not the maid." The difference between a home and an institution is that family members work together to keep a home livable. Mom isn't an employee, Dad isn't the warden, and children aren't freeloading inmates.

Doing chores should be as much a part of the homeschooling curriculum as studying math and science. Any healthy child over the age of three is old enough to pitch in. Our three-year-old is a cleaning demon with the lower kitchen cabinets and the bottom half of the refrigerator door. She can sweep the kitchen floor with a small broom and dustpan. She can empty bathroom wastebaskets, put shoes away, and carry errant dishes to the kitchen. And she's working on putting away silverware from the dishwasher.

Her taller siblings are expected to do much more, and every teenager in our home is expected to pull his or her own weight when it comes to keeping the home and yard neat and clean.

If Mom is feeling like a household servant, things are amiss in the home. Remember: You serve your children best by teaching them teamwork and responsibility. Your job as a parent is to teach, supervise, encourage, correct, and follow through; their responsibility is to learn and do. Read more about homeschooling and chores on the Chores page of the Homeschool Steps Web site at *<www.homeschoolsteps.com/seealso/chores.htm>*.

What About Meal Planning?

Make cooking, setting up, planning, and shopping for meals a family effort. Children should be able to set a table with supervision at age four, and unsupervised by age five. A six-year-old should be able to prepare a very simple cold meal, and a well supervised eight-year-old should be able to safely use a stove. By the age of ten a child should be able to participate in meal planning, and by the age of twelve a child should have no trouble comparison shopping or finding items in a familiar grocery store. Any teenager should be able to independently plan, shop for, and prepare a complete meal.

We provide dozens of child-friendly recipes, advice for cooking in bulk, food storage tips, food safety information, nutrition resources, and more on the Pantry page of the Homeschool Steps Web site, <*www.homeschoolsteps.com/seealso/pantry.htm*>.

Can We Live Off One Income?

In all likelihood, you can live *better* off of one income. Many two-earner households are surprised to discover that the second earner in a family doesn't earn enough to pay for the *costs* of employment.

Look at the math. Suppose your family fits the standard working-family model of a husband and a wife with two young children. Suppose the husband has taxable income of $63,550 and the wife has taxable income of $28,000.[2]

The husband's earnings are taxed at a maximum of 28 percent, but the wife's income moves the couple into a higher tax bracket and is taxed at 31 percent. Moreover, she pays 7.65 percent in social security taxes, an average of 4.3 percent in state income taxes, and a variety of income, unemployment, disability, and miscellaneous taxes, which we generously average out at 2.5 percent.[3] Many employers and most religious faiths expect you to donate a percentage of your income to United Way, community organizations, and your church. Calculate charitable contributions at an additional 5 percent. That's a total of 42 percent—or nearly $12,000—before you even get to the bank.

Childcare at a low-end facility will cost at least $5,200 per year for two children. Your institutionalized children will require more and newer clothing than they would if they were home with

Mommy all day, so add a children's clothing differential of $25 per child a month, or $600 per year.

A working mother needs a reliable automobile and probably can't get by with the $500 junker an at-home mom could use. So add in monthly car payments of $250, gasoline at $15 per week (assuming you live fairly close to your workplace and childcare location) for a total of $780 per year, and increased auto insurance premiums of $600 per year.

Then look at the direct costs of employment. Working mothers can't shuffle in to the office in sweats and a beauty-school haircut. A working wardrobe will cost a bare minimum of $100 per month, dry cleaning will run about $25 per month, and the beautician will add an additional $25 per month.

Finally, add in the "hidden" costs of employment. Fast-food and cafeteria meals at around $5 per day. Contributions to gifts for coworkers who are quitting, getting married, and having babies easily run $25 per month. Consider what we call the "convenience-food differential." You're too tired and too rushed to cook from scratch, so you stop at Taco Bell or open a package of ready-made stir-fry for dinner. Breakfast is cold junk cereal rather than less expensive meals made from scratch. And who has time to comparison shop, clip coupons, or hit all the weekday sales when you're working full-time? You'll be fortunate if you can keep the convenience-food differential below $50 per week.

The grand total? Out of an income of $28,000, you're spending about $28,164 per year for the privilege of working. In other words, you could lie in bed and stare at the ceiling all day and be ahead almost two hundred bucks a year.

And that's assuming you don't give more to charity, you don't live in any of the twenty-five higher-taxed states, and you scrimp on clothing, childcare, the automobile, and all the rest. A working Mom in a generous family in a higher-taxed state would have to earn $35,000 or more just to break even.

Moreover, those figures don't count the additional cost to the primary worker of not having a backup parent at home. If Mom is at work, Dad's job is in jeopardy if he has to take days off to care for a sick child. His lunches and laundry become more expensive if there's nobody available to pack a meal or iron a shirt. If the primary wage earner has to spend time hunting for missing socks, cleaning toilets, and running children to piano lessons—because there's no adult at home keeping things running smoothly—that person becomes less valuable at work, jeopardizing future raises and promotions, and may even risk unemployment.

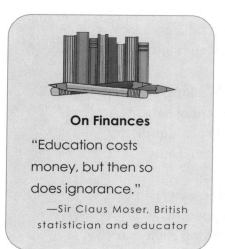

On Finances

"Education costs money, but then so does ignorance."

—Sir Claus Moser, British statistician and educator

So if you could earn, say, $33,200 per year working full-time, subtract the $30,000 or so it costs you to work, and then ask yourself whether it's worth the $12 you'll earn today to be separated from your children, frazzled, stressed, and resentful. Is it worth being estranged from your family, living off Big Macs, and missing your children growing up—for 12 bucks? Is it worth having your children institutionalized, angry, and endangered—for 12 bucks? And is it worth putting your spouse's job at risk—for 12 lousy bucks?

How Do We Earn Extra Money?

We've heard from countless numbers of would-be homeschoolers who tell us that their spouses won't support homeschooling solely because they're worried about finances.

If your family's financial situation requires extra income, consider these homeschool-friendly alternatives:

Moonlight. Your grandmother would remind you that before it became fashionable for women to work outside the home, men did whatever it took to support their families—working two jobs, if necessary. Rather than having two wage earners in the family, it might be easier on everyone if one supportive spouse tends the home, while the other earns two incomes. (Besides, if you require a family income in excess of $84,900—because, for example, you live in California—it's less expensive to have one spouse earn all the money, even if he (or she) has to work a second job. Earnings in excess of that amount are free of social security taxes.)

Work a Second Shift. Many homeschooling families make do by having one spouse work the day shift, while the other works swing or graveyard. That way, children get equal time with both parents and get the benefit of Dad's unique knowledge and talents.

Sell. Find a buyer for the things you own, and the things you create. Sell goods on E-Bay, <*www.ebay.com*>, and at yard sales, craft fairs, farmers markets, and consignment shops.

Live Off the Land. Is your family blessed with a lot of land and friendly zoning laws? Operate a bed-and-breakfast, a u-pick farm, or a tree farm. Do wedding receptions. Board animals. Graze and stable horses. When we lived on five acres in Missouri, we sold the overgrown grass for hay.

Retail. If you have the space and the zoning permits, operate a retail storefront for antiques, farm products, crafts, plants, used books, or any other product you can obtain inexpensively. Your retail operation needn't be expensive. One suburban family we know sells dahlias from a roadside stand in their front yard. Every morning during growing season, the family cuts several bouquets of flowers from their dahlia garden and leaves them on a table with a sign. Passing drivers stop, choose a bouquet, and leave their money. The flowers are always sold out by mid-morning.

Distribute. Multilevel marketing is a significant income source for many families. Opportunity abounds. The Direct Selling Association

<www.dsa.org> has nearly 150 member companies selling everything from vacuum cleaners to encyclopedias to financial advice. Discovery toys, Longaberger baskets, Mary Kay cosmetics, Pampered Chef kitchenware, Stampin'Up! stamping and scrapbooking supplies, Tupperware, and Usborne books are popular party-based companies. Amway, Avon, and Shaklee are well known product lines sold on a person-to-person plan.

Produce. Start a family business that involves your children. Consider cabinetry, crafting, quilting, sculpture, sewing, or Web design. Publish a newsletter or a small magazine.

Do. Start a business doing catering, childcare, cleaning, delivery, lobbying, polling, repair, shopping, or telephone solicitation. Or become a dog walker, event organizer, lobbyist, personal trainer, shopper, or a medical, legal, or broadcast transcriptionist.

Freelance. Consult, cartoon, or paint. Do computer programming, editing, financial counseling, marketing, research, or tax preparation. Become an herbalist, photographer, translator, or writer.

Teach. You and your children can tutor, conduct classes, or train. Whatever you're good at, teach it to someone else.

Entertain. Produce a movie or a play. Sing, dance, juggle, clown, or do magic at conventions, weddings, parties, and bar mitzvahs. Become a motivational speaker.

Invent. If you have a creative bent or technical expertise, patent and market an invention.

Work Very Odd Jobs. Become a secret shopper, a focus-group participant, or a closed-captioning transcriptionist. Sell your blood, bone marrow, or hair. Volunteer to be a research subject. One bilingual mom we know landed an at-home job translating. When her second line rings, it's the phone company or the 911 operator asking her to interpret an incoming call from a Cantonese speaker.

From the Front Lines

For many years, homeschooling mom Janet Hawken was a fitness instructor and her husband Harvey was a highway patrolman. "We worked hard and had little energy left over to spend with our kids," she says.

Then they decided to change their priorities. They landscaped their property, planted a field of evergreens, and got involved with Shaklee, a multilevel nutritional supplement company.

Now Harvey and Janet work from home doing wedding receptions <www .crystalcreekgardens>, distributing Shaklee products, and selling Christmas trees. Not only do they get to spend more time together as a family, they also get to drive new cars, take frequent family trips, and educate their own children.

Can a Single Parent Homeschool?

You can homeschool as a single parent. But unless you're independently wealthy, it takes determination and the goodwill of other people. To homeschool successfully as a single parent requires a three-legged stool of support:

The Other Parent

The first leg of the stool is getting the endorsement of your children's other parent. You could, of course, attempt to homeschool against the wishes of the other parent. But if, instead, you do what it takes to get that support, you won't have to endure court battles, you won't have to deal with being undermined, and you won't have to worry about interference from social workers. For the sake of your kids, avoid squabbling over whatever caused the breakup, and seek reconciliation on this more significant issue: The best education for your children.

If you *are* doing battle with the other parent over homeschooling (or any other issue, for that matter), we strongly advise obtaining the services of a mediator. Don't get lawyers involved in your negotiations; lawyers are trained to be adversarial, and they're expensive. Instead, engage a mediator who will assist you in arbitrating your differences and who will help both of you get what you want. A good mediator will present your case to the other parent, explain your concerns, and help you work through important issues without getting emotional, and without permitting an escalation of grievances.

Help for Working Families

Families with working parents can find additional resources and advice at the Working page of the Homeschool Steps Web site at <www.homeschoolsteps.com/seealso/working.htm>.

Your Support Team

The second leg? You'll need a good support team. In general, a single parent is a working parent, meaning that the kids need a place to be when you're at work. For that reason, we urge single parents to live close to their "support team": supportive family members and friends who will back you up by being a second family to your kids while you're unavailable for parenting. If that support team includes the other parent, terrific. But it's even better if you also have the support of your children's grandparents, aunts and uncles, and adult siblings. We know of one homeschooling situation where two best friends—single moms who live in neighboring apartments—are working together to raise their own and each other's children. While one friend works, the other takes the kids, and vice versa.

The most critical factor is this: Your support team will need to share your commitment to homeschooling. The last thing you need as a single, working parent is a backup who questions your decisions and undermines your parenting. Ideally, your backup will either be in your home while you're working or will provide a safe, nurturing, education-friendly second home where your children feel loved and welcome.

Your Children

The third leg is getting support from your children. Single-parent families are most successful when the children want to be homeschooled, when they're responsible, and when they're appropriately independent. If you're fighting a belligerent child on top of everything else a single parent has to deal with, it might be wiser to be a part-time homeschooler. Educate when the opportunities arise, and simply relax and enjoy whatever time you do have with your child. Life's too brief to spend it fighting every battle.

On Priorities

"What we want is to see the child in pursuit of knowledge, and not knowledge in pursuit of the child."

—George Bernard Shaw
(1856–1950)

What Is Dad's Role in Homeschooling?

The vast majority of homeschooled children are taught primarily by their mother. (In the interest of fairness, there are a few homeschooling families—about half of one percent—with a working mom and a stay-at-home dad.[4])

Families that fit the traditional working dad/at-home mom model often struggle with what role dad should play in homeschooling.

Marji Meyer, head of the School of Abraham Project, has a special interest in the role of homeschooling fathers and has conducted independent research on gender roles in homeschooling. She recently

Table 8.1 A Homeschool Mother's Wish List

What Homeschool Moms Would Like Their Husbands to Do
* Take more time to be involved
* Help with math
* Take over a subject or enrichment project
* Help define goals for homeschool/"Begin with the end in mind"
* Help teach them to work (how to dress, make beds, do dishes, vacuum, mop, rake, wash car, weed garden, care for pets)
* Take time away from business
* Teach obedience
* Call to talk with kids on phone, check on them, let them call him
* Give constructive feedback
* Go with us on field trips
* Hold weekly progress reports with Dad (ask questions, mostly listen)
* Listen to/talk to children about their stories
* Study curricular choices together
* Teach child to listen/concentrate
* Teach nurturing traits
* Come home for lunch
* Give examples and stories of his life
* Inspect child's work
* Jump into an ongoing activity
* Take over science instruction
* Take time to train each child in specific steps of tasks
* Visit Dad's place of work
* Read something someone has written
* Support and praise children
* Teach boys to be men; daughters what to look for in man

Courtesy of the School of Abraham Project <www.schoolofabraham.com>

surveyed a large number of homeschooling moms and asked them to articulate the role their husbands play in home education. Her respondents generated more than 100 ways fathers are—or could be—involved in the education of their sons and daughters.

A summary of Meyer's research appears in Tables 8.1 and 8.2. Within each category, responses are listed in decreasing order of popularity. Where multiple responses generated the same number of "votes," the responses are listed in alphabetical order.

Table 8.2 Involving Dad

General Ways Fathers Are Involved with Homeschool	Moral Support	Assist In School-Related Issues
Spend time with spouse/kids	Really talk to/listen to spouse	Science experiments
Develop a homeschool vision statement	Help teach discipline /responsibility to children	Buy computer
Read to kids	Show interest!/make suggestions	Flash cards for math
Play games (cards, chess, hide and seek, tag, board games, kites, bowling)	Give encouragement	Grade work
Turn off the TV	Discussions around dinner table	Read scriptures
Encourage studying current events	Financial support	Screen books/movies
Help with music	Give mom regular activity or night off	Review curriculum materials
Hikes/bicycle trips	Take kids out for the day	Spelling tests
Hobbies/include kids in what husband is doing ("follow own interests, welcome kids' involvement")	Family outings all together	Build machines with pulleys, motors, gears
Long conversations	Include kids on work and service projects	Help plan school schedule
Visits to theaters and museums	Let Mom soak in tub/ eat M&Ms/ watch movie/relax	Provide transportation
Allow children to visit place of work/talk to colleagues	Take a walk together (husband and wife)	Recommend books
Answer kids' questions		Assign research projects
Attend homeschool conferences		Buy at used book sales/ on the Internet
Building a home (carpentry)		Help kids set goals
Display/really look at kids' pictures/artwork		Read essays
Give another perspective on subject		Teach simulated stock market/responsibility for income/taxes
Sports involvement		Dad's project night
Work two jobs to support family		Teach pledge of allegiance
Listen to kids' stories		Tutor teens
Look for teaching moments		

Table 8.2 Involving Dad, *continued*

Household Help	Values and Principles Dads Help Teach (by Precept and by Example)	Subjects Dads Have Taught

Camping/vacations
Help clean the house
Brush kids' teeth/bath
Dishes
Have meals together
Plant a garden
Play silly games with kids
Cook
Laundry
Family hobbies
Grocery shopping
Pick up own clothes
Watch the kids
	Teach children to strive for
	  excellence
	Emphasize completion of
	  tasks
	Honesty
	Love their mother
	Show appreciation
	Discipline/teach child with
	  poor attitude
	Hug them
	Praise talents
	Pray with and for children/
	  spouse
	Share childhood memories
	  with them
	Teach problem-solving
	  strategies
	Understand personal faith
	Apologize when necessary
	Expect responsibility and
	  follow-through
	Foster a love of learning
	Give them a "vision worth
	  living for"
	Never use profanity
	Patience
	Seek guidance
	Talk to children before
	  disciplining
		Astronomy*
		Bike Riding
		Chemistry/Periodic Table
		Computer Lessons*
		Electricity
		Geography*
		Lego Club
		Math*
		Music
		Physics
		Science*
		Survival Skills
		Woodworking
		
		(*most commonly taught)

Courtesy of the School of Abraham Project <*www.schoolofabraham.com*>

Dealing with Challenges

What's the Downside of Homeschooling?

Nearly every family faces challenges—whether or not they homeschool. In this chapter we discuss ways to overcome objections and challenges that homeschooling parents face.

What If My Spouse Disagrees?

One of the toughest challenges is the issue of what to do when one parent—typically the mother—wants to homeschool while the father wants the children enrolled in public or private school. Families that have resolved this issue say the following ideas have worked for them:

> **Find evidence.** Collect books, articles, and research for the other parent to read. Chapter 1, for example, may provide enough documentary evidence of the success rate of homeschooling to persuade even an adamant spouse.

Start with a trial period. No child has ever died of missing a few months of the third grade! Start with a short-term trial to see how homeschooling works for your family. Our recommendation: Don't promise your children they can return to public school if it doesn't work out. Every homeschool program goes through rough spots. Don't arm a child with ammunition to make those days even harder!

Work together. Jointly develop a plan for what would be acceptable. Compromise. Part-time classes? Participation in after-school sports? A School-at-Home approach that duplicates the traditional classroom? A private tutor? Look for a solution that both parents can live with.

On Educational Systems

"I am beginning to suspect all elaborate and special systems of education. They seem to me to be built up on the supposition that every child is a kind of idiot who must be taught to think."

—Anne Sullivan, tutor and mentor to Helen Keller (1866–1936)

What If My Children Object?

You have two options if your children object. The first: Stay firm. You're the parent. Remember that if your children weren't complaining about homeschooling, they'd probably be complaining about having to bathe, take vitamins, and wear a bike helmet. Some children seem to believe it's their duty to complain. You're the parent because you have more wisdom, experience, and maturity. Just as you wouldn't give in to demands for an all-chocolate dinner, be equally adamant when your children demand anything else that isn't in their best interest—including a form of education that doesn't fit your family's needs or beliefs. We recommend three responses to objections: Belligerence and defiance should be dealt with firmly; ill-natured grumbling should be ignored or sent to another room out of hearing range; and polite requests should be responded to with sincere explanations of why you believe homeschooling is the better way.

The alternative? Sometimes a bad experience is the only way to teach a lesson. A brief stint in public school may be enough to persuade a belligerent child that homeschooling wasn't so bad after all. We know parents who actually threaten their children with public school if they're uncooperative!

What If a Grandparent Objects?

Family harmony is important—but it should never come at the expense of doing the right thing. Remember that your parents and your in-laws already had their opportunity to raise their children. Now it's your turn, and you absolutely must stay true to what you believe is right for your own children.

When responding to questions, be charitable. Sometimes people ask about homeschooling in clumsy or awkward ways. Assume the best intentions and cheerfully explain your reasons for homeschooling.

When confronted by someone who becomes nasty or hostile about your decision to "buck the system," politely but firmly end the debate. Occasionally you may be confronted by someone who simply won't let it go. If such a person is malicious, it may become necessary to actually cut off communication—stop answering phone calls, door knocks, and e-mails—until this individual agrees to stop undermining your parenting decisions.

How Should I Respond to Questions About "Socialization"?

Every homeschooler gets questioned about what old-timers jokingly call the "S" word.

The socialization question has two meanings. Sometimes the questioner is asking simply whether homeschooled children have friends. The answer? Of course! Not only are they free to make friends with neighbor children; they also make friends in their homeschooling groups, in youth organizations such as Scouting and 4-H, on sports teams, in group classes, and at church. Moreover, they are more involved with their own siblings—their built-in "friends for life"—and have more opportunities to form friendships with adults in the community and with members of their extended family. In fact, volumes of research demonstrate that on average, homeschoolers have better social skills and are more mature than their schooled counterparts.[1]

On True Education

"Education is a private matter between the person and the world of knowledge and experience, and has little to do with school or college."

—Lillian Smith, novelist and educator (1897–1966)

Other times, the questioner is asking about the more ominous definition of socialization: Conformity; to be converted or adapted to fit social needs or uses; to be trained for government or group ownership or control; compliance. In other words, the questioner is wondering: "How will your child learn to be a proper cog in the machinery of society if you don't send him to public school?" The best response to this question is to run, screaming, in the opposite direction. If you want to dignify the question with an answer, explain to your questioner that homeschoolers enter college and the workforce at the same or higher rates than their public-school counterparts, and that their achievement levels in college are on par with their peers.[2]

Or for some real fun, quote H. L. Mencken, who said: "The aim of public education is not to spread enlightenment at all: it is simply to reduce as many individuals as possible to the same safe level, to breed a standard citizenry, to put down dissent and originality." Then watch your questioner run, screaming, away from *you!*

Does Homeschooling Damage Public Schools?

This accusation is founded on the strange premise that removing a child from the public-school system costs the schools money. Schools receive government funding based on the number of children enrolled (as well as additional funding for children who come from low-income families or who can be categorized as special needs). When a child doesn't enroll, the school district doesn't receive the money that child would have brought in—typically around $6,000 per child per year.

On Priorities

"When school children start paying union dues, that's when I'll start representing the interests of school children."

—Albert Shanker, longtime president of the American Federation of Teachers

It's all nonsense, of course. If a child isn't enrolled in school, the district isn't required to provide services for that child—services that, presumably, would cost the district the same amount of money it would receive from the state. (On the other hand, if educating a child doesn't actually cost $6,000 a year, then state and federal governments are paying too much, and school districts are profit-making enterprises.)

Don't Families Have a Religious Duty to Public Schools?

Religious families often get this question from their fellow congregants. This question overlooks the fact that public schools are a hostile place for religious discussion or for proselytizing of any kind. A child who states strong religious views in public school is more likely to get disciplined than heard.[3]

At least part of the reason many devout families homeschool is to protect their children from an environment rife with consumerism, drug use, alcohol abuse, early dating, teenage pregnancy, and other corrosive influences on adolescents. These families believe that childhood is a time to prepare and be strengthened for an entire lifetime of religious devotion. Aborting a child's religious education prematurely on the remote chance the child might convert a peer in public school simply doesn't make sense.

How Do I Homeschool a Child with Special Learning Needs?

In every state, children with disabilities—a category that includes children with learning disabilities—have the right to public educa-

On Motivation

"We must view young people not as empty bottles to be filled but as candles to be lit."

—Robert H. Shaffer, former Indiana University dean of students

tional services. In some places, this assistance is freely given even to children who are homeschooled. A progressive, cooperative local school system might provide home tutoring, individual classes, and other adaptations consistent with the child's "IEP," the Individualized Educational Plan legally available to each child with special needs in the United States.

Unfortunately, a number of locations still throw up hurdles, demanding, for example, that children with special needs be enrolled full-time and that they be educated entirely under the jurisdiction of the school system. Most battles in life aren't worth the fight—but if your child requires more help than you can provide, this one may be an exception. Be your child's advocate. Take legal action if necessary to demand that your child be served in accordance with the law, in the "least restrictive" environment—in your case, at home. We list hundreds of resources for special-needs homeschooling, including resources for gifted and talented students, on our Special needs page, <*www.homeschoolsteps.com/seealso/special.htm*>.

How Do I Keep My Child Motivated to Learn?

Your child comes fully motivated for learning. The key is finding an approach that fits your parenting goals, as well as your child's learning needs. The 110 strategies and approaches in Chapters 3 and 4 are bound to motivate even the most reluctant learner. A daughter who is crazy about the Backstreet Boys, for example, might groan and complain over an assigned science project on wave theory, but if you were to suggest that she create a Backstreet Boys notebook, with an in-depth study about how music and sound are created, she might shine. Same science, different strategy, and you've got a motivated learner.

How Do We Stay on Track?

Telephone calls, doctor's appointments, soccer games, and e-mail can distract even a determined homeschooler. Decide from the start that education is going to take precedence over minutiae. Set your school hours, and hold outsiders to your schedule. Let the answering machine pick up phone calls, ignore the doorbell, shut down the e-mail and instant-message software, and reschedule appointments for a time other than school hours. Your dedicated school time might involve only two or three hours a day, three or four days a week, but your kids should know that during this time, at least, they'll have the freedom to read, conduct research, study, and ask questions without having to compete with outsiders for their parents' attention.

What If My Kids Are Different Ages?

If your children are varying ages, you're in luck! The reason human beings don't have children in litters is that living and working with people of multiple ages is beneficial for everyone. Unlike children who are institutionalized in daycare and schools, your children will have the benefit of growing up in a mixed-age setting.

Researchers who have studied mixed-age educational programs say children who regularly interact with older and younger people are better off than those who interact primarily with same-aged peers.

In one study, researchers found numerous advantages to mixed-age education for all participants.[4] Older children benefit because they learn nurturing skills in a real-life context. They also learn tolerance, cooperation, teaching skills, parenting, and social responsibility. Their self-esteem increases. And in teaching a younger child, they master the subject matter. (Interestingly, the study found that arguing is an effective way for children to teach one another. When children thoroughly understand a subject, they spontaneously vary their explanations during the argument until the other child catches on.) A parent can observe as the older children teach to discover whether they have gaps in their learning and to rectify misinformation.

For younger children, there are just as many benefits. Kids with older brothers and sisters have multiple sources of information and models of behavior and are motivated to accelerate their learning to "catch up" with an older sibling.

In same-aged groupings, children tend to bully their peers, but in mixed-age groups, older children tend to facilitate, share, and modify to accommodate younger children. Mixed-age groups are therapeutic for socially immature children, because these children are rebuffed less frequently than when mixing with same-age peers. In mixed-age groups, older children tend to self-regulate their behavior as a model for younger children. Bossiness requiring adult intervention was a problem in either setting. In the mixed-age setting, older children had to learn to deal kindly and effectively with being pestered by a younger child.

When it comes to teaching multiple ages, remember that very few subjects are "sequenced." It's not a problem to teach the history of ancient Egypt or the Constitution to everyone at once. Simply expect more of your more advanced learners.

How Do I Keep Preschoolers Occupied While Teaching Older Children?

Homeschoolers use numerous strategies to occupy their toddlers. Tip one: No toy boxes. Instead, put all the toys away, out of sight, and bring out only two or three toys a day. A Lego set is more fun if it hasn't been seen in awhile, and if the child knows it's only available for the day.

In the same vein, have on hand a dozen or more "quiet packs" that you can distribute and collect throughout the week. Make quiet packs out of gallon-sized resealable plastic storage bags. One day's pack might contain a book, a lace-up shoe, and a watercolor set. Another day's pack might contain a small electronic toy, some crayons, and a coloring book. The third day, your child might get a quiet pack with paper dolls, stackable blocks, and a flashlight. On the fourth day, the pack might contain a book-on-tape, dry-erase markers, and a handheld mirror for drawing on. With practice, your preschoolers can learn to entertain themselves quietly and safely while you spend half an hour with an older sibling.

Here are other ways families deal with toddlers and infants while teaching older children:

For More Information

For more information on research related to homeschooling challenges, visit the Challenge section of the *Homeschool Steps* Web site at <www.home schoolsteps.com/see also/challenge.htm>.

Sling. A good sling—one that hangs over the hip—might keep your infant content during fussy times.

Crafts. A glue stick, Popsicle sticks, beads, string, ribbon, buttons, feathers, construction paper, and other craft items are an inexpensive distraction for older toddlers.

Snacks. Place snack items, such as crackers, peanut butter, raisins, marshmallows, apple slices, cream cheese, sprouts, and dried fruit, in the individual cups of a muffin tin. Let your toddlers use the ingredients to make their own snacks.

Water play. While Mom and the older kids are seated on the bathroom floor, the toddler plays in the bath.

Rice box. Once a child passes the stage of putting objects in the mouth, a plastic wash basin filled with rice or beans or dried peas, along with inexpensive beach toys, can sit on a drop cloth or shower curtain and provide an hour or more of entertainment.

Gooshies. A dry bathtub, a warm porch, or a drop cloth on the kitchen floor are all good locations for finger-painting, play dough, spaghetti eating, finger Jell-O, watercolors, pasting, flour mixing, bubble blowing, and other messy activities.

Library books. An ever-changing stack of colorful books provides endless distraction.

Tapes. Rather than live by a programming schedule, tape episodes of children's television for viewing at times that are convenient for your homeschooling schedule.

Trade off. One older child can teach a toddler while you work with another older child. Teaching can involve more than just reading aloud or drawing pictures together. Let your "student teacher" turn on music and dance with the toddler, build a cardboard house, run circles around the dining table, or do other activities that "get the wiggles out."

Worksheet

Homeschooling presents unique challenges for every family. This worksheet will prompt you to think through the problems your own family might encounter and prepare solutions before they become overwhelming.

1. Virtually every homeschooling parent gets challenged at some point by a family member, a neighbor, or even a stranger about their decision to homeschool. When you think about your extended family, your neighborhood, and other communities to which you belong, which people do you expect might challenge your decision to homeschool?

    _____

    _____

    _____

2. If you are asked about why you're homeschooling, what reasons will you give?

    _____

    _____

    _____

    _____

    _____

    _____

3. If you're challenged by someone who becomes overbearing or hostile, how will you respond?

    _____

    _____

    _____

    _____

    _____

(continues)

4. List the names of each of your children in the spaces below, and think about what special teaching challenges that child might provide. Is the child gifted, learning disabled, significantly older or younger than siblings, easily distracted, a perfectionist, hard to motivate, preparing for college, or studying advanced subjects? After you've completed this task for every child, consider what ways you can accommodate or challenge that child's learning needs. Look through the ideas in this chapter and the supplementary materials online for suggestions.

_____

_____

_____

_____

_____

_____

_____

_____

_____

_____

_____

_____

_____

_____

_____

_____

_____

_____

Finding Support

What Kind of Support Is Available to Homeschoolers?

There are three sources of homeschooling support: other homeschoolers, commercial and government organizations, and charitable community members who believe in helping kids.

How Do I Get Support from Other Homeschoolers?

You can join an existing homeschooling group, or start one of your own. Homeschool groups come in two stripes: support for parents and support for kids.

Parent support groups tend to be social, somewhat educational, and may or may not welcome children. Many of these groups sponsor annual homeschooling conferences with seminars and curriculum fairs for parents. There are also hundreds of online homeschooling support groups that keep in touch and provide support via e-mail.

The other form of homeschool support involves activities or classes for kids, where the primary focus is on academics and building friendships. Some groups meet only for field trips or play dates. Some meet for formal academic classes with professional teachers. Others meet as homeschooling cooperatives, with parents as teachers. And others meet as "clubs" or for "lessons" with a specific focus—debate, rocketry, crafting, scouting, basketball, or band, for example.

How Do I Find a Support Group?

Start by telling people you know about your decision to home-school. Inevitably, they'll know someone else in your area who is homeschooling, and you'll have made your first contact! Call and ask about local homeschooling groups.

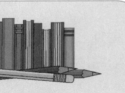

On Educational Tasks

"Getting things done is not always what is most important. There is value in allowing others to learn, even if the task is not accomplished as quickly, efficiently or effectively."

—R. D. Clyde

Inquire with your local school district and state education office about whether or not they know of any homeschooling support groups. Check the public library as well. Many homeschooling groups leave flyers and information packets with local librarians.

And go online to find local support groups. See the Groups page of our companion Web site *<www.homeschoolsteps.com/seealso/groups.htm>* for a comprehensive list of links to homeschooling groups in every state and around the world.

What If I Can't Find a Homeschool Group I Like?

Start one of your own! Sometimes a local group is "great except"—except you have teenagers and they all have six-year-olds; except your family has one religious faith and they have another; except they meet on Tuesdays and you can only meet on Fridays.

Find three or four like-minded families in your area or online, and schedule a lunch date to discuss ways to support one another. Can one mom teach American history while another teaches writing? Will you teach classes or just let the kids play while you talk? Can your kids meet to work on a project or can they study a subject together online? Do you simply want to have "Moms' Nights" or "Parents' Nights" where one or both parents can leave the kids and spend time talking with adults?

It's important when starting a new group to ensure that the founding members share some basic philosophies, to avoid having the group fall apart over disagreements and misunderstandings. During your planning meeting, be sure to discuss potential hurdles such as:

On Trying

"Anyone who has never made a mistake has never tried anything new."

—Albert Einstein

Purpose. Perhaps your primary goal in setting up a group is to give your kids a chance to socialize, with academics playing a secondary role. Or perhaps you're interested primarily in dividing up the task of organizing academic studies or field trips among several families so that each has less of an organizational burden. Your goal could be to learn more about homeschooling, without having children distracting the discussion. Or it might be to socialize with other adults, while your children study or play together independently.

Formality. How rigid and structured do you want to be? More groups have difficulty over this disagreement than any other issue. If you're highly disciplined, you'll find yourself at odds with parents who view group participation as optional or as an amusement. If you're more relaxed, a highly disciplined group will place demands on your family that may make you or your kids miserable.

Inclusiveness. Will your group welcome members of any religious denomination or homeschooling approach? Or would you prefer to have your children strengthened in their religious faith and academic training by group members who share your beliefs and approach?

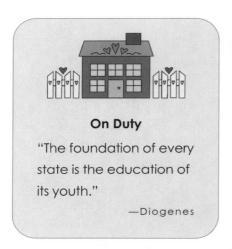

On Duty

"The foundation of every state is the education of its youth."

—Diogenes

Fees. Many groups operate without fees. They have potluck meals or take turns bringing snacks and meet in homes, church buildings, or public libraries for free. Some groups charge nominal fees for photocopying and postage, and some charge a substantial annual fee to cover speakers and other costly services.

After you get started with your small group, you may want to increase your size. Create an informational brochure and leave copies with libraries, school and district offices, the state educational office, grocery store bulletin boards, the education reporter at your local newspaper, and radio and television stations. Notify your statewide homeschooling group and ask to be included on their list of local homeschooling groups. Build a Web site and start an email group. And don't forget to publish your group's contact information on Web sites that list support groups.

Are There Alternatives to Support Groups?

Many families are happy sharing resources with just one other family. They might switch off play dates, pool curriculum, or trade teaching. Just knowing you have a buddy to listen to you when times are tough may be all the support you need.

What Support Is Available from Commercial and Government Organizations?

Commercial enterprises offer tutoring services, umbrella schooling, and correspondence courses. (See Chapter 3 for discussions of using these services as homeschooling strategies.)

Many states and individual schools or school districts offer various forms of academic support, which we address in Chapter 4 under the Hybrid approach. Some schools also allow homeschooled children to use sports facilities, participate in extracurricular programs, and access other resources outside of school hours. In addition, the U.S. government has published several brochures and online articles for homeschooling parents. Locate information about these resources on our Other Support page at *<www.home schoolsteps.com/seealso/othersupport.htm>*.

What Other Support Is Available in My Community?

The list of other support is endless. In addition to inviting field trips, members of your community may be available for mentoring, tutoring exchanges, interviews, and case studies. Community support resources include the public library,

For More Information

For more information on finding, starting, and belonging to homeschooling support groups, visit the Support section of the Homeschool Steps Web site at *<www.home schoolsteps.com/see also/support.htm>*.

parks, community recreation centers, public colleges and universities, and government offices—all of which support your family's efforts to educate. As a taxpayer and a citizen, it's your right to take advantage of whatever resources are available to you.

And let your family give back to the community through volunteer work and political involvement. It'll be the best education you can give your kids!

Checklist for Choosing a Homeschooling Group

❏ The group shares my general beliefs about how structured homeschooling should be.

❏ The group's basic purpose is in line with my family's support needs.

❏ The group meets no more frequently than we have time for.

❏ The group is located within easy driving distance.

❏ If the group welcomes children, there are other kids about the same age as my kids.

❏ I've met a few other group members and feel comfortable with them.

❏ The group shares my beliefs about who may or may not be a member.

❏ I can afford the group's membership fees.

Graduation Guidance

What Happens After Homeschooling?

The transition to adulthood can be a little intimidating. So many choices and opportunities! All that's needed is a bit of preparation.

Unlike the rest of this book where we speak to parents, in this chapter we speak directly to teenagers. Parents will want to read along, of course, but the responsibility for post-homeschooling life lies primarily in the hands of the new adult who will be living it. In this chapter we tell you and your parents what you need to know about life skills, the granting of diplomas, college preparation, college admissions, job training, and the military.

How Should I Prepare for Graduation?

In addition to your academic preparation, which we address under the Scope-and-Sequence strategy in Chapter 3, and your moral and spiritual preparation, be sure you are financially and legally prepared for entering adulthood. This knowledge is critical to your success in adult life. Ask your parents to help you understand the following.

Banking and Investing. Learn how to manage a checking account, investments, credit cards and loans, and find out what the consequences are when any of these items are mismanaged. It may be worth sitting down with a bank employee shortly before your eighteenth birthday to ask in-depth questions about banking terminology, credit applications, and account management.

Budgeting. A minimum-wage paycheck doesn't stretch very far in real life. Your parents may be willing to show you how they budget for your family. In addition, your public library has books on budgeting and personal finance. Have a read, and find out what kind of income you'll need to get by as an adult. Learn about the huge difference between income and take-home pay, and find out how to make those dollars stretch by avoiding unnecessary debt.

Consumer Credit. Consumer credit law is your protection when your credit card number is stolen, when your credit is reported to credit bureaus, and when you apply for loans and credit cards. You should thoroughly understand your rights and responsibilities before you use credit.

Contracts. Before you sign that housing contract or take up that tempting offer on a new cell phone, be sure you have a good understanding of contract law. After you turn eighteen, you're accountable for anything you sign. Don't ever put your signature on a blank document, a document with any blank spaces, or a document you haven't read thoroughly or don't understand.

Criminal Law. There's no such thing anymore as petty crime. Shoplifting, employee theft, and every other criminal act can follow you for years—even if you committed them as a minor. Modern computerized reporting systems can include reports of even the smallest instances of lawbreaking and are easily available to potential employers, creditors, landlords, or anyone else with whom you might have a financial relationship. Don't embarrass yourself or your family with reckless behavior.

Employment Law. Can you be fired? Are you required to join the union? Must you be paid for overtime? Laws vary from state to state. Know your responsibilities and rights as an employee or—if you're the entrepreneurial type—as an employer.

Insurance. If you're driving, or will be driving soon, you probably know more about *auto insurance* than you'd like to know. But there are other kinds of insurance you should know about. As a young person with no dependents, it's not especially important for you to have *life insurance*—but you should understand enough about life insurance to know when you should buy it and what kind you should buy. *Renter's insurance* is an inexpensive way to protect your valuables when you're away at college or living on your own. *Medical insurance,* on the other hand, is expensive. If you're fortunate, you may be eligible for coverage through your parents' insurer as long as you're in college, but eventually you'll need to know about the jungle that is the U.S. health-care system. Even brilliant people with advanced college degrees have trouble understanding all the ins and outs of deductibles, co-pays, limitations, providers, and the other jargon that goes with health-care coverage, so don't feel awkward about asking lots of questions.

Home Management, Maintenance, and Repair. There's nothing like a broken faucet to make you want to call Dad. If you're lucky, your parents will have involved you in the basics of keeping a home in good working order while you were growing up. If not, it's time to ask for lessons in the basics of cooking, carpet cleaning, electrical repairs, plumbing, and all the other management and maintenance tasks that keep a home functioning.

Marriage and Family Law. Through the haze of romance, most young people lose sight of the fact that marriage—and behavior that imitates marriage—brings legal obligations that last a lifetime.

Marrying, setting up a common household, and parenting a child bind you to another human being, legally and ethically. Before taking on the responsibility of another person, know what your obligations involve and be thoroughly committed to keeping them.

Taxes. At a minimum, you should have a complete understanding of simple income tax forms such as the federal 1040EZ and the W4. Your parents may know an accountant or a financial planner who will sit down with you to explain in general terms how items such as charitable contributions, mortgages, business income, and changing family circumstances will affect your tax burden in the future.

How Do I Get a Diploma?

Unless you're homeschooling through a diploma-granting school, it's up to your parents to grant you a high-school diploma. As the administrators of your homeschool, they decide when you've fulfilled the requirements for your degree and have earned the document that makes you an official graduate.

Many homeschooling families get together with other families to plan formal graduation ceremonies for their high-school graduates. At these ceremonies, graduates wear caps and gowns, give commencement speeches, and receive formal diplomas. Other families are more low-key, and award the diploma at a family dinner, a graduation party, or a gathering of extended family.

In any event, your parents can obtain blank diploma forms at stationery stores, or they might opt to have your diploma created by a professional calligrapher or graphic artist.

What About a Transcript?

There are only three uses for a high-school transcript: College admissions, military admissions, and scholarship applications. When you apply for admission to college—usually at the end of your junior year or early in your senior year—you'll probably be asked for a transcript of your high-school work. About two-thirds of American colleges now accept transcripts prepared by parents, or portfolios assembled by students, in lieu of an accredited diploma.[1] Transcripts must cover four full years of high-school work (which may be completed in fewer than four calendar years, if you're on an accelerated track). They should demonstrate that you have received a broad education at a fairly advanced level. We have sample transcripts available on the Transcripts page of our companion Web site at *<www.homeschoolsteps .com/seealso/transcripts.htm>*.

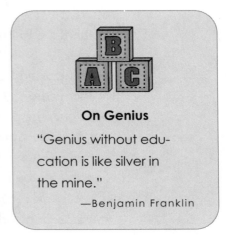

On Genius

"Genius without education is like silver in the mine."

—Benjamin Franklin

The transcript required for the military is less rigorous, but requirements vary depending on the branch of the service (you may or may not need to have the document notarized, for example). For this reason, you may want to discuss specifics with a recruiter before submitting a transcript.

Likewise, some scholarship applications will require a transcript, and requirements may vary. An individual or a small committee generally reviews scholarship applications. Rather than making inquiries that would put a question mark next to your name, it may be wisest to simply prepare a professional-looking document, have it notarized, and have it certified by a local school district if possible. Your transcript should demonstrate competence in whatever academic areas are covered by the subject matter of the scholarship.

What Other Documentation Do I Need?

Colleges, scholarship committees, and some employers may look for additional evidence of your high-school preparation, beyond the documents listed above. During your high-school years you should prepare a portfolio that documents your original research, writing skills, and other areas of academic preparation and experience. Refer to Chapter 3 for an in-depth discussion of Portfolio-Building.

You should also create a résumé that details your employment experience and your volunteer work. Include character references, awards, and a list of your extracurricular activities and research projects.

Should I Earn a GED?

Perhaps a GED is a good idea. In most cases, taking the test is free or involves only a nominal administrative fee, so cost shouldn't be a factor. The deciding factor is whether or not the GED will benefit you in the future.

Different people have different impressions of the GED. Some see it as documentation that you're as capable as any other high school graduate. Others view it with some disdain and see it as evidence that you couldn't cut it in regular high school. Still others see it as evidence that you're self-motivated and creative, and have *superior* ambition and drive.

In any event, the GED doesn't involve a facial tattoo, so completion can be disclosed or not, as it fits your circumstances and needs. There's little valid argument against taking the test, so we recommend that for most students—if only for the practice of taking tests—you go ahead and take the GED. Contact a local community college for information about prep classes (which are free in many locations) and GED administration. We provide links to GED prep resources and other high-school completion tests on our GED page, *<www.home schoolsteps.com/seealso/ged.htm>*

Why College?

The issue of college attendance is actually a fairly controversial one among long-time homeschoolers. Having seen that there's virtually nothing that can't be learned independently, some families see college as a waste of time and money.

Having spent a cumulative total of about twenty-five years in college, we're somewhat sympathetic to the argument. But we still believe the advantages outweigh the negatives. For adult learners, the structure of college classes is strong motivation to continue learning. And there's no arguing against a college degree for the credentials it provides to job applicants and anyone else who wants to be taken seriously in a credential-crazed world.

How Should I Prepare for College Admission?

College Prep is one of the strategies discussed in Chapter 3. There we talk about how to improve basic academic skills, specialize in two or three disciplines, ace your entrance exams, and earn early college credit. Together these accomplishments will virtually guarantee admission to the university of your choice.

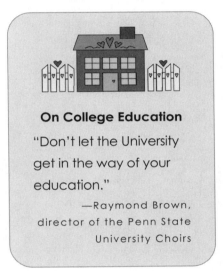

On College Education

"Don't let the University get in the way of your education."

—Raymond Brown, director of the Penn State University Choirs

Once you've been admitted, you'll benefit from some additional preparation. Master study skills such as speed reading (difficult material at high speed with good comprehension), learning to avoiding distractions, note-taking and outlining, graphic organization, and pacing yourself. (See Chapter 3 for more information on the strategies of Outlining and Note-Taking and Graphic Organizers.)

Prepare by knowing why you're attending college and what you wish to obtain from the experience. Some dark, wet winter day when it's tough to get out of bed, you'll need the motivation.

Finally, prepare financially. Even if you're among the fortunate few whose parents are able and willing to fund your education, apply for scholarships and get a job—preferably one in your intended field. Not only will you feel better about yourself for being independent, you'll also have a more impressive résumé, and be more employable, when you graduate.

What If I Want to Go Straight to Work?

On Job Training

"Thanks to my solid academic training, today I can write hundreds of words on virtually any topic without possessing a shred of information, which is how I got a good job in journalism."

—Dave Barry, columnist and author

We recommend it highly—even if you're also attending college. There's no better time in your life to work around the clock. As a young adult, you have the advantage of living in your parents' home, if you wish—assuming you're pulling your own weight with chores and financial contributions and are pleasant to be around—and you're not yet responsible for supporting a family of your own. You're completely free to dive headlong into whatever compels you: starting your own business, working multiple jobs to save up money toward some goal, travelling, volunteering, or anything else you enjoy.

If you want to work toward a vocational career, seek opportunities for apprenticing yourself to a professional in your field. You may wish to consider vocational or technical training, as well. Our Vocational page at *<www.homeschoolsteps.com/seealso/vocational.htm>* contains numerous resources for job training and employment.

Is the Military an Option?

Enrolling in the military is definitely an option. For the time being at least, the military accepts homeschoolers under the same terms it accepts any other high-school graduate. (At the time of this writing, the military was testing a pilot program for admitting homeschoolers. See our Military page at *<www .homeschoolsteps.com/seealso/military.htm>* for updates as the situation evolves.)

The military offers incredible educational and training benefits to new recruits. You might enlist for a single term of service, and have your entire education paid for, or you might choose to stay in the service as a career. After twenty years of military service, you could retire and start a whole new career, while continuing to collect military benefits. It's possible to retire from the military with full benefits as young as age 37.

If you're considering the military, speak to a recruiter around your sixteenth birthday to learn what you need to do to qualify for entry under the most favorable terms. It may be advantageous to you to complete one or two years of community college before entry and have the military pay your way all the way through graduate school. Ask about all your options before enlisting.

For More Information

For additional information on preparing for college and adulthood, as well as research on college admission and success rates for homeschoolers, visit the Graduation section of the *Homeschool Steps Web* site at <www.home schoolsteps.com/see also/graduation.htm>.

Graduation Checklist

❑ I have created a portfolio of my best academic work.

❑ My academic studies have been documented on a transcript.

❑ I have taken, or am fully prepared to take, college entrance exams.

❑ I feel prepared academically for college and/or employment.

❑ I feel prepared emotionally and spiritually for adulthood.

❑ I understand the financial and legal ramifications of adulthood.

❑ I have applied for, or am doing what is necessary to apply for, admission to the military, college, vocational training, or some other clear path to independence.

❑ I am financially prepared to live on my own or to make the financial contributions my parents expect of me if I continue to live at home.

Eight marks? Congratulations! You're ready for graduation!

Epilogue

There you have it—all the steps to homeschooling.

Let's summarize:

Step one is to decide *why* you're homeschooling. Knowing your own mind will steel your resolve when you hit rough patches. Next, know your legal rights and obligations. Educating yourself about the law will help you sleep easy at nights. Third, familiarize yourself with a variety of teaching strategies. Fourth, choose a homeschooling approach that matches your family's beliefs and lifestyle. And fifth, determine a curriculum and gather materials.

After you've mastered these five basic steps, it's time to move to a higher level. As you gain confidence in your teaching abilities, you'll want to broaden the scope of your homeschooling. As step six, we propose the PROJECT Management approach as a template for thinking through your vision.

Step seven is to rethink your homeschool's learning environment. Learn about your child's learning styles, and consider a variety of ways to create a rich environment for education.

The final four steps consider issues that could arise at any point in your homeschooling journey.

Number eight relates to balancing homeschooling with your financial and household obligations. Step nine considers solutions to a list of homeschooling challenges—everything from unsupportive family members to unmotivated children. Step ten is to find support, and the last step, eleven, is to prepare your children for adulthood.

There's one final step that every homeschooler needs to experience: Joy. Absolute joy in seeing a child triumph over challenges and embrace each day with wonder and enthusiasm. Joy in seeing your children laugh together, and debate and learn and teach one another. Joy in drawing your family close about you. And joy in standing shoulder-to-shoulder as you take on the world.

You are a family! Rejoice in one another's company, and take pride in one another's accomplishments.

Now it's time to put this book down and teach your kids. You can do it! Enjoy!

Appendix A:
Homeschooling Laws, State by State

On the following pages, you'll find brief summaries of the homeschooling laws for each U.S. state. This is our interpretation of the laws that were in effect at the time we went to press.

Do not rely on this information for legal advice. Laws are complex, they may change from time to time, and local jurisdictions may interpret the law differently than we have.

To suggest updates, or to see our scoring system or the actual scores for each location, visit our companion Web site at <*www.homeschoolsteps.com /seealso/htm*>. At our site, you'll also find links to legal information for homeschoolers outside of the United States.

See Chapter 2 for an in-depth explanation of homeschooling legalities.

State/ Province	Grade	Compulsory Ages (1)	Notification Requirements (2)	Parental Qualifications (3)	Format (4)
Alabama	A	7–16	One-time enrollment form to local superintendent.	None	Structure as a "church school" is most flexible, and "church" is not defined by law. Private school and tutoring options are heavily regulated.
Alaska	A+	7–16	None	None	None. Restrictive options are available . . . but why?
Arizona	A	6–16, or 8–16 with affidavit at 6.	One-time affidavit of intent with county school superintendent within 30 days of beginning homeschool.	None	Homeschool conducted by custodial parent/ guardian or instruction provided primarily in the home. Private school option is more restrictive.

LEGEND

1. The broader the range, the lower the grade. High grades go to states that leave educational decisions to parents.
2. Notification is usually an unnecessary burden. The less interaction a state demands, the higher the score.
3. In this text, we describe research showing that there's no correlation between a parent's teaching qualifications and a child's educational success. States that have no qualification requirements get the highest scores.
4. Parents should be able to choose the form their homeschooling takes. When states place restrictions on that freedom, the score drops.
5. This category describes ongoing reporting requirements, over and above simple notification. The more burdens the state places, the lower the score.
6. Testing is controversial even among public schoolers. When a state subjects homeschooled children to testing, the score drops.

Reporting Requirements (5)	Testing Requirements (6)	Other Assessments Required/ Accepted (7)	Subject Requirements (8)	Access (9)	Other Requirements (10)
Church school must maintain, but not submit, attendance records.	None	N/A	None for church schools; physical education in all other schools.	Local decision, but concerns over "liability" issues make access unlikely.	None
None	None	None	None	Yes to classes, but restrictions on athletics and ex-tracurricular.	None
None	None	None	Generic: Reading, grammar, mathematics, social studies science.	Guaranteed access to inter-scholastic athletics, but no access to materials. Other decisions are local.	None

7. This category describes alternatives to testing. In states that have no test requirements, this score is neutral. In states that permit an alternative to testing, this score is positive. When states demand an alternative or addition to testing, this score is negative.

8. Parents should be able to decide which subjects they teach. When the state interferes with parental decision making by setting out a required curriculum, this score is negative.

9. We contacted the education department of every U.S. state and the District of Columbia to ask whether home-schooled children can access public school resources, if they wish. We asked about access to standardized testing, academic classes, materials such as textbooks, interscholastic athletics, and extracurricular activities. We also asked about granting diplomas—a rarity, but available in a handful of states. States that guarantee access get high scores. States that restrict access get lower scores. In most locations, most of these decisions are made by local schools or school boards, which generated a neutral score.

10. Other requirements describe record keeping, attendance, and a few miscellaneous requirements. The more burdens, the lower the score.

State/Province	Grade	Compulsory Ages (1)	Notification Requirements (2)	Parental Qualifications (3)	Format (4)
Arkansas	C+	5–17 (may be excused from kindergarten with state-provided form to school district)	Annual letter of intent and signed waiver filed with local superintendent. 14-day waiting period for students withdrawing from public school. Further restrictions for students under disciplinary action. First letter must be delivered in person.	None	None
California	C	6–18	Under School-in-Private-Home option, parent must file annual R-4 affidavit with state superintendent of public instruction. Records become public.	Must be "capable" of teaching. Formal credentialing required under tutor option only.	Most flexible option: Register as a school in a private home. More restrictive or expensive options: Enroll in a public, private, or charter school's independent study program; or have child tutored by a credentialed teacher.
Colorado	D+	7–16	Annual declaration of intent. (First notice must be submitted 14 days prior to beginning homeschool. Habitual truants must provide written description of curricula before approval to homeschool.)	None. (Private tutor option requires teacher certification.)	Instruction by parent or adult relative. Alternative formats (enrolling in a private school that allows home instruction, or using a private tutor) are more expensive and/or more restrictive.

Reporting Requirements (5)	Testing Requirements (6)	Other Assessments Required/ Accepted (7)	Subject Requirements (8)	Access (9)	Other Requirements (10)
None	Grades 5, 7, and 10, through school or through one of 15 educational cooperatives.	By approval	None	Free testing available, diplomas available for PS'ing senior year, other access is a local decision	None
Maintain attendance records, records of course of study for each child, and immunization records or waivers.	None	None	Generic: Instruction in "the several branches of study required to be taught in the public schools" and in the English language.	Hostile treatment of homeschoolers neutralizes what looks like open access.	None
Submit annual attendance records, plus test or evaluation results to public school or independent or parochial school. Maintain permanent academic records of attendance, test/ evaluation results, and immunization records.	Grades 3, 5, 7, 9, and 11. Children scoring at or below 13th percentile must enroll in public/ independent/ parochial school.	Submit evaluation by qualified person in lieu of test. Qualification is lax: A certified teacher, a licensed psychologist, a teacher employed by a Colorado private school, or a person with a graduate degree in education.	Generic: Reading, writing, speaking, math, history, civics, literature, science, the U.S. Constitution.	Open access to athletics and activities, and diplomas are available, but testing may involve a fee.	172 days/year, 4 hours/day.

State/Province	Grade	Compulsory Ages (1)	Notification Requirements (2)	Parental Qualifications (3)	Format (4)
Connecticut	D	5–18 (may opt out to age 7 and at age 16 with annual personal appearance and signed declaration)	Technically none, but State Department of Education requires annual notice of intent, within 10 days of beginning to homeschool.	None	None
Delaware	C	5–16 (may delay start with consent of school)	Homeschool organizations must register with department of education.	None	Three options: (1) Affiliate with homeschool organization, or (2) establish homeschool to satisfaction of local superintendent and board of education, or (3) report to state DofE as a private school.
District of Columbia	B	5–18 (serious debate contemplates lowering compulsory age)	None, unless removing child from public school.	None	Private instruction not affiliated with educational institution.
Florida	C–	6–16	One-time minimal notice of intent.	None	None
Georgia	D+	6–16	Annual declaration of intent on school-district form within 30 days of beginning, and by Sept. 1 in subsequent years.	Parent: High school diploma. Tutor, if any, must have bachelor's degree.	Own children only.

Reporting Requirements (5)	Testing Requirements (6)	Other Assessments Required/ Accepted (7)	Subject Requirements (8)	Access (9)	Other Requirements (10)
Include in notice of intent: subjects to be taught, calendar, and method of assessment.	None	Mandatory annual submission of portfolio for evaluation.	Generic: Reading, writing, spelling, English, grammar, geography, arithmetic, U.S. history, citizenship (including study of town, state and federal governments).	No access to testing, other decisions are local.	180 days/year
Provide annual report of enrollment, student ages, and attendance. Separately, submit annual enrollment form.	Testing may be required under option 2, but is not required of private schools.	None	Same as public schools.	No access to testing, athletics available only with more than half-time enrollment. Other decisions are local.	180 days/year
Maintain accurate record of attendance.	None	N/A	None	Free testing, no other access.	While public schools are in session.
Submit portfolio with 15 days' written notice. Maintain portfolio of records and materials (log of texts and sample work sheets) for two years.	Annual standardized test administered by certified teacher.	In lieu of test, evaluation by certified teacher or licensed psychologist, or by other mutually agreed tool.	None	FCAT test free, other testing restricted; interscholastic extracurricular access guaranteed; other decisions are local	None
Monthly attendance forms sent to superintendent. Maintain test results for three years.	Nationally standardized tests in grades 3, 6, 9, and 12.	N/A	Generic: Reading, language arts, mathematics, social studies, science	No access to testing, other decisions are local.	180 days/year; 4.5 hours/day. Children out of home without written "excuse" are subject to arrest by truant officer.

State/ Province	Grade	Compulsory Ages (1)	Notification Requirements (2)	Parental Qualifications (3)	Format (4)
Hawaii	D	6–18	Simple declaration of intent to local school principal. Resubmit at junior high and high school entrance ages.	None (Alternate education program requires bachelor's degree.)	Most flexible option: Operate a home school. Less flexible option: Superintendent-approved appropriate alternative educational program.
Idaho	A–	7–16	None	None	Child must be "comparably instructed."
Illinois	A+	7–16	None	None	Private school, no registration.
Indiana	B	7–18	One-time enrollment report, available online.	None	Private school, no registration.
Iowa	B–	6–16	Annual "Competent Private Instruction Report Form"; 2 copies to local school district by 1st day of school or within 14 days of withdrawal from school.	None (Supervised and tutoring options require teaching license.)	Homeschool by parent is most flexible. Alternatives (supervision by licensed teacher, or instruction by private tutor) are more restrictive.

Reporting Requirements (5)	Testing Requirements (6)	Other Assessments Required/ Accepted (7)	Subject Requirements (8)	Access (9)	Other Requirements (10)
Maintain record of planned, structured curriculum, with complex assessment and bibliographical requirements.	School-paid testing in grades 3, 6, 8, and 10.	Private testing may be used in the alternative to school-paid testing. Submit mandatory annual progress report, including assessment (test, written evaluation or portfolio).	Suggested sequence, not mandated.	Open access to college entrance exams.	None
None	None	N/A	Same as public schools.	Free testing, access to classes, qualified access to athletics and activities; other decisions are local.	Same attendance as public schools.
None	None	N/A	Extensive: Language arts, biological and physical sciences, math, social sciences, fine arts, health and physical development, honesty, justice, kindness, moral courage	Access to classes, restricted access to athletics and activities. Other decisions are local.	Suggested: 176 days/year.
Maintain attendance records, which must be submitted upon request.	None	N/A	"Equivalent" instruction.	May be a fee for testing, qualified access to classes, concerns over liability issues in athletics and activities.	180 days/year.
None	Annual standardized test. (No testing requirement for supervised or tutoring options.)	In lieu of test, may submit portfolio for review.	None	Free testing with dual enrollment, but children can dual enroll for anything—even recess. Athletics and activities are guaranteed access. Local decision on diplomas.	148 days/year

State/Province	Grade	Compulsory Ages (1)	Notification Requirements (2)	Parental Qualifications (3)	Format (4)
Kansas	A–	7–18	Register name and address of school. No approval required.	Competence (Board may not define or evaluate competence.)	Operate as a nonaccredited private school. (Alternatives: Operate as satellite of an accredited private school, or for high school grades, obtain religious exemption from state board of education.)
Kentucky	B+	6–16	Annual notice to local school board.	None	Qualify as a private school. No approval necessary.
Louisiana	B	7–17	Annual notice of intent to state department of education within 30 days.	None	Least-restrictive format: Operate as a private school, which requires application and approval. (Alternatively, operate under the more restrictive option of obtaining approval as a homeschool from board of education.)

Reporting Requirements (5)	Testing Requirements (6)	Other Assessments Required/ Accepted (7)	Subject Requirements (8)	Access (9)	Other Requirements (10)
None	None	N/A	None (alternative forms may require particular subjects).	All decisions are local.	186 days/year or 1,116 hours/year; 1,086 hours for senior year.
Maintain, but do not submit, attendance register and scholarship reports.	None	N/A	Generic: Reading, writing, spelling, grammar, history, mathematics, civics	All decisions are local.	185 days/year, or the equivalent of 175 six-hour days.
Annual attendance report. (Under board of education option, must show "satisfactory" evidence of public school equivalency.)	None, as private school. (Under board-approval option, testing may be required to show equivalency.)	N/A	Meets and maintains a sustained curriculum or specialized course of study of quality at least equal to that prescribed for similar public schools, including the Declaration of Independence and the Federalist Papers.	Free testing, but no athletics. Other decisions are local.	180 days/year.

State/ Province	Grade	Compulsory Ages (1)	Notification Requirements (2)	Parental Qualifications (3)	Format (4)
Maine	C+	7–17	Under private school option: Annual notification to state department of education. (Homeschool option requires extensive state-developed 'application' to two offices at least two months prior to start of each homeschool year. Application must be approved by commissioner prior to beginning homeschool program. Denied applications must be resubmitted within deadlines, and are reviewed by state-level advisory board.)	Teacher certification, or designation as "Tutor" with assistance from certified teacher, public school, approved home instruction program, or approved homeschool support group.	Least-restrictive format (operation as a nonapproved private school) requires teaching at least two unrelated students. (Parents who want to teach their own children without affiliating with an organization must obtain approval from the local school board and the commissioner of the state department of education.)
Maryland	F	5–16 (exemption to age 6 available)	One-time notice of intent indicating which option a family is using (portfolio review or instruction through approved correspondence or church school).	None	Most flexible—but highly intrusive—option: Establish a qualifying home school. (Other options are less intrusive, but require instruction through a bona fide church school or through a state-approved nonpublic school or correspondence course.)

Reporting Requirements (5)	Testing Requirements (6)	Other Assessments Required/ Accepted (7)	Subject Requirements (8)	Access (9)	Other Requirements (10)
None. (Under homeschool option, annual declaration of intent must include thorough plan of instruction. Maintain extensive records.)	None. (Homeschool option requires annual standardized test.)	May submit annual academic assessment by certified teacher in lieu of test.	Extensive list: English, language arts, math, science, social studies, physical and health education, library skills, fine arts, Maine studies (in one grade between grades 6 and 12), computer proficiency (in one grade between grades 7 and 12).	May be a fee for testing, qualified access to classes, full access to athletics and activities.	175 days/year. Special education students subject to additional considerations.
Maintain a portfolio of educational materials, subject to review.	None. (Church or correspondence schools may impose testing requirements.)	Mandatory portfolio reviews up to three times per year. SofD standard: Superintendent determination that student is not receiving regular, thorough instruction in conformity with regulations. (Not required under church/ correspondence- school option.)	Regulated list: "Regular, thorough instruction" in the same subjects as the public schools, including English, math, science, social studies, art, music, health, physical education. (Under church/corre- spondence option: Requirements prescribed by program.)	Free testing, possible diploma, other decisions are local.	"Sufficient duration to implement the instructional program."

State/ Province	Grade	Compulsory Ages (1)	Notification Requirements (2)	Parental Qualifications (3)	Format (4)
Massachusetts	F	6–16	Make complex application, and obtain advance approval from local school committee or superintendent. Each locality sets its own standards and may require annual notice. Failure to obtain approval obligates child to attend public school.	School committee may examine the competency of the parents to teach their children, but may not require certification, advanced degrees, or college degrees.	None
Michigan	A+	6–16	None	None	Organized educational program, no registration. (A more restrictive "non-public school" option is available, but if confers no advantages.)

Reporting Requirements (5)	Testing Requirements (6)	Other Assessments Required/ Accepted (7)	Subject Requirements (8)	Access (9)	Other Requirements (10)
The school committee must have access to textbooks and lesson plans, but "only to determine the types of subjects to be taught and the grade level of the instruction for comparison purposes with the curriculum of the public schools." Neither the school committee nor the superintendent may dictate "the manner in which the subjects will be taught."	Annual standardized test administered by a "neutral party."	In lieu of testing, submit an annual "progress report" or a home visit. Parent chooses method of assessment. Requirements for progress report vary from district to district.	Extensive: Reading, writing, English language and grammar, geography, arithmetic, drawing, music, history, U.S. constitution, citizenship, health (including CPR), physical education, good behavior.	No access to testing, other decisions are local.	Committee may inquire about number of hours and days. (Public schools require 180 days/year, 900 hours/year at elementary level and 990 hours/ year at secondary level.)
None	None	N/A	Generic: Reading, spelling, math, science, history, civics, literature, writing, English grammar.	Free testing; limited access to classes; other decisions are local.	None

State/Province	Grade	Compulsory Ages (1)	Notification Requirements (2)	Parental Qualifications (3)	Format (4)
Minnesota	F	7–16	Annual notification to local superintendent, by October 1.	Teaching license in field and grade taught, passing score on teacher competency exam, or direct supervision by licensed teacher to avoid additional testing requirements. Bachelor's degree or instruction under approved umbrella school to avoid quarterly achievement reports. If none of the above are met, then family is subject to additional testing and reporting requirements.	None
Mississippi	B+	6–17	Annual "certificate card" to school attendance officer. No waiting period.	None	None

Reporting Requirements (5)	Testing Requirements (6)	Other Assessments Required/ Accepted (7)	Subject Requirements (8)	Access (9)	Other Requirements (10)
1. Include with notification of intent proof of compliance with parental qualification requirements. 2. If parent doesn't meet one of the teacher qualification exemptions, the family must also submit quarterly achievement reports. 3. Undergo either an annual home visit from superintendent, or refuse home visit and submit, in lieu of visit, documentation (class schedules, copies of materials used for instruction, and description of method used to assess student achievement indicating that the subjects required are being taught) that demonstrates compliance with law.	Annual nationally norm-referenced standardized achievement examination. Children who score below the 30th percentile, or who score a full grade below children of the same age must undergo an evaluation for learning problems.	Parents who don't meet teaching qualifications must additionally assess their children in subject areas not covered by the test.	Extensive: Reading, writing, literature, fine arts, math, science, history, geography, government, health, physical education.	Fee for testing; access to classes; no access to daytime activities; other decisions local.	None
Include with "certificate card" a simple description of the type of education children are receiving.	None	N/A	None	No access to anything.	Whatever "number of days that each [home] school shall require for promotion from grade to grade."

State/Province	Grade	Compulsory Ages (1)	Notification Requirements (2)	Parental Qualifications (3)	Format (4)
Missouri	C+	7–16	None required. Law contains implied threat of investigation unless parents submit notice of intent within 30 days of establishment and on Sept. 1 each year thereafter.	None	No more than four children are unrelated, and no receipt of fees, tuition, or other renumeration.
Montana	B	7–16 (or completion of eighth grade, if later)	Annual notice of intent filed with the county superintendent.	None	None
Nebraska	C–	7–16	One-time notice of intent to homeschool, 30 days in advance of starting. Annual statement of exception based on religious beliefs or interference with parental decisions.	None for parents; hired tutor must meet unspecified qualifications.	Private school, no registration.

Reporting Requirements (5)	Testing Requirements (6)	Other Assessments Required/ Accepted (7)	Subject Requirements (8)	Access (9)	Other Requirements (10)
Maintain logbook of subjects taught and activities engaged in, portfolio of child's academic progress, and record of evaluations of child's progress; or other written, credible evidence equivalent to above. Submission of logbook is a defense to charges of educational neglect.	None	N/A	Generic: Reading, math, social studies, language arts, science.	Fee for testing, qualified access to classes, no materials access, regulated access to athletics and activities.	1,000 hours/year; at least 600 hours in the five required subjects; 400 of these 600 hours must occur at "the regular homeschool l ocation."
Maintain attendance and immunization records; must be available for inspection by county superintendent upon request.	None	N/A	Same "basic instructional program" as the public schools.	Free testing, other decisions are local.	180 days/year, 4 hours/day for grades 1–3 and 6 hours/day for grades 4–12
Birth certificate for first year. Annual proof that home meets health, fire, and safety standards; that child has met attendance requirements; that program meets educational standards. Annual statement that parents believe individuals monitoring program are qualified.	None enforced, though law gives board of education a testing and visitation option.	N/A	Generic: Language arts, math, science, social studies, health.	No athletics, other decisions are local.	Elementary: 1,032 hours/year; secondary: 1,080 hours/year. Compliance with immunization requirements.

State/Province	Grade	Compulsory Ages (1)	Notification Requirements (2)	Parental Qualifications (3)	Format (4)
Nevada	C–	7–17	Annual request for exemption.	Teacher certification, or use of approved correspondence course, or consultation with licensed teacher or three-year homeschooling veteran, or waiver. Qualification requirements waived if child makes "reasonable educational progress in his educational plan" for one year.	None
New Hampshire	F	6–16	One-time notice of intent filed with private school principal, the state commissioner of education, or the local superintendent within 30 days of withdrawing from public school.	None	Planned and supervised instructional and related educational activities, including a curriculum and instruction. May instruct own children only by agreement of educational authorities.

Reporting Requirements (5)	Testing Requirements	Other Assessments Required/ Accepted (7)	Subject Requirements (8)	Access (9)	Other Requirements (10)
Include with request for exemption: Written evidence of teacher qualifications; educational plan including learning goals, teaching methods, and a description of the instructional materials; calendar; typical weekly instructional schedule; birth certificate or other proof of identity.	None (as of Sept. 1997)	N/A	Equivalent instruction of the kind and amount approved by the state board of education, including U.S. and Nevada constitutions	Free testing, qualified access to classes, no athletics, but activities are open. Other decisions are local.	180 days/year; grades 1 and 2: 240 minutes/day; grades 3–6: 300 minutes/day; grades 7–12: 330 minutes/day.
Include with notice of intent list of the subjects to be taught, along with name of an established correspondence school or commercial curriculum provider, if any; table of contents or other material that outlines the scope of and instructional sequence for each subject, and a list of textbooks or other instructional materials used. Maintain, for two years after ending instruction, a portfolio of records and materials, including a log of reading materials used, samples of writings, worksheets, workbooks, or creative materials used or developed by the child.	Annual standardized test or state student assessment test with SofD cutoff of 40 percent. Results are submitted to state.	In lieu of test, submit annual academic assessment by certified teacher or other agreeable means.	Extensive: Science, math, language, government, history, health, reading, writing, spelling, constitutional history of New Hampshire and the United States, art and music appreciation.	Free testing, other decisions are local.	None

State/Province	Grade	Compulsory Ages (1)	Notification Requirements (2)	Parental Qualifications (3)	Format (4)
New Jersey	A	6–16	None	None	Child must receive "equivalent" instruction, which means academic, and not social, education. Burden is on state to demonstrate that education is not equivalent, and unless there is compelling evidence that a child is receiving no education at all, the state doesn't interfere.
New Mexico	C	5–18	Annual notarized state-developed form within 30 days of starting, and by April 1 of each subsequent year. No approval requirement.	GED or high school diploma	None
New York	F	6–17 (Birthdays determine, not ages. Maximum: 5.75–17.99)	Annual notice of intent to home-school by July 1 or within 14 days of starting home-school.	None	School at home or in building that meets building codes.

Reporting Requirements (5)	Testing Requirements	Other Assessments Required/ Accepted (7)	Subject Requirements	Access (9)	Other Requirements (10)
None	None. No testing available through public schools.	N/A	No oversight, so generic list is, essentially, only a recommendation: U.S. and NJ history, citizenship, civics, geography, safety, physical education. Also recommended, but not required: sexual assault prevention, health.	Local decisions on everything.	None
Include with declaration of intent annual calendar of instructional days, immunization records, or statement of religious/conscientious objection.	None (new law)	N/A	Generic: Reading, language arts, math, social studies, science	Possible fee for testing, no athletics, restricted access to activities, other decisions are local.	Same attendance as public schools.
Submit complex annual individualized home instruction plan, subject to review and approval by superintendent of schools. Also submit quarterly reports of hours of instruction, description of material covered, grades or written narrative of progress, written explanation of any failure to comply with plan. Failure to submit adequate plan of instruction obligates child to attend public or authorized private school. Maintain attendance records; submit to school district upon request.	Submit annual commercially published norm-referenced achievement tests, administered at school or at home by certified teacher, by consent of superintendent. Sword of Damocles mark: 33 percent.	Alternative to mandatory testing: In grades 1–4, 6, 8: Written narrative evaluation by certified teacher based on portfolio and interviews. Parent-pay, and by consent of superintendent.	Extremely detailed, complex scope and sequence set forth by state.	Free testing, no athletics, other decisions are local.	180 days/year, with 5 (grades 1–6) or 5.5 (upper grades) hours of instruction per day.

State/Province	Grade	Compulsory Ages (1)	Notification Requirements (2)	Parental Qualifications (3)	Format (4)
North Carolina	B+	7–16	One-time notice of intent with name of school, name of administrator submitted to state division of nonpublic education.	GED or high school diploma	None
North Dakota	F	7–16	Annual notarized statement of intent on state-developed form, 30 days/14 days(?) prior to start of public school term. Additional requirements for autistic children.	Bachelor's degree, teacher certification, pass National Teachers' Exam, or high school diploma with weekly monitoring and biannual submission of reports by certified teacher.	For high school-diplomed parents, monitoring must continue until child scores above 50th percentile for two consecutive years.
Ohio	D–	6–18	Annual notice of intent to home-school.	GED or high school diploma, or assurance that parent is working under supervision of person with Baccalaureate degree.	None
Oklahoma	B	5–18	None	GED or high school diploma, or assurance that parent is working under supervision of person with Baccalaureate degree.	Educate in "good faith."

Reporting Requirements (5)	Testing Requirements (6)	Other Assessments Required/ Accepted (7)	Subject Requirements (8)	Access (9)	Other Requirements (10)
Maintain attendance and immunization records.	Annual standardized test covering English grammar, reading, spelling, and mathematics. Results may be inspected by state, but need not be submitted.	None	None	Restricted access to classes, no competitive athletics or activities, other decisions are local.	Nine calendar months/year.
Include with declaration of intent proof of identity and immunizations, and a list of planned public school courses or extracurricular activities. Maintain an annual record of courses taken by each student, including copies of academic progress assessments and results of nationally standardized achievement tests.	Grades 4, 6, 8, and 10. Professional assessment and plan of remediation for scores below 30th percentile.	None	Extensive: English language arts, including reading, composition, creative writing, English grammar, spelling; mathematics; social studies, including U.S. Constitution and U.S. history, geography; government; science, including agriculture; physical education; health, including physiology, hygiene, disease control, the nature and effects of alcohol, tobacco, and narcotics.	Free testing, access to classes, athletics, activities, diplomas.	175 days/year, 4 hours/day.
Outline of curriculum and textbooks attached to notice of intent, for informational purposes only.	Annual standardized test, with results sent to superintendent.	Alternative to testing: Submit annual written narrative indicating that a portfolio of child's work has been reviewed by certified teacher.	Extensive: Language arts, geography, U.S. and Ohio history, government, math, health, physical education, fine arts, first aid, science.	Free testing; restricted access to athletics; other decisions are local.	900 hours/year.
None	None	N/A	Generic: Reading, writing, math, science, U.S. and Oklahoma citizenship.	No access to anything.	175 days of instruction per year.

State/Province	Grade	Compulsory Ages (1)	Notification Requirements (2)	Parental Qualifications (3)	Format (4)
Oregon	C–	7–18	One-time notice to education service district; annual notice if child is participating in public-school activities.	None	None
Pennsylvania	D–	8–17	Annual notarized declaration of intent registered with local school district.	Affidavit of high school education (Extension alternative has no requirement.)	Homeschool program is least expensive, most independent option. (Other choices—hire a certified private tutor or operate as an extension of a private school—are more expensive.)

Reporting Requirements (5)	Testing Requirements (6)	Other Assessments Required/ Accepted (7)	Subject Requirements (8)	Access (9)	Other Requirements (10)
None	Parent-pay testing in grades 3, 5, 8, and 10, plus 18 months following withdrawal from public school. SofD cutoff: Failure to achieve "satisfactory" test results.	Restrictive additional requirements for handicapped children, giving districts the power to order children into public school for failure to make satisfactory progress.	None	Qualified access to athletics and activities; other decisions are local.	None
Annual declaration of intent must include outline of the educational objectives arranged by subject matter, evidence of immunization, evidence of receipt of "appropriate" medical services.	Grades 3, 5, and 8.	Mandatory annual assessment by certified teacher/ psychologists. Portfolio, interviews with children. Subject to review of superintendent.	Extensive. Elementary: English, including spelling, reading, writing; arithmetic; science; geography; U.S. and Pennsylvania history; civics; safety education, including continuous instruction in the dangers and prevention of fires; health and physiology; physical education; music; art. Secondary: English, including language, literature, speech, composition; science; geography; social studies, including civics, world history, U.S. and Pennsylvania history; math, including general mathematics, algebra, geometry; art; music; physical education; health and safety education, including regular and continuous instruction in the dangers and prevention of fires. Such courses of study may include, at the discretion of the supervisor of the home education program, economics; biology; chemistry; foreign languages; trigonometry; or other age-appropriate courses as contained in chapter 5 (Curriculum Requirements) of the State Board of Education.	Free testing, diplomas with college credit, other decisions are local	?

State/Province	Grade	Compulsory Ages (1)	Notification Requirements (2)	Parental Qualifications (3)	Format (4)
Rhode Island	D–	6–16	Must obtain approval by the school committee of the town wherein the child resides.	None, but local school board has authority to make demands.	As defined by local school boards.
South Carolina	C	5–17 (may be excused from kindergarten with written notice to school district)	None	High school diploma or GED.	Least-hassle alternative: Join an association for homeschools that has at least 50 members. Other options (going through local school district or through the South Carolina Association of Independent Home Schools) have more requirements and/or higher cost.

Reporting Requirements (5)	Testing Requirements (6)	Other Assessments Required/ Accepted (7)	Subject Requirements (8)	Access (9)	Other Requirements (10)
Submit an attendance register.	Local school officials may require testing or other evaluation.	At the discretion of local school board.	Extensive: Reading, writing, geography, math, U.S. history, history of Rhode Island, the principles of American government. Shall be taught in the English language. Constitution and government of Rhode Island and of the United States. Health and physical education.	Free testing, guaranteed access to materials, restricted access to athletics, other decisions are local but access is "encouraged."	Attendance "substantially equal" to public schools.
Each association must annually report number and grade level of members to local school districts. Maintain evidence of regular instruction, including a plan book, diary, or other record indicating subjects taught and activities in which the student and parent-teacher engage; a portfolio of samples of the student's academic work; and a semi-annual progress report including attendance records and individualized documentation of the student's academic progress in each of the basic instructional areas.	None. (Local school option requires annual Basic Skills Assessment Program.)	None	Generic: Reading, writing, math, science, social studies; also composition and literature in grades 7–12.	Possible fee for testing, no athletics or activities, other decisions are local.	180 days/year. (Local school board option also requires 4-1/2 hours/day.)

State/ Province	Grade	Compulsory Ages (1)	Notification Requirements (2)	Parental Qualifications (3)	Format (4)
South Dakota	D–	6–16 (children under 7 can be excused)	Annual notarized application for excuse, using a state-provided form.	None	No individual may instruct more than 22 children. Secretary of the Department of Education and Cultural Affairs may investigate and determine whether the instruction is being provided. Failure to provide instruction is grounds for the school board, upon 30 days notice, to revoke the excuse from school attendance.
Tennessee	F	6–17	Annual registration with local education authority by August 1 or be subject to fine. Students affiliated with church school need not register annually until high school.	Bachelor's degree required to teach high school-aged students; high school diploma for lower grades. Parents whose children are affiliated with a church school need only a high school diploma.	Register with LEA, or affiliate with a church school, most of which are pricey and require families to sign a statement of adherence to a particular religious faith.
Texas	A–	6–17	None	None	Operate a bona fide homeschool, which is considered a homeschool.
Utah	B+	6–18	Annual request for home exemption.	Unenforced possibility that school board can consider basic educative ability of parent in granting request to homeschool.	None

Reporting Requirements (5)	Testing Requirements (6)	Other Assessments Required/ Accepted (7)	Subject Requirements (8)	Access (9)	Other Requirements (10)
Submit birth certificate. Maintain attendance and evidence showing academic progress, which are a defense against assertions of educational neglect.	Grades 2, 4, 8, and 11. SofD cut-off: "Less than satisfactory" academic progress.	None	Generic: Basic skills of language arts and math. All instructions shall be given so as to lead to a mastery of the English language.	Free testing, guaranteed access to materials, no high school athletics or competitive activities, other decisions are local.	Equivalent period of time as in the public schools.
Submit proof of vaccinations and of receipt of other health services required by law.	Grades 5, 7, and 9, 10, 11, 12. SofD testing level in upper grades: Less than one year behind grade level/ average.	None	Strict curriculum requirements for high school-aged children. Church school-affiliated children are exempted.	All decisions are local.	4 hours/day for same number of days as required for public schools. Church school-affiliated high school students must register with LEA.
None	None	N/A	Generic: Written curriculum from any source, covering reading, spelling, grammar, math, good citizenship.	No access to testing, other decisions are local.	Cooperate with any reasonable inquiry from an attendance officer.
None	None	N/A	Generic: Language arts, math, science, social studies, art, health, computer literacy, vocational education.	All decisions are local.	180 days/year, 4 $5^1/_2$ hours/day ($4^1/_2$ for 1st grade; $2^1/_2$ for kindergarten).

State/ Province	Grade	Compulsory Ages (1)	Notification Requirements (2)	Parental Qualifications (3)	Format (4)
Vermont	D	7–16	Annual enrollment notice on state-provided form. Submission subject to approval from commissioner.	None	May teach children residing in own home, plus maximum of two children from one additional family.
Virginia	F	5–18 (may be delayed one year if parent believes child is not mentally, physically, or emotionally prepared to attend school)	Annual notice of intent. (Religious exemption permits a one-time notice of intent.)	Bachelor's degree, or Board-qualified teacher, or have student enrollment in approved correspondence course or in division superintendent-approved program of study. (Must meet state learning objectives, and prove that parent is able to provide "adequate education".) No requirements under religious exemption; parent or teacher under private tutor exemption must hold teacher certification.	Standard home-school option applies to all except for observants of particular religious faiths and those using hired tutors.

Reporting Requirements (5)	Testing Requirements (6)	Other Assessments Required/ Accepted (7)	Subject Requirements (8)	Access (9)	Other Requirements (10)
Annual enrollment notice must include outline of course of study, along with assessment of handicap for each child not previously enrolled in school.	Submit annual standardized test results.	Submit annual assessment by certified or approved teacher, report and portfolio from commercial curriculum provider, or report prepared by parents along with portfolio of child's work.	Generic: Reading, English, science, math, social studies (citizenship, history, U.S. and VT government), physical education, health, fine arts.	Free testing, access to classes, qualified access to athletics and activities; other decisions are local.	175 days/year. Special education students subject to additional considerations.
Annual notice of intent must include description of the curriculum and documentary evidence of compliance with parental qualification standards. Upon request by division superintendent, submit immunization records or affidavit of exemption on religious or medical grounds. (Religious exemption format requires extensive documentary evidence proving sincere belief in a religious faith that has a bona fide opposition to public schools; affidavit from religious expert concurring with parents' opposition, and letters from other acquaintances vouching for sincerity of belief.)	Annual test with SofD score above the 40th percentile.	Submit annual assessment indicating to satisfaction of division superintendent that child is achieving adequate level of education progress.	Generic: Curriculum or program of study that includes the state's Standards of Learning for math and language arts.	No athletics or activities, other decisions are local.	180 days/year.

State/ Province	Grade	Compulsory Ages (1)	Notification Requirements (2)	Parental Qualifications (3)	Format (4)
Washington	B–	8–18	Annual declaration of intent, using state-developed form. File by Sept. 15.	Complete 45 hours of college credit or college level course in home education; or obtain approval from local school superintendent; or undergo weekly supervision from certified teacher.	May teach own children only.
West Virginia	D–	6–16	One-time notice of intent filed with county board of education at least two weeks prior to withdrawal from public school.	High school diploma and at least four years' more instruction than most academically advanced child. (Four-year rule waived until June 2003.) (Board-approval option requires that parent "Be deemed qualified" by local educational authorities.)	Establish a homeschool. (Alternative format, obtaining board approval, has entirely subjective requirements. Second alternative allows a group of homeschools to organize as a single alternative school subject to a different set of requirements.)
Wisconsin	B–	6–18	Annual affidavit on a specific government form to Department of Public Instruction by October 15. Call 1-888-245-2732, ext. 1, and request form PI-1206. Form must be received prior to withdrawal from public school.	None	One family unit only.

Reporting Requirements (5)	Testing Requirements (6)	Other Assessments Required/ Accepted (7)	Subject Requirements (8)	Access (9)	Other Requirements (10)
Maintain records of test scores or annual academic progress assessments, immunization records, other records relating to instructional and educational activities. No requirement to submit records unless student returns to public school.	Annual standardized test administered by qualified person. Not submitted.	Annual academic assessment by certified teacher in lieu of test. Not submitted.	None	Access to testing, classes, athletics, activities. Other decisions are local.	None
None	By June 30, annual standardized test administered by school or county-authorized person, not parent. If scores fall below 40th percentile for three consecutive years, student must enroll in public/private school.	In lieu of test, submit annual academic assessment by certified teacher or other agreeable means.	Generic: English, grammar, reading, social studies, math.	Free testing, no athletics or activities, other decisions are local.	None (approval option requires 180 days).
None	None	N/A	Generic: Sequentially progressive curriculum of fundamental instruction in math, reading, language arts, social studies, science, health.	Possible fee for testing, qualified access to classes and athletics, other decisions are local.	875 hours of instruction per year, during same hours as local public schools.

State/Province	Grade	Compulsory Ages (1)	Notification Requirements (2)	Parental Qualifications (3)	Format (4)
Wyoming	A	7–16	Annual submission of curriculum to local board to demonstrate compliance.	None	One family unit only.

Reporting Requirements (5)	Testing Requirements (6)	Other Assessments Required/ Accepted (7)	Subject Requirements (8)	Access (9)	Other Requirements (10)
None	None	N/A	Generic: Sequentially progressive curriculum of fundamental instruction in reading, writing, mathematics, civics, history, literature, science. Exemptions for religious objections.	Free testing, access to classes, may be a fee for athletics and activities.	175 days/year.

Appendix B: Ideas for Educational Field Trips

Field trips are among the sixty teaching strategies described in Chapter 3. Following is a list of more than 250 field trip ideas. We suggest the usual—zoos, farms, and museums—as well as dozens of ideas you might never have considered.

All-Time Favorites: Parent's workplace.

Agriculture: Farms, ranches, dairies, food-processing plants, orchards, vineyards, farmers markets, grocery stores, greenhouses, fields, fisheries/hatcheries, florists, tree farms.

Armed Services: Military recruiting stations, military bases, large-scale military equipment, docked ships, historic military sites, U.S. Coast Guard, National Guard Armory, civil air patrol.

Arts: Music stores, ceramics studios, graphic arts studios, movie sets, photography studios, ballets, operas, concerts, theatre, recitals, museums, symphonies, orchestras, bands, readings and book signings, library events, bookstore events, performing arts centers. Visit behind the scenes, and interview artists, writers, and musicians one-on-one.

Business and Industry: Banks, check-clearing centers, chambers of commerce, museums of local industries, home businesses, malls, retail outlets, service businesses (software development, engineering, architecture, design, advertising, marketing, public relations), warehouses, restaurants, factory/plant tours, bakeries, gas stations, auto mechanics, construction sites, lumber yards, refineries, mills.

Communications: Television stations, newspapers, radio stations, Internet server farms, satellite transmitters, broadcast towers, telephone companies, post offices, publishers, printers, bookstores.

Education: Public libraries, college libraries, college and university campuses, schools for the blind or deaf, college lectures, symposia, colloquia, other campus events.

Emergency Services: Fire stations, hospitals, university hospitals, ambulance services, emergency clinics, emergency communications centers (911).

Events: Exhibitions, state/county fairs, festivals, parades, street fairs.

Government: Legislators, lawyers, judges, lobbyists, politicians, administrators, courthouses, jails, state capitol buildings, federal reserve, U.S. mint, city halls, courthouses, legislative sessions, legislative committee meetings, supreme court sessions, trials, city council meetings, school board meetings, zoning meetings, polling places, caucus meetings, rallies, marches, protests.

Health Services: Doctor's offices, health departments, medical labs, dentist's offices, ophthalmologists/optometrists, hospital baby nurseries, surgical centers, nursing homes and shut-ins (deliver cards and treats), mental hospitals.

Historical Trips: Local historical museums, battle sites, depots, memorials, statues, old neighborhoods, famous homes, local historical sties, trails, roads, tracks, buildings, cemeteries, family history libraries.

Home and Garden: Residential construction sites, historical homes, model homes and apartments, parade of homes, furniture stores, craft stores, driving tour of historic and upscale neighborhoods, hardware and lumber stores, plant nurseries, electricians, plumbers.

Husbandry: Dog, cat, or horse shows; zoos; petting farms; stables; kennels; animal shelters; aquariums; marine biology centers; veterinarian's offices; emergency animal hospital/clinics.

International Experiences: Ethnic markets, international district in big cities, day trips across state or national borders, international festivals, ethnic restaurants.

Law Enforcement: Police departments, K9 units, sheriff stations, fingerprinting units, crime labs.

Local: Local tourist attractions, both in your own community and in nearby cities.

Nature Walks: Bodies of water, large and small (lakes, rivers, swamps, keys, bogs, ocean, streams, sound, tide pools); deserts; mountains; forests; meadows; canyons; bluffs; flats.

Outdoor Recreation: Ice skating, canoeing, rafting, biking, hiking, skiing. Consider conservationist visits to recycling centers or drop-off sites, government environmental agencies, Greenpeace, or other ecologically sensitive groups.

Preserved Lands: Botanical gardens, forestry services, national parks, state parks, campgrounds, reservations, local parks, wildlife preserves, greenbelts.

Religion: Tours and visitors centers at temples, mosques, cathedrals, churches, reading rooms, seminaries and missions; service within a community of faith; service with welfare and service missionaries; interviews with theologians of your own and other faiths; tours of historically and theologically significant religious sites; religious services of various faiths.

Science Trips: Weather forecasting stations (check with local radio and television stations), planetariums, science centers and museums, archaeological digs, geological displays (cliffs, glaciers, mining sites, river beds).

Service Organizations: Goodwill, Deseret Industries, Salvation Army, homeless shelters, American Red Cross, soup kitchens, food banks (bring donations of canned goods), blood banks, children's homes and shelters, hospices, long-term care centers.

Sports: Professional sports practices, training camps, college sports events (women's field hockey and other less-popular sports may allow free admission to games), training facilities.

Transportation: Buses, trains, cable cars, trolleys, ferries, airports (large and small) and other local means of public transportation, switching yards, shipyards, docks. Don't be content to just take a ride; ask for tours of depots, terminals, and ports to find out how they keep people and goods on the move.

Utilities: Switching stations, sewage treatment plants, hydroelectric dams, power plants, coal mines, wind turbines, nuclear plants.

Appendix C: Web Sites Referenced in This Book

Throughout this text, we've described numerous Internet resources for homeschooling. Here's a quick summary of what you can find online.

Chapter 1: Introduction

Homeschooling Research: *<www.homeschoolsteps.com/seealso/research.htm>*

Reasons for Homeschooling: *<www.whywehomeschool.com>*

Number of Homeschoolers: *<www.homeschoolsteps.com/seealso /number.htm>*

Free Homeschooling: *<www.hsfree.com>*

Chapter 2: The Legal Gamut

State by State Laws: *<www.homeschoolsteps.com/seealso/states.htm>*

Homeschooling Outside the USA: *<www.homeschoolsteps.com/seealso /international.htm>*

Parental Qualifications: *<www.homeschoolsteps.com/seealso /qualifications.htm>*

General Legal Information: *<www.homeschoolsteps.com/seealso/legal.htm>*

Record Keeping Software: *<www.homeschoolsteps.com/seealso/records.htm>*

Performance on Standardized Tests: *<www.literatefolk.com/assessment>*

Private Testing Services: *<www.homeschoolsteps.com/seealso/testing.htm>*

Chapter 3: Teaching Strategies

Online Classes: *<www.homeschoolsteps.com/seealso/classes.htm>*

Placement Testing: *<www.homeschoolsteps.com/seealso/placement.htm>*

Rubrics: *<www.homeschoolsteps.com/seealso/rubrics.htm>*

Scope and Sequence: *<www.homeschoolsteps.com/seealso/sequence.htm>*

Critical Reading: *<www.literatefolk.com/literarydevices.htm>*; *<www.homeschoolsteps.com/seealso/critical.htm>*

Logic and Rhetoric: *<www.homeschoolsteps.com/seealso/rhetoric.htm>*

Socratic Questioning: *<www.homeschoolsteps.com/seealso/socratic.htm>*

Field Trips: *<www.homeschoolsteps.com/seealso/virtual.htm>*

Kitchen Science: *<www.homeschoolsteps.com/seealso/kitchen.htm>*

Research Techniques: *<www.literatefolk.com/research.htm>*

Expert Resources: *<www.homeschoolsteps.com/seealso/experts.htm>*

Literature-Based Learning: *<www.literatefolk.com/readinglist.htm>*

Media-Supported Learning: *<www.homeschoolsteps.com/seealso /tv.htm>*

Web-Based Education: *<www.homeschoolsteps.com/seealso /webed.htm>*

Documentaries: *<www.homeschoolsteps.com/seealso/documentaries.htm>*

Essays: *<www.homeschoolsteps.com/seealso/essays.htm>*

Forensics: *<www.homeschoolsteps.com/seealso/forensics.htm>*

Broadcasting: *<www.homeschoolsteps.com/seealso/broadcast.htm>*

Presentations: *<www.homeschoolsteps.com/seealso/presentations.htm>*

Scrapbooking: *<www.literatefolk.com/scrapbooking>*

Self-Publishing: *<www.homeschoolsteps.com/seealso/publishing.htm>*

Theses and Dissertations: *<www.homeschoolsteps.com/seealso /thesis.htm>*

Awards: *<www.homeschoolsteps.com/seealso/awards.htm>*

Competitions: *<www.homeschoolsteps.com/seealso/compete.htm>*

Strategies: *<www.homeschoolsteps.com/seealso/strategies.htm>*

Chapter 4: Approaches and Philosophies

Theory Backgrounders: *<www.homeschoolsteps.com/seealso /theories.htm>*

Accelerated Learning: *<www.homeschoolsteps.com/seealso /accelerated.htm>*

Delayed Schooling: *<www.homeschoolsteps.com/seealso/delayed.htm>*

Natural Learning: *<www.homeschoolsteps.com/seealso/natural.htm>*

Tutoring Resources: *<www.homeschoolsteps.com/seealso/tutoring.htm>*

Approaches and Philosophies: *<www.homeschoolsteps.com/seealso /approaches.htm>*

Chapter 5: Curriculum and Materials

Online Safety: *<www.homeschoolsteps.com/seealso/safety.htm>*

Recommended Reading: *<www.homeschoolsteps.com/seealso /reading.htm>*

Commercial Reference Materials: *<www.homeschoolsteps.com/seealso /reference.htm>*

Online Dictionaries: *<www.m-w.com>*; *<www.dictionary.com>*

Online Encyclopediae: *<www.britannica.com>*; *<www.bartleby.com>*

Commercial Curriculum and Materials Suppliers: *<www.home schoolsteps.com/curriculumproject>*

Scope and Sequence Resources: *<www.home2school.com>*; *<www.homeschoolsteps.com/seealso/sequence.htm>*

Used Curriculum Resources: *<www.homeschoolsteps.com/seealso/used.htm>*

Craft Your Own Materials: *<www.literatefolk.com/tools>*

Free Online Academic Resources: *<www.hsfree.com>*

Unit Studies: *<members.aol.com.donnandlee/SiteIndex.html>*;
<www.andwhatabout.com/articles/unit_study_101.htm>;
<homeschooling.about.com/library/weekly/aa051601a.htm>

Lesson Plans: *<www.cstone.net/~bcp/BCPIntro2.htm>*;
<www.LessonPlanz.com>;
<k12.msn.com/LessonConnection/Teacher.asp>

Worksheets: *<www.evan-moor.com/freeidea.htm>*;
<www.ezschool.com/example/EZTrack2?Name=index>;
<www.learningpage.com>

Freebies: *<www.homeschoolsteps.com/seealso/products.htm>*;
<www.geocities.com/Heartland/Oaks/9122/subject.html>;
<www.geocities.com/tolerance_diversity/HomeschoolerFreebies.html>;
<www.weeklyfreebie.com>

Free Software: *<www.zdnet.com/downloads/home.html>*;
<www.pcworld.com/downloads/browse/0,cat,546,sortIdx,1,00.asp>;
<www.freewarefilez.com/Educational>

Classes: *<www.barnesandnobleuniversity.com>*; *<www.free-ed.net>*;
<www.learningshortcuts.com>

Chapter 6: Gaining Confidence

Moral Foundation: *<www.homeschoolsteps.com/seealso/religion.htm>*;
<www.homeschoolsteps.com/seealso/inspire.htm>

Confidence to Homeschool: *<www.homeschoolsteps.com/seealso/confidence.htm>*

Advanced Teaching: *<www.homeschoolsteps.com/seealso/advanced.htm>*; *<www.homeschoolsteps.com/seealso/science.htm>*;
<www.homeschoolsteps.com/seealso/kitchen.htm>

PROJECT Management: *<www.literatefolk.com/project>*

Transitioning: *<www.homeschoolsteps.com/seealso/adjustment.htm>*

Chapter 7: A Learning Environment

Learning Styles: *<www.homeschoolsteps.com/seealso/styles.htm>*

Testing Resources: *<www.homeschoolsteps.com/seealso/inventory.htm>*; *<www.homeschoolsteps.com/seealso/iq.htm>*; *<www.homeschoolsteps.com/seealso/placement.htm>*

Teaching: *<www.homeschoolsteps.com/seealso/planning.htm>*

Rubrics: *<www.homeschoolsteps.com/seealso/rubrics.htm>*

Motivation: *<www.homeschoolsteps.com/seealso/competition.htm>*

Scheduling: *<www.homeschoolsteps.com/seealso/schedule.htm>*

A Learning Environment: *<www.homeschoolsteps.com/seealso/teaching.htm>*

Learning Styles Products: *<www.homeschoolsteps.com/seealso/vak.htm>*

Chapter 8: The Balancing Act

Naming Your School: *<www.homeschoolsteps.com/seealso/naming.htm>*

Free Products: *<www.homeschoolsteps.com/seealso/freebies.htm>*

Getting Organized: *<www.homeschoolsteps.com/seealso/organize.htm>*; *<www.homeschoolsteps.com/seealso/chores.htm>*; *<www.homeschoolsteps.com/seealso/pantry.htm>*

Working Families: *<www.homeschoolsteps.com/seealso/working.htm>*

Chapter 9: Dealing with Challenges

Socialization: *<www.homeschoolsteps.com/seealso/friends.htm>*

Admissions: *<www.homeschoolsteps.com/seealso/admit.htm>*

Witnessing: *<www.whywehomeschool.com>*

Mixed-Age Teaching: *<www.homeschoolsteps.com/seealso/mixed.htm>*

Homeschooling Challenges: *<www.homeschoolsteps.com/seealso /challenge.htm>*

Chapter 10: Finding Support

Homeschooling Groups: *<www.homeschoolsteps.com/seealso /groups.htm>*

Commercial and Government Support: *<www.homeschoolsteps.com /seealso/othersupport.htm>*

Finding Support: *<www.homeschoolsteps.com/seealso/support.htm>*

Chapter 11: Graduation

Transcripts: *<www.homeschoolsteps.com/seealso/transcripts.htm>*

GED and High School Completion: *<www.homeschoolsteps.com /seealso/ged.htm>*

Vocational Training: *<www.homeschoolsteps.com/seealso/vocational.htm>*

Military: *<www.homeschoolsteps.com/seealso/military.htm>*

College Prep and Graduation: *<www.homeschoolsteps.com/seealso /graduation.htm>*

Notes

Chapter 1: Getting Started

1. We discuss the concept of unschooling in Chapter 4 and deschooling in Chapter 6.

2. Konzal, Jean, Ph.D. (Undated) "Gender Roles: Is Education the Problem or Solution?" History of Education Course at the College of New Jersey. An interesting article on the role of public education in shaping gender roles in the latter half of the twentieth century. Available online at *<www.tcnj.edu/~konzal/gender_web.htm>*.

3. In the news recently: *The (London) Times* reports school administrators in one American school replaced children's Ritalin with sugar pills, in a ploy to steal the psychotropic drug for resale on the black market. (Bone, James. "Ritalin sold in playgrounds." *The (London) Times,* November 28, 2000. *<www.thetimes .co.uk/article/0,,42518,00.html>*.

   Other administrators may not be so nefarious, but their insistence on the administration of Ritalin to schoolchildren can be downright Orwellian. In one case, New York school administrators reported a family to child protective services when they decided to take their seven-year-old son off Ritalin because of its side effects. The child was suffering sleeplessness and a loss of appetite. The parents are now on a statewide list of alleged child abusers, and have been told child welfare workers will take their child away if they don't continue administering the drug. (Karlin, Rick. "Ritalin Use Splits Parents, School." *Albany Times-Union,* Section A1, Sunday, May 7, 2000.)

   Another New York couple was visited by child protective services investigators who were checking into anonymous allegations that they'd taken their son off Ritalin and other drugs because of side effects. The same article reports that as many as 3.8 million schoolchildren are diagnosed with ADD/ADHD, according to the American Academy of Pediatrics. At least 2 million take Ritalin, a stimulant, for symptoms such as inattentiveness, impulsivity, and occasional hyperactivity. ("Land of the Free." *USA Today,* August 16, 2000.)

   A Michigan medical examiner blames the death of a fourteen-year-old boy on long-term use of Ritalin. The examiner says changes occurred in the small blood vessels that supply the heart. Child psychiatrists and psychologists who prescribe the drug are angry over the allegation. ("Experts doubt medical examiner's finding that Ritalin led to boy's death." CNN.com, via AP wire, April 17, 2000.)

In a strongly worded editorial in *The Libertarian*, Vin Suprynowicz, a nationally syndicated libertarian columnist and author and the assistant editorial page editor of the *Las Vegas Review-Journal,* suggests school administrators operate a kind of official, tax-supported dope monopoly that threatens to take children away from parents should they refuse to go along with the "mind-numbing nostrums which our schoolmasters themselves now press on nearly a quarter of our young boys, the better to keep those valuable but restless butts planted in their seats." (Suprynowicz, Vin. "Pharmaceutical blackmail." *Libertarian*, August 2000 *<http://www.thelibertarian.net/2000/vs000818.htm>*.)

See dozens of related articles in the *Detroit News*, available online at *<www.detnews.com/1998/metrox/ritalin>*.

How widespread is the perception that overactive children need "treatment"? It's become part of the common vernacular. Humor columnist Dave Barry includes this item in his parody Year in Review for the Year 2000: "In medicine, the American Academy of Pediatrics reports that it has finally tracked down seven-year-old Matthew Parmogaster, believed to be the only remaining boy in the United States not being treated for attention deficit hyperactivity disorder (ADHD). A team of camouflage-wearing doctors is able to creep close enough to the youngster to bring him down with Ritalin-tipped blowgun darts." (Barry, Dave. "Dave Barry's Yearbook." *Miami Herald,* December 31, 2000.)

4. For a prescient view of the founding of the homeschooling movement, read "Twenty-one Ways Public Schools Harm Your Child," a 1957 editorial from the publisher of the *Orange County Register*. Available online at *<www.sepschool.org/edlib/v3n2/21ways.html>*, it's a fascinating read.

5. One of the most horrifying accounts of indoctrination—the term in use at the time was "rehabilitation"—of children to fuel the political ends of tyranny is found in a 1998 study of German education during the Second World War. In "Hitler's Unwanted Children: Children with Disabilities, Orphans, Juvenile Delinquents and Nonconformist Young People in Nazi Germany," researcher Sally M. Rogow describes attempts by the Hitler regime to enforce conformity on freethinking children. The article is available online at *<www.nizkor.org/ftp.cgi/people/r/rogow.sally/hitlers-unwanted-children>*.

6. A recent survey of homeschoolers on a large Internet mailing list found that nearly 20 percent are not required to, or choose not to, have any interaction with their local school district. The survey had responses from 165 homeschoolers. (Homeschool Reviews Poll, January 2000 *<www.yahoogroups.com/group/0-homeschoolreviews>*.)

7. Ray, Brian D. (2001) "Active and Visible in American Life" *<http://www.nheri.org/98/research/fact3b.html>*.

8. Bunday, Karl M. (1995 and regularly updated) "Homeschooling Is Growing Worldwide." Learn in Freedom! *<learninfreedom.org/homeschool_growth.html>*.

9. Ibid.

10. Lines, Patricia M. (1999) "Homeschoolers: Estimating Numbers and Growth." National Institute on Student Achievement, Curriculum, and Assessment, Office of Educational Research and Improvement, U.S. Department of Education, Web Edition, Spring 1999 (www.ed.gov/offices/OERI/SAI/homeschool).

11. Bielick, Stacey, Kathryn Chandler, and Stephen Broughman. (2001) "Home Schooling in the United States: 1999" National Center for Education Statistics. This government study puts the number of homeschoolers at 850,000 in 1999. It also covers race, household income, and reasons for homeschooling*<nces.ed .gov/pubs2001/HomeSchool>*.

12. The eight states with school-age populations that exceed the population of homeschoolers are California, Texas, New York, Florida, Illinois, Pennsylvania, Ohio, and Michigan. Michigan's school-age population exceeds the homeschooling population by only 11 percent. (Based on U.S. Census figures for July, 1999, estimating numbers of children aged five to eighteen *<www.uscensus.gov>*.) Because many U.S. states have compulsory education age ranges much narrower than five to eighteen, the homeschooled population may actually outnumber the school-aged population more dramatically than these figures would indicate.

13. Fisher, Keri. (1999). "A Homeschooling Primer: The ABCs of Teaching Kids at Home." Family.com, November 1999. *<family.go.com/Features/family_1999_11 /dony/dony119homeschool/dony119homeschool.html>*

14. Gold, LauraMaery. (published since 1999) "Why We Homeschool." A weekly column that includes reports on homeschooled children winning national academic competitions. Archived online at Why We Homeschool *<www.whywe homeschool.com>*.

15. Knowles, J. Gary. (1991) "We've Grown Up and We're Okay." The University of Michigan. Paper presented at the 13th National Conference of the New Zealand Association for Research in Education, subtitled "An Exploration of Adults Who Were Home-Educated as Students" Knowles's research demonstrates that homeschoolers are able to attend college and find employment without any particular difficulty. *<http://www.geocities.com/Athens/Acropolis/7804/a05.htm>*.

16. Ray, Brian D. (1999) "Facts on Homeschooling." National Home Education Research Institute *<www.nheri.org/98/research/general.html>*

17. Rudner, Lawrence M. (1999) "Scholastic Achievement and Demographic Characteristics of Home School Students in 1998." Education Policy Analysis Archives, Volume 7, Number 8, March 23, 1999. Published online through the ERIC Clearinghouse on Assessment and Evaluation, College of Library and

Information Services, University of Maryland, College Park *<epaa.asu.edu/epaa /v7n8>*. In a study using more than 20,000 homeschoolers taking the Iowa Tests of Basic Skills or the Tests of Achievement and Proficiency, Rudner found that homeschooled students earned exceptionally high scores. Median scores were typically in the 70th to 80th percentile.

See also Brian Ray's study "Strengths of Their Own." (The National Home Education Research Institute, 1997) This study found that homeschoolers scored, on average, in the 87th percentile on the Iowa Test of Basic Skills, and in the 80th percentile on the Stanford Achievement Test, while public schoolers averaged in the 50th on both. (A summary is available online at *<www.nheri.org/ 98/research/book.html>,* or read an Education Week report on the study at *<www.edweek.org/ew/vol-16/25home.h16>.)*

And finally see Patricia Lines's "Home Schooling" (ERIC Digest, Number 95, 1995). In this government-funded ERIC Clearinghouse study, Lines asserts that "virtually all the available data show that the group of home-schooled children who are tested is above average. The pattern for children for whom data are available resembles that of children in private schools." (Available online at *<www .ed.gov/databases/ERIC_Digests/ed381849.html>.)*

18. Both Ray's 1997 study and Rudner's 1999 study found that a quarter of home-schooled students are enrolled one or more grades above their age-level public and private school peers.

19. Ray, 1997.

20. Ray, 1997.

21. Ray, 1999.

22. Read more about homeschooling for free in our first home education book, *Homeschool Your Child for Free.* The main Web site for the book is found at *<www.hsfree.com>.*

Chapter 2: The Legal Gauntlet

1. For example, a Michigan court ruling on behalf of homeschoolers wherein the judge declared, "It is the natural, fundamental right of parents and legal guardians to determine and direct the care, teaching, and education of their children." (MCLA § 380.10) A Missouri court said of the state's former homeschool law: "This statute represents a prime example of legislation which yields an unacceptable amount of discretion to officials charged with enforcement. The statute, therefore, does not comply with due process requirements, and is unconstitutionally vague." (Ellis v. O'Hara, 612 F.Supp. 379 (D.C. Mo. 1985))

2. Lines, Patricia M., PhD. (2000) "Homeschooling Comes of Age." *The Public Interest.* No. 140, (Summer): 74-85. On the subject of parental teaching qualifications, researcher Lines says: "Significantly, a handful of studies suggest that

student achievement for homeschoolers has no relation to the educational attainment of the homeschooling parent. This is consistent with tutoring studies that indicate that the education level of a tutor has little to do with the achievement of a tutored child. One explanation might be that the advantages of one-to-one learning outweigh the advantages of professional training." Find links to this and related studies on the Qualifications page of our companion Web site, *<www.homeschoolsteps.com/seealso/qualifications.htm>*.

3. We list research showing that homeschooled children perform as well as or better than their public-schooled counterparts on the Assessment page of the Literate Folk Web site at *<www.literatefolk.com/assessment>*.

4. See past issues of *Why We Homeschool News* for numerous instances of public-schoolteachers and administrators caught cheating on the administration of standardized tests. *<www.whywehomeschool.com>*

5. Two organizations that have been prominent in arguing for homeschooling rights are the Rutherford Institute *<www.rutherford.org>* and the American Center for Law and Justice *<www.aclj.org>*. The American Civil Liberties Union *<www.aclu.org>*, on the other hand, has fought against issues such as parental rights and equal access to public facilities, and is unlikely to be a proponent for families and home education.

6. Source: Family Oriented Learning Co-operative *<www.expage.com/page/folclegal>*.

Chapter 3: Teaching Strategies

1. A Dr. Frederick Goodwin, former director of the National Institute of Mental Health, is widely quoted as saying, "You...can change their [children's] IQ measure in different ways, perhaps as much as 20 points up or down, based on their environment." *<www.infoline.org/Parents/Infants/Development/Beginnings/Infant Brain.asp>*.

   Other studies that have demonstrated a link between environment and early learning:

   > Durkin, Dolores. (1966) *Children Who Read Early.* New York: Teachers College Press.

   > Taylor, Denny and Catherine Dorsey-Gaines. (1988) *Growing Up Literate.* Portsmouth, NH: Heinemann.

2. Lawrence, Dorothy Lockhart. (2001) "Using Music in the Classroom." Lockhart Lawrence Studios. *<www.advancedbrain.com/article6.html>*. Lawrence reviews and summarizes numerous studies on the connection between music and advanced learning.

3. Assigning grades is a controversial practice in the homeschooling community. Some families reject the notion of grading children, believing that doing so is

meaningless and degrading. In other families, however, grading works just fine. Some children enjoy working for grades, and are highly motivated to earn tangible parental approval. If grades motivate your kids, go ahead and give it a try—but don't be afraid to switch to a new motivator if grading stops being fun.

4. Garlikov, Rick. (Undated) "Using the Socratic Method." <*www.garlikov.com /teaching /smmore.htm*>.

5. Abelman, R. (1992) *Some Children Under Some Conditions: TV and the High Potential Kid.* Storrs, CT: The National Research Center on the Gifted and Talented. <*www.ed.gov/offices/OERI/At-Risk/giftab1.html*>.

6. Eighty percent of elementary teachers use worksheets at least once a week. That number falls to 60 percent in the upper grades. KNEA President Christy Levings and Director of Instructional Advocacy Peg Dunlap. (2000) "Findings from Kansas State Department of Education Survey of Teachers." Comp. <*www.knea .org/strengthen/qualityPD.html*>.

Chapter 4: Approaches and Philosophies

1. Other religious traditions add additional support for the model. Mormon theology, for example, adds a center component to the Alpha and Omega description of Jesus Christ: the great "I Am" (D&C 38:1. See also John 8:58 and Exodus 3:14). In the Mormon model, then, Christ is—from eternity to eternity—"Alpha," "I Am," and "Omega" . . . the quintessence of the Ages and Stages philosophy.

An Islamic hadith (tradition) has the angel Jibril (Gabriel) sitting before the Prophet and testing him on his understanding of the most significant components of Islam. The stranger "dressed in white without any sign of travelling," places his knees against the knees of the Prophet. "What is Islam?" the stranger asks. The Prophet cites various acts of worship. "You have spoken the truth," the stranger replies. "What is Iman?" The Prophet responds that Iman is belief in G-d, his angels, his books, his messengers, and other standards of belief. You have spoken the truth," the stranger says again. "What is Ihsan?" The Prophet answers that Ihsan is awareness of the omnipresence of God. When the Prophet demonstrates understanding of these three principles—Islam (submission or performance), Iman (faith), and Ihsan (goodness)—he is subsequently asked a question about the Day of Judgment, the answer to which is known only to God. Finally, he is asked to describe the signs of the hour of judgment. He answers in highly symbolic language, demonstrating the highest level of understanding. In our model, submission is the childlike Alpha, faith is the intermediate Iota, and goodness is the mature Omega.

The Buddhist tradition explains existence in terms of *santai*—three aspects of existence that together explain all earthly phenomenon. This quantum-physics view of the world describes phenomena as nonsubstantial at the Alpha end and as transitory at the Omega end. The central aspect—called, ironically, the Middle Way—is life, the continuity between the non-substantial beginning and the transitory end.

2. The Swann's Accelerated Learning independent study program uses Calvert School for grades 1 though 8, the American School for high school, Brigham Young University for undergraduate degrees, and California State University at Dominguez Hills for graduate degrees.

   Contact the Calvert School at <*www.calvertschool.org*>, 105 Tuscany Rd., Baltimore, MD 21210; phone: (410) 243-6030; e-mail: <*inquiry@calvertschool.org*>.

   The American School can be contacted at <*www.americanschoolofcorr.com*>, 2200 East 170th Street, Lansing, IL 60438; phone: (800) 531-9268 or (708) 418-2800/2814.

   Brigham Young University's Department of Continuing Education offers accredited high school, associates, and bachelor's degrees through independent study. Contact Continuing Education at <*ce.byu.edu*>, 206 Harman Continuing Ed Building, Box 21514, Provo UT 84602; phone: (800) 914-8931; fax: (801) 378-5817; e-mail: <*indstudy@byu.edu*>.

   California State University at Dominguez Hills offers seven academic degrees and five certificates without ever coming to campus. Courses are taught online and, in some cases, using TV/Internet broadcasts. Contact the Division of Extended Education at <*dominguezonline.csudh.edu*>; 1000 East Victoria Street, Carson, CA 90747; phone: (310) 243-3741; fax: (310) 516-3971; e-mail: <*midl @csudh.edu*>.

3. Jefferson wrote: "Is it a right or a duty in society to take care of their infant members in opposition to the will of the parent? How far does this right and duty extend? To guard the life of the infant, his property, his instruction, his morals? The Roman father was supreme in all these. We draw a line, but where? Public sentiment does not seem to have traced it precisely. . . . It is better to tolerate the rare instance of a parent refusing to let his child be educated, than to shock the common feelings and ideas by the forcible asportation and education of the infant against the will of the father . . . What is proposed . . . is to remove the objection of expense, by offering education gratis, and to strengthen parental excitement by the disfranchisement of his child while uneducated. Society has certainly a right to disavow him whom they offer, and are permitted to qualify for the duties of a citizen. If we do not force instruction, let us at least strengthen the motives to receive it when offered." (Letter of Thomas Jefferson to Joseph Cabell, Note to Elementary School Act, September 9, 1817, reprinted in *Writings of Thomas Jefferson* [Memorial Edition 1904] volume 17, page 423.) The word "asportation" is a legal term meaning, "The felonious removal of goods from the place where they were deposited."

4. Mettes, Ben. (1995) "Integrated Learning—The Forbidden Alternative." Quintessence Ply. Ltd. On the Web at *<www.optionality.net/mag/feb95a.html>*.

Chapter 5: Curriculum and Materials

1. WebTV *<www.webtv.com>* and Compaq's comparably priced iPaq *<www.compaq .com/products/iPAQ>* are available in major discount stores (Wal-Mart, Fred Meyer, ShopKo, etc.) and most electronic retailers (Circuit City, Best Buy, and many others.) When we went to press, AOL and Samsung were developing a competitive product called AOLTV.

2. Contact Juno *<www.juno.com>* toll free at 1 (800) 654-5866 for software and installation information. The software can be downloaded for free over the Internet, or it can be obtained from Juno for a $10 shipping charge. NetZero software can be ordered online for free at *<www.netzero.net>* or over the phone for $10 by calling 1 (800) 333-3633. Software for DotNow can be downloaded free from the Web at *<www.dotnow.com>* or by phone for $7 at 1 (515) 253-9999 ext. 10.

3. Commercial reference materials are reviewed on the Reference page of the Homeschool Steps Web site, *<www.homeschoolsteps.com/seealso/reference.htm>*. The noncommercial resources mentioned in this chapter are explained in greater depth in our first homeschooling book, *Homeschool Your Child for Free <www.hsfree .com>*.

4. Popular traditional curricula include A Beka *<www.abeka.com>*, Milliken Publishing *<www.millikenpub.com>*, Core Curriculum of America *<www.core -curriculum.com>*, and many others. Visit the Curriculum Review Project for more information about traditional curricula. It's on the Web at *<www.home schoolsteps.com/curriculumproject>*.

5. Some of the better-known correspondence programs are American School of Correspondence *<www.americanschoolofcorr.com>*, Bob Jones University *<www .bju.edu>*, and the University of Nebraska Independent Study High School *<www.unl.edu/ISHS>*. You'll find many others, along with reviews and contact information, at the Curriculum Review Project at *<www.homeschoolsteps.com /curriculumproject>*.

6. Most single-subject curriculum products are available directly from publishers. The best known is Saxon Publishers *<www.saxonpub.com/home>*, which produces a popular series of math texts and phonics texts. Castlemoyle Publishing *<www.castlemoyle.com>* produces writing and spelling books. Five in a Row *<www.fiveinarow.com>* is a popular unit-study program. There are hundreds of other single-subject publishers reviewed at the Curriculum Review Project, *<www.homeschoolsteps.com/curriculumproject>*.

You'll also want to consider offerings from both national and local retailers. The Elijah Company *<www.elijahco.com>* distributes a catalog stuffed with educational products and homeschooling advice. Rockman's Trading Post *<www.rocksandminerals.com>* offers science materials, kits, and more. Kids Art *<www.kidsart.com>* offers a catalog of art materials. Generic homeschooling product catalogs are also available from Curriculum Associates *<www.curriculumassociates.com>*, J. L. Hammett *<www.hammett.com>*, and many others, all compiled at the Curriculum Review Project.

7. Umbrella programs are offered by schools around the world. Some of the best-known national umbrella schools are Clonlara *<www.clonlara.org>* and Compuhigh *<www.compuhigh.com>*. Washington State's Chrysalis School *<www.chrysalis-school.com>* is typical of local umbrella schools. The Curriculum Review Project describes numerous similar programs.

8. Two of the many tutorial services available are Schola Classical Tutorials *<www.schola-tutorials.com/internet.htm>* and Escondido Tutorial Service *<www.gbt.org>*. We review these, and many others, at the Curriculum Review Project.

9. In Chapter 3 we discussed a teaching strategy called "Scope-and-Sequence," which is an organized way of planning a comprehensive curriculum. You'll find additional scope-and-sequence resources, including links to the learning standards for each U.S. state, at the Sequence page of the Homeschool Steps Web site *<www.homeschoolsteps.com/seealso/sequence.htm>*.

10. Several popular scope-and-sequence books are included on the Reading page of the Homeschool Steps Web site at *<www.homeschoolsteps.com/seealso/reading.htm>*.

11. ALA Library Fact Sheets. Fact Sheet 1 *<www.ala.org/library/fact1.html>* and Fact Sheet 6 *<http://www.ala.org/library/fact6.html>* provide information about library usage in the United States.

Chapter 6: Gaining Confidence

1. Read the archives of "Why We Homeschool News" for several articles about the large number of public-school teachers—or would-be teachers—who fail tests of basic academic skills. The archives also document numerous instances of "dumbed down" tests and decreased standards that are nothing more than desperate attempts by shorthanded administrators to lower the threshold of academic requirements for teaching. You'll find the archives online at *<www.literatefolk.com/wwhs>*.

2. Numerous free resources for teaching and understanding the scientific method are located on the Science page of Homeschool Steps at *<www.homeschoolsteps.com/seealso/science.htm>*.

3. We discuss the Kitchen Science strategy in more detail in Chapter 3. Find resources for teaching kitchen science" on the Kitchen page of Homeschool Steps at <www.homeschoolsteps.com/seealso/kitchen.htm>.

4. Commercial laboratory products for homeschoolers are reviewed in the Curriculum Review project. It's online at <www.homeschoolsteps.com/curriculumproject>.

5. We review numerous resources related to deschooling and decompression on the Adjustment page of the Homeschool Steps Web site at <www.homeschoolsteps .com/seealso/adjustment.htm>.

Chapter 7: A Learning Environment

1. Keefe, J. W. (1979) "Learning Style: An Overview." *NASSP's Student Learning Styles: Diagnosing and Prescribing Programs* (pp. 1–17). Reston, VA: National Association of Secondary School Principals. In *ERIC Digest* ED341890 <www .ed.gov/databases/ERIC_Digests/ed341890.html>.

2. Silver, Harvey F., Richard W. Strong, and Matthew J. Perini. (2000) "So Each May Learn: Integrating Learning Styles and Multiple Intelligences." Trenton, NJ: Silver Strong & Associates. Online at <www.ascd.org/readingroom/books /silver00book.html>.

3. Garlikov, Rick. (Undated) "Learning Styles?" Online at <www.garlikov.com /teaching/Lstyles.htm>.

4. e.g., Educator Tom Rogers's discussion of what he calls his grand experiment in "high-powered learning environments" at Intuitor, a guide for parents of gifted and talented children. <www.intuitor.com>. Rogers's research and experiments suggest—not surprisingly—that children who are raised in information-rich homes do better academically than those who are raised in more barren environments.

5. *Schoolhouse Rock* and other products for visual, auditory, and kinesthetic learners are reviewed on the VAK page of the Homeschool Steps Web site at <www.homeschoolsteps.com/seealso/vak.htm>.

Chapter 8: The Balancing Act

1. Other tips for using resealable plastic bags and disposable storage containers are found on the Ziploc Web site at <www.ziploc.com> and on the Glad site at <www .glad.com>.

2. Yes, we know plenty of working women who earn more than their husbands. And there are even a few homeschooling dads out there who stay home and teach their children while Mom is the primary breadwinner. If that's the system that works best for your family, don't let anyone stop you. But be aware that you'll be in the minority of homeschoolers!

3. See calculations at the Working page of the Homeschool Steps Web site at *<www.homeschoolsteps.com/seealso/working.htm>*.

4. Dunn, Jim. (1998) "When Dad Homeschools: From Breadwinning to Baking." *Home Education Magazine* (May–June) *<www.home-ed-magazine.com/HEM/HEM 153.98/153.98_art_dad.html>*.

Chapter 9: Dealing with Challenges

1. Basham, Patrick. (2001) "Home Schooling: From the Extreme to the Mainstream." Vancouver, BC: The Fraser Institute. The author, a senior fellow at the Cato Institute, conducted an extensive review of homeschooling studies and found that "academic and socialization outcomes for the average home schooled child are superior to those experienced by the average public school student." Read this, and more than a dozen other research studies on the subject of socialization, online at our companion Web site, *<www.homeschoolsteps.com/seealso /friends.htm>*.

2. Galloway, Rhonda A. Scott. (1995) "Home Schooled Adults: Are They Ready for College?" Paper presented at the Annual Meeting of the American Educational Research Association. ERIC Document ED384297. Galloway's investigation found that homeschoolers do as well or better than their schooled peers on college admissions examinations and that their achievement levels in college are similar to those of their peers. Read additional research on the subject of college admissions, employment, and college success on the Admit page, *<www.home schoolsteps.com/seealso/admit.htm>*.

3. The author's *Why We Homeschool* news column documents numerous cases of students being mocked, chastised, suspended, or expelled for wearing clothing making religious statements, making speeches expounding a religious point of view, reading religious books, or wearing religious symbols in public schools. The archives are available online at *<www.whywehomeschool.com>*.

4. Katz, Lilian G. (1995) "The Benefits of Mixed-Age Grouping." The Clearinghouse on Elementary and Early Childhood Education. ERIC-EEEC Document EDO-PS-95-8. Katz describes her own research and reviews a number of similar studies in this excellent report. Find this article, and additional research on mixed-age education, on our Mixed page at *<www.homeschoolsteps.com/seealso /mixed.htm>*.

Chapter 11: Graduation Guidance

1. Pink, Daniel H. (2001) "School's Out: Get Ready for the New Age of Individualized Education." *Reason Online*, October 2001 *<reason.com/0110/fe.dp.schools .shtml>*.

Index

About the Authors

LauraMaery Gold is the homeschooling mother of seven, ranging in age from babyhood to adulthood. She operates one of the largest homeschooling lists on the Internet and writes a weekly Internet column on homeschooling. She is also the author of a number of books on technology, religion, and business. She and her husband, Dan Post, teach their children through an eclectic curriculum of free educational resources, the scope of which grows as the children's interests develop. The former managing editor of several overseas editions of *PC World* and other technology publications, LauraMaery earned her law degree from London's Wolverhampton University. She did her graduate work in journalism at the University of Missouri at Columbia. Her undergraduate studies were in family financial planning and counseling. While living in Taiwan and Hong Kong, she studied Chinese. She and her family now live in Kent, Washington, where the children are finally getting to spend time with their grandparents, aunts, uncles, and cousins.

Joan M. Zielinski is the mother of four—one of whom is LauraMaery. Joan, a professional educator for nearly thirty years, recently retired to undertake volunteer work in literacy education. She is a former Teacher of the Year for the Kent School District, one of the largest districts in Washington State. She earned her bachelor's degree in Arts Education from the University of Washington, and her associate's degree in Art form Green River Community College. She and her husband, Stan, are also licensed dog show judges and raise champion St. Bernards.

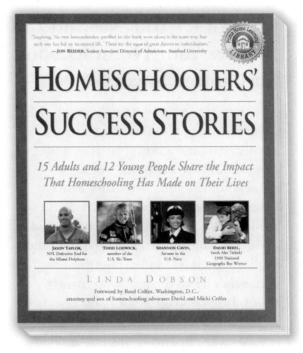

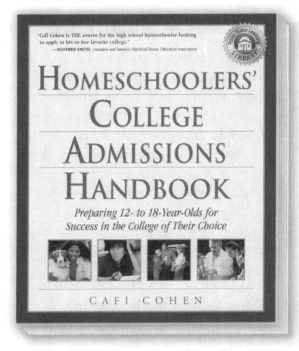

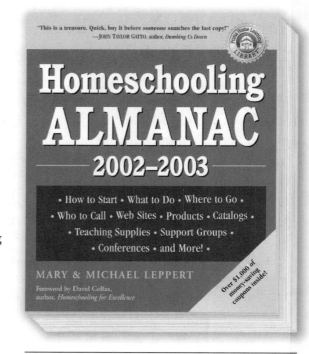